HEALTH PSYCHOLOGY

PSYCHOLOGY OF EMOTIONS, MOTIVATIONS AND ACTIONS

Additional books in this series can be found on Nova's website under the Series tab.

Additional E-books in this series can be found on Nova's website under the E-books tab.

PUBLIC HEALTH IN THE 21ST CENTURY

Additional books in this series can be found on Nova's website under the Series tab.

Additional E-books in this series can be found on Nova's website under the E-books tab.

PSYCHOLOGY OF EMOTIONS, MOTIVATIONS AND ACTIONS

HEALTH PSYCHOLOGY

RYAN E. MURPHY
EDITOR

Nova Science Publishers, Inc.
New York

LIBRARY OF CONGRESS CATALOGING-IN-PUBLICATION DATA
Health psychology / editor, Ryan E. Murphy.
p. cm.
Includes index.
 ISBN 978-1-61728-981-1 (hardcover)
1. Medicine and psychology. I. Murphy, Ryan E.
R726.5.H43227 2010
616.08--dc22
2010026173

Published by Nova Science Publishers, Inc. ✦ *New York*

CONTENTS

PREFACE

Health psychology is concerned with understanding how biology, behavior, and social context influence health and illness. Recent advances in psychological, medical, and physiological research have led to a new way of thinking about health and illness. This book presents topical research gathered from across the globe in the study of health psychology, including leisure and depression in midlife; the benefits of humor on health and pain; hypnosis for the treatment of chronic pain; benefit finding relating to better emotional health in heart patients; blaming parents for their children's weight issues.

Chapter 1-The two studies reported herein examined the construct validity and reliability of a brief 12-item version of the Situational Humor Response Questionnaire (SHRQ; Martin & Lefcourt, 1984). In this research, separate samples of participants were administered the SHRQ, several other humor and laughter measures, as well as scales related to daily stress, mood, and perceived physical symptomatology. The results from both studies indicate that, with few notable exceptions, the 12-item version was comparable in performance to the 21-item version. Specifically, the brief version was found to have acceptable levels of reliability and construct validity, be correlated with higher levels of extraversion, optimism, happiness, vigor, positive mood and lower levels of negative mood, and stress. Further, sex differences were absent and both measures were found to moderate the relationship between stress and physical symptoms, positive mood, as well as vigor. As predicted, high scores on the two SHRQs and stress measures were associated with greater levels of vigor, positive mood, and less physical symptomatology. The 12-item SHRQ appears to be a useful measure for those interested in a quicker assessment of this valuable humor construct.

Chapter 2-Racial and ethnic minority groups are known to experience poor health status and increased health risks, which are remarkably consistent across a range of illnesses and health care services, even when social determinants are controlled. These disparities occur in the context of cultural differences between physicians and patients. A considerable body of research indicates cultural barriers and biases on the part of physicians affect clinical recommendations resulting in lower quality of services and thus contributing to health disparities. The response has been an emphasis on cultural competency training for physicians. Unfortunately, that response, while needed, does not adequately address the cultural gap between physicians and patients and does not necessarily result in culturally competent care. Studies conducted with an eye towards addressing health disparities and formulating an evidence based cultural competency intervention are described in this chapter. It is suggested that cultural competency judgments may be quantified using patient rather than physician reports, and that this largely overlooked measurement strategy may enhance research within this area of inquiry. The relationship of the cultural competency construct and variables such as satisfaction with the medical encounter has been proven to be important to health care behaviors and is examined in this chapter. Finally, as a strategy to address health disparities by empowering patients, the implementation of a simple intervention which would address communication barriers between African American patients and their physicians is reviewed.

Chapter 3-Racial and ethnic minority groups are known to experience poor health status and increased health risks, which are remarkably consistent across a range of illnesses and health care services, even when social determinants are controlled. These disparities occur in the context of cultural differences between physicians and patients. A considerable body of research indicates cultural barriers and biases on the part of physicians affect clinical recommendations resulting in lower quality of services and thus contributing to health disparities. The response has been an emphasis on cultural competency training for physicians. Unfortunately, that response, while needed, does not adequately address the cultural gap between physicians and patients and does not necessarily result in culturally competent care. Studies conducted with an eye towards addressing health disparities and formulating an evidence based cultural competency intervention are described in this chapter. It is suggested that cultural competency judgments may be quantified using patient rather than physician reports, and that this largely overlooked measurement strategy may enhance research within this area of inquiry. The relationship of the cultural competency construct and variables such as satisfaction with the medical encounter has been proven to be important to health care behaviors and is examined in this chapter. Finally, as a strategy to address health disparities by empowering patients, the implementation of a simple intervention which would address communication barriers between African American patients and their physicians is reviewed.

Chapter 4- The purpose of this study is to explore the contributing effects of hypnosis on a cognitive-behavioural therapy intervention for the treatment of chronic pain in patients with fibromyalgia.

The study is structured in four sections. Firstly, it introduces what fibromyalgia is, why it has become a current concern for health psychology and what are the more effective treatments for this syndrome. Specifically, individual and group cognitive-behavioural therapy as part of a multidisciplinary treatment are described as commonly recognised as an effective psychological treatment in fibromyalgia patients. Also, a brief review on the use of clinical hypnosis to reduce both acute and chronic pain is offered, noting that there are only few studies that focus on fibromyalgia-related pain.

Secondly, the methods and procedures of this study are specified. A sample of patients with fibromyalgia were randomly assigned to one of the two treatment conditions: 1) Cognitive-behavioural group therapy treatment; or 2) Cognitive-behavioural group therapy treatment with hypnosis. The contents of each psychological treatment program are carefully described. To assess the efficacy of the designed treatment programs, some outcome measures were taken before and after the treatment. These variables were: pain intensity, pain quality, anxiety, depression, functionality, and some sleep dimensions such as quantity, disturbance, adequacy, somnolence, and problems index.

Thirdly, the main results from this study are exposed. The analysis shows clinically significative improvements in both psychological treatment groups. However, patients who received cognitive-behavioural group therapy plus hypnosis showed greater improvement than those who received cognitive-behavioural group therapy without hypnosis.

And finally, a conclusion on the evidences described, some limitations to be considered in following studies and some recommendations on the treatment of patients with fibromyalgia are followed.

Chapter 5- The use of technology to treat common health problems, such as chronic insomnia, is a growing trend in the health psychology field. The experience of persistent insomnia, as defined by a difficulty with falling asleep, staying asleep, and/or early morning awakening, coupled with sleep-related daytime impairment affects a large number (10%) of adults (Morin, LeBlanc, Daley, Gregoire, & Merette, 2006). Those with chronic insomnia are at an increased risk for a number of health problems (Elwood, Hack, Pickering, Hughes, & Gallacher, 2006; Crum, Storr, Chan, & Ford, 2004) and laboratory based studies show that restricting the sleep of healthy individuals to 50 to 75% of that normally obtained often produces unrecognizable impairments in vigilance and working memory (Van Dongen, Maislin, Mullington, & Dinges, 2003). The two main treatments for chronic insomnia consist of cognitive behavioral therapy and pharmacotherapy, however, consumers often express a preference for cognitive behavioral therapies (Morin, Gaulier, Barry, & Kowatch, 1992; Vincent & Lionberg, 2001). In response to this need, a variety of intervention websites and handheld microcomputer devices have been developed to provide cognitive behavioral intervention to those with this problem. Additionally, the potential use of telehealth to treat individuals with this problem will be discussed. This paper will review these new technologies and highlight the evidence base for these approaches. Additionally, considerations regarding who might most benefit from using these supports will be examined, as will receptivity to these innovations. Implications of the use of technology for the delivery of cognitive behavioral therapy services will be discussed.

Chapter 6- Objective

The purpose of this study was to determine whether benefit finding was related to better emotional health in cardiac patients following cardiac rehabilitation. Benefit finding refers to the ability to find something positive or grow in response to a stressful event.

Design

Participants were cardiac patients (21% female and 22% ethnic minority) in a 12 week cardiac rehabilitation program. Benefit finding was assessed before and after the rehabilitation program. The main hypotheses were that benefit finding would predict increased positive emotion and decreased negative emotion at follow up when controlling for baseline emotion and other potential predictors of emotional health. The main outcome measures were positive and negative emotion following the rehabilitation program.

Results

Path analyses showed that benefit finding was related to more positive emotion and less negative emotion at follow-up when controlling for other predictors of emotion at follow up. In addition, positive reframing coping and income were related to more positive emotion, ethnic minority status was related to more negative emotion, and tangible social support was related to less negative emotion at follow-up.

Conclusion

Benefit finding may improve emotional health during cardiac rehabilitation. Health psychology interventions should focus on enabling cardiac patients to find more benefits in the process of coping with and recovering from heart disease.

Chapter 7- In recent years, the so-called "fatness epidemic" has been subjected to critical examination by different researchers questioning the biomedical definition of fatness as a self-induced health risk and focusing on the discrimination and blame directed at fat people. Attention has also been paid to the ways fat people themselves interpret and account for their fatness in the prevailing negative atmosphere, but the viewpoints of *the parents of fat children* have received less attention. As the primary caretakers, parents are often the ones blamed for their child's weight and are easily viewed as somehow "improper" parents. It is therefore important to look at the ways these parents interpret and manage the ambient messages implying their deviance from the norms of "good" parenthood. In this chapter, my aim is to take this subject up for discussion by presenting an analysis of the interviews of two mothers whose children have been determined to be "overweight" or "obese" by health care. These interviews are part of my current study concerning the ways the parents of Finnish fifth-graders discuss their children's health and their own role and responsibilities as parents. These two interviews stood out as clear exceptions to the other interviews, for they revolved around the issues of the child's weight and the blaming of the parents. I will present a close reading of these two interviews and analyze the multiple ways the mothers discursively and rhetorically managed the blame and tried to position themselves as worthy parents.

Chapter 8- Over the past few decades, there has been a shift from an emphasis on medical paternalism to the recognition of the importance of an informed patient. A balance may be achieved by encouraging patients and physicians to share decision making. Patients' trust in their physician has been suggested as a crucial factor influencing patients' willingness to participate in decision making. Investigating which variables influence trust in physicians and in heath care institutions, therefore, becomes more essential than ever. Our aim in this chapter is to examine the conceptual issues and empirical research regarding patients' trust in the different constituents of the health care system. First, we explain the meaning of trust and provide an overview of the instruments that have been developed to measure the concept. Second, we describe different types of trust and some of the variables that influence each of them. Third, we explain the impact of trust in health care systems and discuss the elements of trust that may be particularly important in this context. Finally, we describe several relevant results that emerge from a review of the literature on the topic and open avenues for future research. We conclude that empirical research clearly complements theory and suggests that developing a trustworthy health care system requires more than competent physicians. More importantly, it needs health workers that have the motivation and capacity for empathetic understanding of patients, as well as institutions that sustain ethical behaviors and so provide a basis for trust.

Chapter 9- The key problem in Internet-delivered interventions is high rates of attrition: people leave the website before actually using it. The aim of this chapter is to better understand compatibility between design and user needs. Thereby we can improve the public health impact of Internet-delivered interventions targeting health risk behaviours (e.g., a sedentary lifestyle, high fat intake, and cigarette smoking) by retaining website visitors' attention through "interactional richness" and thus creating a more positive user experience. Such a positive user experience leads to increased "e-retention" (i.e., the actual use of the intervention by the target group once they access its website). Previous studies assessed and favourably evaluated the efficacy of Internet-delivered interventions without considering use data, whereas the public health impact of an intervention largely depends on the actual use of the intervention website by the target group. Furthermore, the development and application of theories regarding e-retention is timely, since no such theories currently exist. I therefore developed an integrative theoretical framework that provides a theory-driven solution for a practice-based problem with direct applications within the mushrooming field of Internet-delivered interventions.

Chapter 10- The author aimed to explore middle-aged people's subjective leisure experiences, and to further examine associations of such experiences with their depressive symptoms in a Chinese society--Taiwan. Known correlates of depression such as demographics, physical health and social support, were taken into account. Face-to-face interviews were conducted to collect data using structured questionnaires from a national representative sample of community older people ($N = 1143$, aged 45-65). Using hierarchical multiple regression, it was found that (1) being female, had lower family income were demographic risk factors of depression; (2) worse physical health, lack of independent functioning in ADL, and disability were related to more depressive symptoms; (3) greater social support was related to less depressive symptoms; (4) having controlled for all the above effects of demographics, health, and social support, positive leisure experiences in terms of satisfaction and meaningfulness were independently related to fewer depressive symptoms. The benefits of meaningful leisure pursuits for successful midlife transition and prospective ageing were discussed.

In: Health Psychology
Editor: Ryan E. Murphy, pp. 1-36

ISBN 978-1-61728-981-1
© 2010 Nova Science Publishers, Inc.

Chapter 1

FOR THE HEALTH OF IT: A BRIEF VERSION OF THE SITUATIONAL HUMOR RESPONSE QUESTIONNAIRE (MARTIN & LEFCOURT, 1984)

Dave Korotkov, Ian Fraser, Mihailo Perunovic, and Marvin Claybourn*

Department of Psychology, St. Thomas University
Fredericton, New Brunswick, E3B 5G3

ABSTRACT

The two studies reported herein examined the construct validity and reliability of a brief 12-item version of the Situational Humor Response Questionnaire (SHRQ; Martin & Lefcourt, 1984). In this research, separate samples of participants were administered the SHRQ, several other humor and laughter measures, as well as scales related to daily stress, mood, and perceived physical symptomatology. The results from both studies indicate that, with few notable exceptions, the 12-item version was comparable in performance to the 21-item version. Specifically, the brief version was found to have acceptable levels of reliability and construct validity, be correlated with higher levels of extraversion, optimism, happiness, vigor, positive mood and lower levels of negative mood, and stress. Further, sex differences were absent and both measures were found to moderate the relationship between stress and physical symptoms, positive mood, as well as vigor. As predicted, high scores on the two SHRQs and stress measures were associated with greater levels of vigor, positive mood, and less physical symptomatology. The 12-item SHRQ appears to be a useful measure for those interested in a quicker assessment of this valuable humor construct.

---

* Address correspondence to: korotkov@stu.ca

INTRODUCTION

"Laughter is the best medicine, says the old adage – but how much truth is there to the saying?"

- Mindess, Miller, Turek, Bender, & Corbin (1985, p. 109)

Since comedy is – again – in some way about tragedy, one of its functions is to alleviate the pain we would constantly be suffering were we to concentrate on the tragedy that characterizes life on this planet. Humor is a social lubricant that helps us get over some of the bad spots. It is a humanizing agent. You know, it's strange – we will accept almost any allegation of our deficiencies – cosmetic, intellectual, virtuous – save one, the charge that we have no sense of humor.

- Allen (In Allen & Wollman,1998, p. viii)

The current vogue surrounding the therapeutic consequences of humor and laughter owes much to the ascent of holistic medicine in the 1970s, as well as to Norman Cousins' incredible story about his recovery from a disabling disease. In 1976, Cousins chronicled his trials with the potentially fatal disorder, Ankylosing Spondylitis, a chronic, inflammatory, collagen disease of the connective tissue. His story was subsequently published in the 1979 book, *Anatomy of an Illness as Perceived by the Patient: Reflections on Healing and Regeneration* (see also Goldstein, 1987, p. 2). While hospitalized and in considerable pain, Cousins found hospital routines to be additional stressors that appeared to exacerbate his condition. Realizing that such a negative atmosphere could only worsen his state, and with the aid and cooperation of his physician, Cousins moved out of the hospital and sought his own antidote: humor and vitamin C. Therapy consisted of watching old movie clips of Candid Camera, the Marx Brothers, and reading humorous books, while ingesting massive does of vitamin C. The apparent effect of this treatment was astounding. According to Cousins (1979),

It worked. I made the joyous discovery that 10 minutes of belly laughter had an anesthetic effect and would give me at least two-hours of pain-free sleep. When the pain-killing effect of the laughter wore off, we would switch on the motion-picture projector again, and, not infrequently it would lead to another pain-free sleep interval.

While Cousins' cause-effect claims concerning the apparent health enhancing effects of humor and laughter could easily be dismissed given other alternative explanations (e.g., history, regression to the mean; see Cook & Campbell, 1979), the holistic value of humor and laughter was just beginning to be considered a serious subject of research for many scholars (e.g., Cann, Holt, & Calhoun, 1999; Kuiper & Nicholl, 2004; Lefcourt & Martin, 1986; Martin, 2001; Martin & Lefcourt, 1983; Saraglou & Scariot, 2002; Simon, 1988; Svebak, 1974; Svebak, Jensen, & Götestam, 2008; Tűmkaya, 2007). For example, there is now a journal devoted exclusively to the study of humor (i.e., Humor: International Journal of Humor Research), scholarly societies and associations (e.g., The International Society for Humor Studies), humor and humor writing improvement courses/programs and books (Allen & Wollman, 1998; Klein, 1989; Nevo, Aharonson, & Klingman, 1998; Peter & Dana, 1982), as well as a keen multidisciplinary interest from scholars in such areas as psychology (e.g.,

Comisky, Crane, & Zillmann, 1980; Ziv, 1979), anthropology (e.g., Apte, 1985; Butovskaya & Kozintsev, 1996), linguistics (e.g., Oring, 1992; Salvatore, 1994), computer science (e.g., Dormann & Biddle, 2006; Mihalcea & Strapparava, 2006), communication studies (e.g., Brock, 2004; Meyer, 1997), biology (e.g., Fry, 1994; Watson, Matthews, & Allman, 2007), sociology (e.g., Zijderveld, 1995; Kulpers, 2006), social work (e.g., Mik-Mayer, 2007; Moran & Hughes, 2006), politics (e.g., Lewis, 2006; Morris, 2009), business (Lee & Lim, 2008; Rogerson-Revell, 2007), and nursing (e.g., Dean, 1997; Hulse, 1994; Simon, 1988). As Martin et al. (2003) point out, the study of humor is also likely to garner increased attention in light of several recent developments in the growing area of positive psychology (e.g., Peterson & Seligman, 2004).

Although the history of humor and health research is replete with other landmark moments (e.g., Freud, 1905; see Martin, 2007, p. 20 for a fascinating history of humor), a second key and relatively recent event occurred only a few years post-Cousins with the publication of a series of studies by Martin and Lefcourt (1983, 1984; see also Lefcourt & Martin, 1986) on the sense of humor as a stress and mood modifier. In their research, Martin and Lefcourt found that humor and laughter were linked to the attenuation of the relationship between life stress and mood disturbance. Since their classic set of studies, other researchers have come forth to proclaim both the virtues and vices of mirth (e.g., Abel, 1998, 2002; Guiliani, McRae, & Gross, 2008; Kerkkänen, Kuiper, & Martin, 2004; Moran & Hughes, 2006).

In general, despite some claims or qualifications to the contrary (e.g., Boyle & Joss-Reid, 2004; Kuiper & Nicholl, 2004; Martin, 2001, 2002), the view that humor and laughter produce therapeutic effects on health by reducing stress has been well received (e.g., Burridge, 1978; Cassell, 1973; Ellis, 1977; Martin, 2002; McGhee, 1979, p. 227; Nehemour, McClusky-Fawcell, & McGhee, 1986). For example, Cassell (1974) had suggested that humor could be used as a monitoring tool for evaluating the efficacy of therapy, client progress, and a client's reaction to the environment. Cassell further suggested that humor could serve as an aid to the coping process. Albert Ellis (1977), the founder of rational-emotive-behavior therapy, suggests that humor can help to minimize cognitive, behavioral, and emotional distress. Cognitively, humor lends insight to the inflexible or rigid client. Behaviorally, it encourages relaxation and reduces anxiety. Emotively, it brings enjoyment and pleasure, and helps the client to construe life more positively. Along similar lines, in a literature review by Martin (2002; see also Martin, 2001 and Svebak, Martin, & Holmen, 2004), humor and laughter may extend their effects on physical health through four possible mechanisms: (1) through systemic physiological change (e.g., production of endorphins); (2) through positive affective states (e.g., positive mood, joy); (3) through stress moderation; and (4) by raising social support levels to help buffer stress.[1] The following theories, though not fully inclusive, elaborate on these processes and effects.

---

[1] According to Martin (2002), these mechanisms have yet to be adequately tested. More theoretical and methodologically rigorous studies need to be conducted.

THEORIES OF HUMOR: AROUSAL, INCONGRUITY, SUPERIORITY/DISPARAGEMENT, AND BEHAVIORAL

On a golf course, one golfer is choking another to death. A third
golfer nonchalantly walks over and says to the aggressor, "Pardon
me, sir, but your grips' all wrong."

- Gollob & Levine (1967)

In their book, *Humor and Life Stress: Antidote to Adversity*, Lefcourt and Martin (1986, p. 4; see also Berger, 2010, Ferguson & Ford, 2008, Haig, 1988, and Martin, 2007) categorized several theories of humor according to Eysenck's (1942) 3-type classification model.[2] Within each system (i.e., Arousal, Incongruity, Superiority/Disparagement), varying degrees of emphasis are placed on the affective, cognitive, and conative (motivational) components, respectively. Although these theories address different aspects of humor and laughter, the classificatory types (theories) nonetheless do not reflect the total humor experience. For example, the behavioral implications, consequences, and antecedents (e.g., stimulus control and behavioral function) of humor and laughter as well as various phenomenological processes (e.g., cognitive appraisal; see e.g., Dixon, 1980 and Vollrath, 2001) are not objectively spelled out across these models. Thus, to complement or extend our discussion, and given its prominence as a model for understanding individual behavior idiographically, we also include the behavioral model as a fourth potential explanatory framework, in particular, for the creation, experience, and maintenance or stability, as well as the generalization of the humor and laughter responses.

I. Arousal Theories

The first category reflects the view of those theorists who have argued that humor and laughter reduces physiological arousal or tension in stressful situations; that is, humor and laughter can modify one's perception or construal and felt experience of arousal (e.g., Freud, 1905, 1928).[3] One significant theoretical model comes from the comprehensive work of Sigmund Freud (1905, 1928; see also Apter & Smith, 1977, Berlyne, 1972, Dixon, 1980, Kline, 1977, Lazarus & Folkman, 1984, Vaillant, 2000, and Wyer & Collins, 1992 for other arousal based models). In general, Freud presented his theory of humor in two distinct publications. The first publication, a book entitled, *Jokes and Their Relation to the Unconscious* (Jokes), was written in 1905 and dealt primarily with four mirth related entities: the joke, wit, the comic, and humor. The second publication was a paper simply entitled, *Humour* (Freud, 1928).[4]

---

[2] We define humor and laughter in the section that follows.

[3] Consider the inverted-U model where optimal arousal is reflected at mid-point in the curve. Extremes at both ends reflect decrements in the criterion (e.g., pleasure; see Berlyne, 1972); thus the goal is to find the optimal level to enhance one's positive emotional experience.

[4] According to Levine (1969, p. 3), Freud seems to be the only theorist to have viewed humor as a fundamental psychological process that exemplifies one of the two motivational bases for all behavior. Thus, according to Freud, "The dream serves preponderantly to guard against pain while wit serves to acquire pleasure; in these two

As part of Freud's grander theory of personality, he believed that the structure of personality is configured by three interrelated states or constructs, the id, the ego, and the superego. From this model, Freud (1936) argued that several conflicts can take place between these three structures, one of which involves the id and ego. Technically, the id (functioning in accordance with the pleasure principle) may give rise to a psychic impulse that needs to be gratified but is barred from expression by the ego (functioning in line with the reality principle). To *filter* the id's demands, the ego employs various defence mechanisms.[5] Humor/laughter reflects one such mechanism(s). That is, we can often more easily handle distress or anxiety if we adopt a humorous or playful attitude (McGhee, 1979, p. 32).

Freud further contended that laughter and comedy are a function of three separate theories based on psychic economy. Generally, Freud believed that comedy helps to release any nervous energy that has built up in the nervous system, with the resultant laughter acting as the release valve (see Haig, 1988). In particular, he was careful to distinguish the wit from the comic, and humor (Grieg, 1969). In considering wit, Freud made reference to various *joke-work* techniques, the intrapsychic phenomena of creating the joke (e.g., condensation; "alcohol-idays"), each of which allows the individual to express forbidden and repressed sexual and aggressive impulses.[6,7] In other words, psychic energy is not expended for inhibition (i.e., it is economized) and pleasure is derived from the gratification of the instinct (see Kline, 1977, p. 9). This description of wit can be seen in the following jokes (see Mindess, Miller, Turek, Bender, & Corbin, 1985): (1) "Is sex dirty? Yes....if its done right" (sex joke); and (2) "Male: What do I have to do to get a kiss? Female: Chloroform" (hostile joke). According to a Freudian analysis, each joke type represents a psychological mechanism or gateway to help satisfy the needs of the id.

The second distinction Freud made was that of the comic. Generally, the comic has to do with the various nonverbal sources of mirth (e.g., slapstick comedy) in which the observer of the actor experiences a build up of psychic energy, while expecting the expected to occur (e.g., "To be a good nurse, you must be absolutely sterile"; Klein, 1989). Laughter ensues when the unexpected occurs or when the expected does not happen. With the comic, it is the mental or ideational energy that is saved as opposed to inhibitory energy as in wit or the joke. In sum, the pleasure of the comic lies in the economy of expenditure in thought (Grieg, 1969, p. 273).

The final and most relevant distinction that Freud made, was that of humor. While wit represents a savings of inhibitory energy, the comic, mental or ideational energy, humor represents an economizing of emotional or affective energy. Essentially, when confronted with adversity the ability to perceive humorous elements in the situation or to view the situation from an altered perspective, allows one to discharge psychic energy in the form of laughter. Humor therefore diverts the distressful affect from conscious attention.[8] Put

---

aims, all of our psychic activities meet" (as cited in Levine, 1969).

[5] See Vaillant's (2000) discussion of humor as an adaptive and mature defence mechanism

[6] For his 1905 text, Freud borrowed from his widely acclaimed work, The Interpretation of Dreams (Sulloway, 1979, p. 356). While reading the proof for Dreams, Wilhelm Fliess commented to Freud that his dream analyses were full of jokes. After deliberating on this insight, Freud subsequently proposed that the technical components of jokes were similar to those found in dreams. Thus the analogy between dream-work and joke-work was born.

[7] As alluded to, joke-work is similar to dream-work, albeit with a number of qualifications. One major difference is that in a joke the meaning must be intelligible, whereas in a dream the meaning is meant to be hidden.

[8] Interestingly, when Freud was asked to sign a sworn statement as a requirement to leave Nazi Germany, he invoked the power of word play. Richard Simon Keller (1977) graphically illustrates this in the following:

differently, when confronted with an intense situation, some of this primed emotion is suddenly diverted, thus freeing the psychic energy as laughter. Humor tries to withdraw the idea of painful affect from one's conscious or mindful attention. When this happens, it overcomes the defence automatism (see Grieg, 1969). In this sense, humor is a defence mechanism that allows one to see the funny side of a stressful encounter (e.g., accident). An example of this gallows type of humor (see also *Broken Humor*; Haig, 1988, p. 22) is exemplified in the case of a murderer who is about to be hanged. When asked if he has any last words, the murderer replies, "Could I have a scarf for my neck, I don't want to catch cold?"

In sum, Freud's theories of wit, the comic, and humor represent three distinct explanations or psychic mechanisms of mirthfulness with each emphasizing the notion of economy of expenditure. Respectively, these economies are of inhibition (wit), upon ideation or through cathexis (comic), and finally, of affect (humor). While his theory offers some intriguing hypotheses and appears to be the most impressive single volume devoted to a psychological analysis of humor (Kline, 1977), support for Freud's theory is limited and inconsistent. While some analytic research continues, the psychoanalytic theory of humor has been largely abandoned. However, as Martin (2007, p. 41) emphasizes, early tests of Freud's theory tended to focus less on humor, a model with significant implications for the stress-coping process. Further, there appears to be some indirect support for various aspects of Freud's model (see Martin, 1998, 2007).

Just as Freud's model can be construed as based on arousal (tension) reduction, other arousal based models are of value here. For example, evidence from Berlyne's important work (e.g., 1972) provides additional support for the arousal perspective. Basing his work on the inverted-U model, Berlyne argued that an optimal level of arousal is associated with high levels of pleasure. However, as Martin (2007, p. 62) further points out, while arousal appears to be linearly related to emotional enjoyment, there is little support for the inverted-U relationship between arousal and pleasure. Berlyne's work is important for its support of humor as a "complex, physiological-based interaction between cognition and emotion."

II. Incongruity Theories

The second set of theories, those related to the Incongruity Model, focuses on cognition and less (but not wholly abandoned) on the socio-emotional aspects of humor. Incongruity theorists have contended that humor is healthy because it allows one to broaden, modify, or shift perspective of, for example, a demanding or stressful encounter. By shifting perspective, one distances the self from the distressing event. Thus, humor is a function of the juxtaposition, reframing, or restructuring of two normally different or disparate ideas,

---

"I, Prof. Freud, hereby confirm that after the Anschluss of Austria to the German Reich, I have been treated by the German authorities and particularly by the Gestapo, with all the respect and consideration due to my scientific reputation, that I could live and work in full freedom, that I could continue to pursue my activities in every way I desired, that I found full support from all concerned in this respect, and that I have not the slightest reason for any complaint." Earnest Jones, who reports this incident in his biography of Freud, and was himself instrumental in getting Freud out of Austria, explains "Freud had, of course, no compunction about signing it, but he asked if he might be allowed to add a sentence which was: "I can heartily recommend the Gestapo to anyone."

concepts, or situations in an unexpected manner (Lefcourt & Martin, 1986). Koestler (1964) echoes this theme through his *Theory of Bisociation*. According to Koestler, bisociation refers to "the juxtaposition of two normally incongruous frames of reference or the discovery of various similarities and analogies implicit in concepts normally considered remote from each other." Consider the following joke, which demonstrates this juxtaposition: "I used to snore so loud that I would wake myself up. But I solved the problem. Now I sleep in the next room" (last sentence or punchline reflects a violation of expectation; Mindess et al., 1985).

Koestler further believed that humor, scientific discovery, and art were each a function of bisociation. The reason why humor elicits laughter while art and scientific discovery do not, has more to do with the emotional context or situation in which these activities normally take place or occur. While art and science are elicited in neutral or positive emotional contexts, humor is brought on by aggression or low-grade anxiety. Similarly, O'Connell (1976; see also Abel, 2002, Kant, 1790, Nerhardt, 1976, and Suls, 1983) has argued that humor is beneficial because it allows the individual to distance him- or herself from the tension provoking situation. By distancing oneself, the individual changes his or her frame of reference (reframing), thereby minimizing one's negative experience of the stressful encounter.

The incongruity model appears to be generally supported as an *essential perspective of humor*. Although incongruity has been difficult to define and there has been some controversy as to whether incongruity resolution is a necessary condition for an affective experience, the model has contributed much to our understanding of the cognitive-perceptual underpinnings of humor (Martin, 2007, p. 72).

III. Superiority/Disparagement Theories

Superiority or Disparagement theories are among the oldest of the humor theories (e.g., Aristotle, Plato). Generally, these theories suggest that humor enhances feelings of self-control, mastery, self-esteem, and confidence, in addition to minimizing the threat that may accompany a stressful event, demand, or situation. According to this view, one's sense of superiority results from the humorous disparagement of oneself (e.g., *I can be such an idiot. For example, just the other day when I saw a 'do not cross' the street sign, I thought it meant not to get mad at the traffic guard*) or others (e.g., *He's so dumb that when he showers, he puts the shower cap on after he turns off the water, just to keep his hair dry*). Thus, in one sense, humor can reflect a form of aggression towards another (male/female, ethnic groups, etc.; Martin, 2007, p. 44) or towards the self. One major proponent of this view is Jacob Levine (1977; see also Gruner, 1997). From a developmental perspective, Levine (p. 129) believes that humor is a necessary element in both growth and peak mastery processes. At each stage of development, the child learns that humor is a source or antecedent of pleasure that allows him or her to reexperience the mastery of earlier periods in life. As an adult, these early sources of gratification and mastery have been consolidated and are therefore more difficult to recognize or detect. Whether distressed or relaxed, humor represents its own assertion of mastery or control over the environment. For example, Levine argues that humor is often used to reduce anxiety. Because humor is thought of as a learned drive, it represents an attempt at mastery (or competence attainment) when experiencing anxiety or tension. For example, consider the joke of the man who is facing a firing squad and is asked if he would like a last cigarette. "He replies, no thanks, I am trying to quit" (p. 130). In this example, it is the man's attempt at quitting that represents his need for mastery or superiority despite the looming threat.

In his critique of the superiority model, Martin (2007, p. 53) points out that while aggression can play a role in humor, little evidence exists concerning the pervasive influence of disparagement in *all* forms of mirth (vs. Gruner, 1997); that is, not all forms of humor are based on disparagement. However, while the superiority view has to a large extent been replaced by the incongruity model, the former may still serve some theoretical purpose in helping researchers to understand the impact of humor in mastering life's demands (see our subsequent discussion of social-cognitive theory and humor production).

IV. Behavioral Models

The last model that may help to shed additional light on the humor and laughter experience reflects a *second force* in psychology, the behavioral approach. Interestingly, despite offering several plausible hypotheses and mechanisms for construing mirthful behavior, there has been relatively little discussion or research concerning the behavioral model. While in some ways it may be construed of in a conative or motivational sense given, for example, the concepts of reinforcement and establishing operations, the behavioral model (e.g., operant perspective) views humor and laughter as learned functions of the environment (e.g., three-term contingency; *antecedent* – humorous cue → *behavior* – joke telling → *consequence* – reinforcement/social laughter → behavioral maintenance and generalization → repeat telling of joke across contexts; see e.g., Epstein & Joker, 2007). Despite little acknowledgment as a viable model to explain individual differences in humor and laughter, its benefits have been recognized, at least somewhat within the clinical context (e.g., the use of humor in systematic desensitization; Richman, 1996; Ventis, Higbee, & Murdock, 2001; see also Cassell, 1973 and Ellis, 1977).[9]

More specifically, the production of humor and laughter can in part be explained by such concepts as the setting event (e.g., positive mood, context), stimulus control (e.g., predictable or antecedent cues to be humorous), and reinforcement (see also establishing operations). For example, a joke produced in the presence of others (i.e., controlling stimuli/discriminative stimuli) may lead to reinforcement (e.g., an observer's smile and/or laughter). Theoretically, its production and reinforcement may be modified, strengthened, or weakened by an establishing operation (i.e., abolishing, motivating; e.g., deficit or excess in social contact) or be contextually influenced by a setting event (e.g., humor produced only in response to specific others or when experiencing a positive mood; that is, a discriminant and controlling stimulus). Further, given extinction and spontaneous recovery processes, the production of humor may wax and wane and wax (i.e., intermittent or variable behavior) depending on various situational cues. Thus, generalization or maintenance of the humor response or its

---

[9] Grossman (1977) makes reference to the reinforcement model, albeit somewhat implicitly. For example, Grossman states,

It is essential to point out the limitations of the use of jokes. The joke is no more that 'magic pill' than any other therapeutic technique in our armamentarium. The favourite joke is not always directly connected with a patient's problems: on many occasions it may merely be a joke that was heard and repeated with success. The reward of laughter might be enough to make this a joke that the patient might repeat on all occasions. The reward is what makes the joke a favourite and not its personal meaning.

creation, may occur spontaneously or through training, and intermittent reinforcement (see e.g., Martin & Pear, 2007, p. 201).

While these dynamics may reflect the production of humor and laughter and describe its intermittent and continuous rates of responding, the behavioral model (e.g., positive behavioral support) also provides for a functional understanding of behavior that may explain some of the processes or reasons underlying the humor, stress, and health status relationship. Thus, in partial accord with other theories, we *further* speculate that the behavioral purposes underlying humor and laughter may be viewed as multifunctional; that is, the payoff for both humor use and laughter has several functions or purposes, including, to obtain attention (e.g., social reinforcement), to engage in a needed activity (social activity), to escape or avoid a demand or instructional cue (e.g., social threat), and to decrease or increase sensory overload/ underload, respectively (e.g., tension reduction; see e.g., Durand, 1999).[10] While these assumed functions of humor have yet to be tested, at least to our knowledge, the functional model deserves further scrutiny (see Martin & Pear, 2007, O'Neill et al., 1997 and Luiselli & Cameron, 1998 for related behavioral examples of the functional model).

More research is also warranted for both Pavlovian (e.g., laughter as an unconditioned reflex to a conditioned/unconditioned stimulus) and social-cognitive models (e.g., humor self-efficacy). For example, a vast body of research suggests that self-efficacy is linked to health, health behavior, and adjustment (see e.g., Bandura, 1997, p. 259).[11] From this, one intriguing question concerns the role of humor and laughter efficacy in confronting the demands of various stressors. Given the variability and relative instability of humor use and response, it is not clear how confident (i.e., high self-efficacy) some individuals are in their use of humor, in their use of humor to combat stress, in their beliefs about the benefits of humor (i.e., outcome expectations), in their ability to learn the technical aspects of humor generation from others through for example, modeling and observational learning, as well as in their ability to self-regulate or control their use of humor (e.g., deliberate/controlled versus passive/automatic humor use), including its perception.[12] In any case, the behavioral model (i.e., behavioral function, social-cognitive theory) proposes that individuals may use humor and laughter (a) to escape/avoid stress, (b) to decrease/increase sensory over/underload, (c) to obtain attention which may have health enhancing effects, (d) as a needed social activity, (e) reflexively, and (f) to self-regulate their use of humor in response to stress. All of these are vital and competitive hypotheses.[13]

---

[10] O'Neill et al. (1997) and others expand on these functions. For example, in relation to problem behavior, O'Neill et al. suggest that there are 6 possible functions of behavior that include, (1) *Positive Automatic Reinforcement* (i.e., to obtain internal stimulation), (2) *Positive Reinforcement: Social* (i.e., to obtain attention), (3) *Positive Reinforcement: Tangible/Activity* (i.e., to engage in an activity or obtain a tangible), (4) *Negative Automatic Reinforcement* (i.e., to escape/avoid internal stimulation), (5) *Negative Reinforcement: Escape Motivated Social* i.e., to escape/avoid attention), and (6) *Negative Reinforcement: Escape Motivated Task* (i.e., to escape/avoid tasks, activities).

[11] Grossman makes further reference to social learning in relation to humor and therapy:
It may also be that some jokes that are reported as favourites are more a function of social learning and may reflect problems of cultural groups, not specifically those of the individual who repeats them. This does not, however, preclude the possibility that the social problem is not a troublesome one of the patient. In addition, some people's problems may be so complex that many kinds of jokes reflect some aspect of their personality.

[12] We are currently testing such a model.

[13] See Epstein and Joker (2007) for a discussion of a *Threshold Theory of the Humor Response*. Their discussion also provides further insight into behaviorism, humor, and laughter.

SUMMARY OF THEORETICAL EXPLANATIONS FOR THE BENEFITS OF HUMOR

In summary, although not fully inclusive, four general models may help to explain the role of humor in coping.[14],[15] The arousal model (e.g., Berlyne, 1972; Freud, 1905, 1928) suggests that humor helps to relieve excess levels of psychological/physical tension or arousal. The incongruity models (e.g., Koestler, 1964) provide us with a cognitive-perceptual understanding of the role of expectancy violation as a precursor of, for example laughter, which may itself influence the experience of positive affect. Superiority models (e.g., Gruner, 1997; Levine, 1977) suggest that feelings of competence and mastery over the environment result from the disparagement of others or one's self. The last model suggests that humor and laughter may serve several behavioral functions (e.g., escape, avoidance). While the behavioral model appears to share some features with the general arousal approach (e.g., sensory overload reduction), it also distinguishes itself from the other perspectives by its focus on the objective external determinants and outputs (i.e., excesses and deficits) of behavior, as well as the many functions that humorous behavior may be linked to. Social-cognitive and Pavlovian models may also be of use in furthering our understanding of humor. We next examine how humor and laughter have been measured to help test some of these theoretical hypotheses.

MEASUREMENT OF HUMOR AND LAUGHTER

> A patient says to his therapist, 'Thank you doctor for curing
> my kleptomania. Is there anything I can ever do to repay you?'
> The doctor replies, 'Well…. If you ever relapse, could you pick
> up a video recorder for my son?'

> - Dunkelblau (1987, p. 309)

Although many definitions of humor exist, it is generally accepted that humor "represents a rather complex higher-order cognitive-emotional process, whereas laughter is a reflex-like physiological-behavioral response" (Lefcourt & Martin, 1986, p. 31). Expanding on this, Martin (2007, p. 5) suggests that,

> humor is a broad term that refers to anything that people say or do that is perceived as funny and tends to make others laugh, as well as the mental processes that go into both creating and perceiving such an amusing stimulus, and also the affective response involved in the enjoyment of it.

Thus, four elements or components help to define the humor experience, the social context, a cognitive-perceptual process, an emotional response, as well as the vocal-

---

[14] See Vollrath (2001) and Friedman (2008) for a discussion of the various mechanisms and pathways linking personality to health (e.g., stress appraisal, genetics, health behavior). These models may also hold some credence in explaining the processes linking trait humor to health and illness.

[15] We speculate on the role of these models for our study in the Conclusion section.

behavioral expression of laughter (Martin, 2007). Several other authors have proposed more specific definitions and taxonomies (see Ruch, 1998, p. 6 for a discussion of several taxonomies related to humor; see also Hehl & Ruch, 1985; Levine & Rakusin, 1958; Moody, 1978). To some extent, the effects of humor and laughter on stress and health are determined by the different ways in which mirthfulness has been operationalized.

One construct issue that appears to be a source of confusion or bewilderment for some researchers, concerns the number and types of humor and laughter measures in use. For example, according to Ruch (1998), the following eight types of humor measures have been utilized since the early 1970s: (1) Informal surveys, joke telling techniques, diary methods (e.g., Humor Initiation Scales; Bell, McGree, & Duffey, 1986); (2) Joke and cartoon tests (e.g., 3 WD Humor Test; Ruch,1992); (3) Questionnaires, self-report scales (e.g., Situational Humor Response Questionnaire, Martin & Lefcourt, 1984); (4) Peer-reports (e.g., Test of the Sociometry of Humor; Ziv, 1984); (5) State measures (e.g., State-Trait Cheerfulness Inventory-State part; Ruch, Kohler, & van Thriel, 1997); (6) Humor Tests for Children (e.g., Children's Mirth Response Test; Zigler, Levine, & Gould, 1966); (7) Humor scales in general instruments (e.g., COPE; Carver, Scheier, & Weintraub, 1989); and (8) Miscellaneous and unclassified tests of humor (e.g., Wittiness Questionnaire; Turner, 1980). While particularly impressive in their sophistication and scope, it is important to note that many of these scales assess different aspects of the humor experience such as humor style (e.g., Martin et al., 2003), appreciation (e.g., Herzog & Strevey, 2008), initiation, expression, production, or creation (i.e., Zweyer, Velker, & Ruch, 2004), coping humor (e.g., Martin, 1996), joke preference (e.g., Mindess et al.), humor motivation and communication (e.g., Feingold & Mazzella, 1993), personal liking of humor (e.g., Svebak, 1974), comprehension or *getting the joke* (Semrud-Clikeman, & Glass, 2008), and perception or sensitivity to humorous cues (e.g., Bonanno & Jost, 2006; Cann & Etzel, 2008; Eysenck, 1972; Hehl & Ruch, 1985; Levine & Rakusin, 1959; Martin et al., 2003; Moody, 1978; Svebak, 1974, 1996). As might be expected, the intercorrelations amongst these measures have often been found to be moderate in size but stronger than in relation to various nonhumor related constructs (e.g., physical health). One well known and widely used questionnaire in particular, the *Situational Humor Response Questionnaire* (SHRQ: Caldwell, Cervone, & Rubin, 2008; Martin, 1996; Martin & Lefcourt, 1984), is a case in point.

The SHRQ is a 21-item habit related measure constructed to measure individual differences or behavioral tendencies in humorous responding across a range of situations (see Martin, 1996 and Ruch & Deckers, 1993). Its psychometric characteristics are respectable with reported estimates of internal consistency ranging from .70 to .83 and a one-month test-retest reliability of .70. The SHRQ has also been found to be free of any social desirability bias (Martin & Lefcourt, 1984; see also Martin, 1996 and Ruch & Deckers, 1993) and has been linked to other measures of humor (e.g., affiliative and self-enhancing humor; Martin et al., 2003), and personality characteristics such as psychoticism and extraversion (e.g., Ruch & Deckers, 1993), in addition to morale, perceived health (Simon, 1988), bodily preoccupation, health utilization behavior (Kuiper & Nicholl, 2004), immune function (Martin & Dobbin, 1988), depression, self-esteem (Kuiper & Borowicz-Siibenik, 2005), burnout (Fry, 1995), general health (Simon, 1988), and mood disturbance (Martin & Lefcourt, 1984; see also Martin, 1996). According to Martin (1996), in a review of the SHRQ and the Coping Humor Scale, the SHRQ has been found to moderate or buffer the impact of stress on various mood and health related states such as depression, mood balance, positive affect, and indirectly, immune function. Further, those who laugh and smile across a variety of situations tend to use more effective and realistic cognitive appraisals, have a healthier self-concept and high self-esteem, use a variety of defense mechanisms, report greater levels of optimism and feelings of coherence, as well as higher levels of intimacy in social interaction.

For the researcher and clinician interested in using the SHRQ as part of one's assessment or survey package, the current version may not be appropriate for *some* test situations. For example, despite its impressive psychometric characteristics and modest scope, the SHRQ requires the participant to respond to several lengthy, pleasant and unpleasant situations with unusually long response options. These options also vary across the questionnaire. For example, the stem for question 9 reads, "If you were watching a movie or T.V. program with some friends and you found one scene particularly funny, but no one else appeared to find it humorous, how would you have reacted most commonly?" Using a Guttman-like set of response options, the participant would then respond to a multiple choice scale ranging from *a* – "I would have concluded that I must have misunderstood something or that it wasn't really funny" to, *e* – "I would have laughed heartily." Thus, a less cognitively complex and time consuming measure would be useful, in for example, mass testing situations, or in other contexts where time is of the essence. As Marshall et al. (1994) point out, researchers must often make a choice between brevity and comprehensiveness in the selection of their measures. The same case can be made for the measurement of humor. In this case, we examine the SHRQ.

Given these limitations and to complement the full measure, two studies are reported herein detailing the development of a brief 12-item version of the SHRQ. In study 1, the items were selected and subjected to a principal components analysis to assess its construct validity. We also examined its correlates and tested for differences in responding between men and women. In study 1 as in study 2, the brief version was compared to the full 21-item version. Further, in study 2, the data were subjected to a principal components analysis, as well as a moderated regression analysis. Within the context of stress moderation, it was predicted that both the brief and extended versions would be found to buffer the relationship between perceived stress and health; that is, participants who self-report as responding with humor and laughter across a wide variety of situations and when under high stress, would also report fewer health concerns.

STUDY 1: METHOD

Participants, Procedure, and Measures

Twenty-five male and 65 female (N = 90) first year psychology students with a mean age of 20.17 years (SD = 2.90) participated in this study. Data collection took place in small groups.[16]

---

[16] A smaller version of this data set was used in a study conducted by Korotkov (1991). The present study and the 1991 study differ in several respects. For example, in Korotkov, an additional humor measure, the Conformist Humor Rating Measure (see below) was not available; the stress and health measures described herein were excluded as well. Further, the results reported in our research were analyzed in greater depth and with different analytic techniques (e.g., multiple regression). And last, the SHQ measure used in Korotkov differs from the one used herein.

The questionnaires were randomized to help offset potential order effects. Upon completion of the test, participants then rated the tracks. Participants were tested in groups over a two-week period.

Measures

The following measures were administered to all participants:

1) The Situational Humor Response Questionnaire (SHRQ; Martin& Lefcourt, 1984)

As discussed in the introduction, this 21-item scale defines sense of humor "as the frequency with which the individual smiles, laughs, or otherwise displays amusement in a variety of situations." The 21-items are summed to give a total score. Those with high scores tend to laugh and use more humor in a variety of situations.

2) Humor Initiation and Responsiveness Measure (HIRM; Bell, McGhee, & Duffy, 1986; cited in Nahemour, McCluskey-Fawcett, & McGhee, 1986)

This 7-item scale includes both humor initiation and response. Of the seven items, six pertain to different aspects of humor initiation. For instance, "How often do you use puns in an attempt to create your own humor?" The items on this index are summed to give a total initiation score, with high scores indicating higher levels of humor production. The seventh item deals with humor responsiveness (HR): "How often do you have a strong belly laugh of the type that lasts 5 seconds or more?"

3) The Sense of Humor Questionnaire (SHQ; Svebak, 1974)

This 21-item measure assumes that humor production and appreciation consists of three separate qualities: (i) Metamessage Sensitivity – reflects the ability to perceive various humorous cues in the environment. A sample item is, "I must admit that I am usually slow at noticing humorous points or catching onto jokes"; (ii) Personal Liking of Humor – refers to the subjective liking and enjoyment of humor (e.g., "A humorist is typically perceived by others as a person who lacks the courage of his convictions"); and (iii) Emotional Permissivness – refers to the extent to which an individual expresses his or her emotions (e.g., "If I have an unrestrained fit of laughter, I often have misgivings that others thought I was a bit of an exhibitionist"). All three measures are scored on a four-point scale ranging from 1 = Strongly Disagree to 4 = Strongly Agree.[17]

---

[17] Because of concerns surrounding the internal consistency of the SHQ, three items from each of its subscales (i.e., Personal Liking of Humor, Metamessage Sensitivity, and Emotional Permissiveness) with the highest corrected item-total correlations were selected and subsequently combined into a composite measure (α = .60: see Svebak, Martin, & Holmen, 2004). Examination of the correlation matrix (see Table 1of study 1) found that, in line with previous studies (e.g., Svebak, Götestam, & Jensen, 2004), this 9-item SHQ measure tended to be more correlated with the other humor variables and less so with the stress and symptom measures. Thus, for the purposes of this research, this 9-item scale appears to reflect a broad personality construct related to the sense of humor (i.e., emotional expression, liking, and sensitivity to humorous cues).

4) The Coping Humor Scale (CHS; Martin & Lefcourt, 1983)

The CHS is a 7-item measure that directly assesses the extent to which participants report having used humor as a coping device against stress. A sample item is, "It has been my experience that humor is a very effective way of coping with problems." Participants are required to rate the extent of agreement or disagreement on a 4-point Likert-type scale from 1 = *Strongly Disagree* to 4 = *Strongly Agree.* To obtain a total score, all items are summed (two items are reverse scored). High scores reflect a greater tendency to use humor as a coping strategy.

5) Conformist Humor Rating Measure

In contrast to the other humor questionnaires, a behavioral or conformist measure of laughter was included. In constructing this measure, two judges (one male, one female) *initially* rated the degree of mirth in 46 randomized auditory comedy tracks on a seven-point index from 1 = *Not Funny at All* to 7 = *Very Funny.* For ethical reasons, sexual, ethnic, sexist, or sick humor tracks were excluded. From this, the top (scored) 19 auditory tracks were selected and randomized. Each track varied by time and artist (e.g., Robin Williams, Steve Martin). In the actual testing sessions, participants were required to rate each track on the forementioned 7-point scale. Total time for presentation of the tracks was approximately 45 minutes. The cassette tape was played on a prosonic fm/sw/am detachable component system, d2-way speaker system. Alpha was found to be .87 (overall mean = 82.17, SD = 14.65) when the full sample was tested. Higher self-reported scores indicate greater levels of humor appreciation or responsiveness.

6) The Daily Hassles Scale (DHS; Kanner, Coyne, Schaefer, & Lazarus, 1981)

The DHS is a 117-item inventory containing various minor nuisances, which participants respond to based on the past month. Each participant was required to rate the items on a 3-point scale ranging from, 1 = *Somewhat Severe* to 3 = *Extremely Severe.* The DHS frequency score (DHF) was used in all analyses. Items on this measure pertain to the following life areas: work, family, finances, environment, social activities, and health. As some researchers have expressed concern over several health-related items within the DHS, 9 such items were removed (i.e., "trouble relaxing," "trouble making decisions," "physical illness," "side effects of medication," "sexual problems that result from physical problems," "difficulties seeing or hearing," "not enough personal energy," "loneliness," "nightmares"). High scores reflect greater levels of daily stress.

7) The Health Opinion Survey (HOS; MacMillan, 1957)

This abridged 10-item symptomatology inventory was originally designed to screen for persons in the general population who suffer from various neurotic tendencies. Participants are required to rate each item on a 1 (*Never)* to 5 (*Nearly all the time) scale*, to indicate the degree to which a symptom was experienced during the past two weeks. All indicators are summed to yield a total symptomatology score. Examples of such items include, "How often have you had trouble getting to sleep or staying asleep," and "How often have you been troubled by a headache or pain in the head?"

RESULTS

Item Selection & Descriptive Statistics

To develop a brief measure of the SHRQ that would take an average person about roughly half the time to complete, nine situational items from the original measure were first selected based on the highest corrected item-total correlations. In keeping with the theoretical orientation of the original instrument, the three nonsituational questions from the SHRQ were also included. In sum, the 12-items selected for use were: 3, 7, 8, 9, 10, 11, 12, 14, 15, 19, 20, and 21 (see Martin & Lefcourt, 1984 for a copy of the 21-item questionnaire).[18] The 12-item version was found to have an alpha of .72 (men = .80, women = .70), well within previous research estimates of the 21-item scale (e.g., Lefcourt & Martin, 1983). The alpha coefficient for the 21-item measure was found to be .78 (men = .84, women = .75). The means, SDs, as well as a correlation matrix for each of the variables can be found in Table 1. As Table 1 indicates, the 12-item measure was found to be highly correlated with the 21-item measure (r = .94).

Table 1. Means, standard deviations, and intercorrelations for each of the Study 1 variables (N = 90)

Variables	1	2	3	4	5	6	7	8	9
1. Sex	-								
2. S-12	.04	-							
3. S-21	.03	.94**	-						
4. CR	-.25*	.44**	.50**	-					
5. HIRM	-.14	.39**	.43**	.36**	-				
6. SHQ	-.06	.30**	.28**	.26*	.42**	-			
7. CHS	.10	.23*	.26*	-.08	.22*	.18†	-		
8. DHF	.25*	-.04	-.04	.06	-.02	-.15	.06	-	
9. HOS	.31**	-.09	-.07	-.07	-.03	-.24*	.03	.45**	-
Mean	-	34.33	61.66	82.17	18.62	28.14	19.83	26.85	21.70
SD	-	5.78	9.08	14.65	4.90	3.66	2.84	14.28	6.21

Note. S-12 = 12-item SHRQ, S-21 = 21-item SHRQ, CR = humor ratings of audio tracks, HIRM = Humor Initiation and Response Measure, SHQ = Sense of Humor Questionnaire, CHS = Coping Humor Scale, DHF = Daily Hassles Frequency, HOS = Health Opinion Survey, SD = Standard Deviation.
† $p < .10$, two-tailed.   * $p < .05$, two-tailed.   ** $p < .01$, two-tailed.

---

[18] With the exception of items 19, 20, and 21, the remaining situational items are scored in a positive direction. Item 19 reflects the extent to which the individual prefers other individuals with a similar sense of humor. Item 20 is a nonsituational question that requests the respondent to indicate the frequency with which they laugh when compared to an average individual. Item 21 assesses the extent to which the person is consistent from situation to situation in their use of humor. See Lefcourt and Martin (1986, p. 23; see also Martin & Lefcourt, 1984) for a more detailed discussion concerning these items.

Construct Validity

To provide a more stringent test of the SHRQ's divergent and convergent validity, two Principle Components Analyses (PCA) with promax rotations were carried out using each of the humor, stress, and health measures. For each analysis, three components emerged. When the 12-item SHRQ was used, the following three component structure was found (.40 loading cut-off): (1.) the humor response item (λ = .94), the 12-item SHRQ (λ = .69), the Humor Initiation Measure (λ = .58); (2.) daily hassles frequency (λ = .85), the Health Opinion Survey (λ = .85); and (3.) the Coping Humor Scale (λ = .94), and the Sense of Humor Questionnaire (λ = .43). The total variance accounted for by this solution was 67.64 percent. Similarly, when the 21-item SHRQ was used in place of the 12-item SHRQ, the following (similar) components emerged: (1.) the humor response item (λ = .96), the 21-item SHRQ (λ = .73), the Humor Initiation Measure (λ = .56); (2.) daily hassles frequency (λ = .85), the Health Opinion Survey (λ = .85); and (3.) the Coping Humor Scale (λ = .94), and the Sense of Humor Questionnaire (λ = .45). The total variance accounted for by these components was 68.46 percent.

SHRQ Correlates

Two stepwise multiple regression analyses were next carried out using the 12- and 21-item SHRQ versions as separate criterion variables. Each of the humor, hassles, and symptomatology scales were entered as predictors into each regression equation. The results from both analyses were similar although the percentage of variance accounted for in the criteria differed somewhat. When the 12-item SHRQ served as the criterion, the humor response item (β = .44, p < .001) and the Coping Humor Scale (β = .27, p < .01) were found to be significant (R^2 = .25). Similarly, when the 21-item SHRQ was the criterion variable, the humor response item (β = .50, p < .001), and the Coping Humor Scale (β = .31, p < .001) were once again found to be statistically significant (R^2 = .33).

Sex Differences

The main effects of sex, humor (12- and 21-item SHRQ), and their interactions were also examined in relation to each of the humor and health variables. No significant main effects or interactions were found (all ps > .10) suggesting that the two versions were responded to similarly by both men and women.

DISCUSSION

With few notable exceptions, the results indicated that the 12-item SHRQ performed in a manner similar to that of the 21-item measure. As expected, both measures diverged from the stress and health scales while converging with other measures of humor and laughter. The 12-item SHRQ was also highly correlated with the 21-item SHRQ and possessed an acceptable level of internal consistency comparable to previous studies. Lastly, no sex differences were found for either of the two versions.

The purpose of study 2 is to validate these findings with a larger sample and with different measures of stress and health. Given its reported health enhancing effects as a personality measure, we also tested a direct effects model of humor (main effects: 12- and 21-item SHRQ) on health as well as stress moderator model.

STUDY 2: METHOD

Participants, Procedure, and Measures

Data were collected from 541 university students (n_{men} = 207, n_{women} = 334, 2 did not indicate sex) with a mean age of 20.45 years (SD = 4.13).[19] As in the first study, the following measures were administered to participants in a classroom setting: a demographics questionnaire (i.e., sex, age), the 21-item SHRQ (Martin & Lefcourt, 1984), and a one-item question from the HIRM (i.e., "How often do you have a strong belly laugh of the type that last 5 seconds or more": Nahemow et al., 1986). The other measures were unique to Study 2 and were administered in large classroom settings. These measures included the following:

1) Daily Hassles (DHS-56; see e.g., Delongis, Folkman, & Lazarus, 1988)

To measure daily stress, a 56-item measure was administered to participants. Based in part on Delongis et al. (1988), each participant rated the extent to which 56 hassles (e.g., social, academic) were experienced during the past month. Participants used a 4-point rating scale for each item (0 = *None, not applicable* to 3 = *A great deal*). High scores reflect more daily stress.

2) The Inventory of College Students' Recent Life Experiences (ICRLES17; Korotkov, in press-a and b; see Kohn, Lafreniere, & Gurevich, 1990 for the full measure)

A second measure of daily stress was based on a 17-item version of Kohn et al.'s 40-item student hassles measure (e.g., *time pressures*). Each participant responded to the items using a four-point scale ranging from 1 = *Not at all part of my life* to 4 = *Very much part of my life.* All items are summed to form a total stress score. As with the DHS-56, high scores indicate greater levels of stress (during the past four weeks).

3) Short-form Perceived Stress Scale (PSS; Cohen & Williamson, 1988)

A third measure of stress was also included as part of the test battery. The short version of the PSS is comprised of 4-items (e.g., "In the last month, how often have you felt that things were going your way?") in which participants rate their perceived stress levels using a 5-point scale that ranges from 0 = *Never* to 4 = *Very often*. All items are summed to form a total perceived stress score (i.e., high scores = greater perceived stress).

---

[19] A small subset of these variables were analyzed and recently published in Korotkov (in press-a and b). In Korotkov (in press – a and b), optimism, humor, happiness, and vigor were not incorporated into the study; similarly, one of the stress measures' also differed (i.e., DHS-56 vs. DHS-85). Further, distinct hypotheses, study rationale, and analyses, differed as well.

4) The Memorial University of Newfoundland Scale of Happiness (MUNSH; Kozma, Stones, & McNeil, 1991)

The MUNSH is a 24-item measure designed to assess levels of trait happiness. Each of the items (e.g., "The things I do are as interesting to me as they ever were") are rated on the following 3-point scale: *1* (?), *0* (No), and *2* (Yes). High scores reflect greater levels of happiness.

5) The Memorial University of Newfoundland Mood Scale (MUMS; see Kozma et al., 1991 and McNeil, 1987)

A 23-item version of the MUMS was used to measure positive (8 items; e.g., "pleasant") and negative (8 items; e.g., "downhearted") mood, as well as vigor (7 items; e.g., "peppy"). Each adjective was rated on the following 3-point scale: 2 = *Yes, I did feel*, 1 = *Cannot decide*, and 0 = *No, I did not feel*. High scores on each measure reflects higher self-reported feelings of positive and negative mood, and vigor.

6) Dispositional Optimism (OPT; see e.g., Scheier & Carver, 1987)

Optimism was measured by a two-item scale adapted from Scheier and Carver (1987). Both items are rated on a 5-point scale from 0 = *Strongly Disagree* to 4 = *Strongly Agree*.

7) Extraversion (EXT)

Based on Table 1 of McCrae and Costa (1985; see Korotkov, in press - a and b), a 10-item, 9-point bipolar adjective checklist was used to measure extraversion (e.g., 1 = "Talkative" to 9 = "Quiet"). High scores on the extraversion measure reflect a tendency towards extraverted behavior.

8) Memorial University of Newfoundland Symptomatology Scale (MUSS; Korotkov, 2000)

To measure symptomatology, a 10-item perceived symptomatology scale was administered to participants. Each of the symptoms (e.g., "Hands trembling," "Headache") are rated on a 5-point scale that ranges from 0 (*Not at all*) to 4 (*Extremely*). All items are summed to form a total symptom score (i.e., high scores = higher levels of symptomatology).

RESULTS

Descriptive Statistics

The means, SDs, as well as a correlation matrix for each of the variables can be found in Table 2. As Table 2 indicates, the SHRQs were strongly correlated with each other ($r = .92$), with the personality and mood measures, but less so with the stress and symptom measures. The alpha coefficient for the 12-item version was found to be .69 (men = .67, women = .71) and .78 (men = .78, women = .79) for the full measure. Despite these variations, as a following section will detail (*Sex Differences*), no sex differences were found.

Table 2. Means, standard deviations, and intercorrelations for each of the Study 2 variables

Variables	1	2	3	4	5	6	7	8	9	10	11	12	13	14
1. Sex	-													
2. Age	-.03	-												
3. S-12	-.01	-.07	-											
4. S-21	-.01	-.11*	.92**	-										
5. MUNSH	-.15**	.06	.23**	.26**	-									
6. EXT	.10*	-.12**	.36**	.38**	.27**	-								
7. OPT	-.10*	.09*	.33**	.36**	.56**	.29**	-							
8. DHS-56	.02	-.01	-.07	-.09†	-.35**	-.07	-.25**	-						
9. ICSRLE	.05	-.17**	-.16**	-.17**	-.51**	-.10*	-.39**	.61**	-					
10. PSS	.14**	-.11*	-.23**	-.22**	-.64**	-.17**	-.49**	.45**	.62**	-				
11. MUSS	.23**	-.09*	-.16**	-.15**	-.45**	-.11	-.37**	.47**	.51**	.51**	-			
12. NMD	.09*	-.10*	-.21**	-.22**	-.62**	-.24**	-.43**	.32**	.52**	.61**	.50**	-		
13. PMD	-.06	.07†	.30**	.33**	.65**	.38**	.52**	-.25**	-.42**	-.59**	-.40**	-.57**	-	
14. Vigor	-.20**	.04	.31**	.33**	.55**	.36**	.47**	-.19**	-.35**	-.52**	-.47**	-.46**	.77**	-
Mean	-	20.45	33.12	60.2	8.51	65.01	7.06	43.22	21.59	6.88	8.31	18	27.34	25.25
SD	-	4.13	5.39	9.1	9.59	11.67	1.88	20.34	8.25	2.97	6.6	5.52	5.24	5.38

Note. S-12 = 12-item SHRQ, S-21 = 21-item SHRQ, MUNSH = Memorial University of Newfoundland Scale of Happiness (MUNSH), EXT = Extraversion, OPT = Optimism, DHS-56 = Daily Hassles Scale – 56, ICSRLE = Inventory of College Students Recent Life Experiences (ICSRLE-17), PSS = Perceived Stress Scale, MUSS = Memorial University of Newfoundland Symptom Scale, NMD = Negative Mood, PMD = Positive Mood, SD = Standard Deviation

† $p < .10$, two-tailed.   * $p < .05$, two-tailed.   ** $p < .01$, two-tailed.

Construct Validity

To determine whether both versions of the SHRQ would load on the same component as the personality and positive mood measures but diverge from the stress, negative mood, and symptom measures, two PCAs with promax rotations were used. With the exception of the MUNSH, the results generally supported these expectations. In both analyses, two components were found. When the 12-item SHRQ was used, the 17-item Inventory of College Students Recent Life Experiences (λ = .91), the 56-item daily hassles measure (λ = .85), the Memorial University Symptom Scale (λ = .81), the Perceived Stress Scale (λ = .79), the Memorial University of Newfoundland Scale of Happiness (λ = -.67), negative mood (λ = .66), and positive mood (λ = -.42) all loaded on the first component with λ = .40 as the cut-off. The second component was comprised of the one-item humor measure (λ = .75), the 12-item SHRQ (λ = .73), extraversion (λ = .73), vigor (λ = .56), positive mood (λ = .56), and optimism (λ = .41). A similar pattern was found when the 21-item SHRQ was used. Component 1 was comprised of the following variables: the 17-item Inventory of College Students Recent Life Experiences (λ = .91), the 56-item daily hassles scale (λ = .85), the Memorial University Symptom Scale (λ = .81), the Perceived Stress Scale (λ = .79), the Memorial University of Newfoundland Scale of Happiness (λ = -.66), negative mood (λ = .66), and positive mood (λ = -.41). As in the first analysis, the following variables loaded on component 2: the 21-item SHRQ (λ = .75), extraversion (λ = .74), the humor response item (λ = .73), positive mood (λ = .57), vigor (λ = .57), and optimism (λ = .43).

SHRQ Correlates

A set of stepwise multiple regression analyses were once again run to assess the independent correlates of both SHRQs. Both humor measures were regressed on the humor, personality, stress, symptom, and mood variables. In the first analysis, the humor response item (β = .29, $p < .001$), optimism (β = .18, $p < .001$), extraversion (β = .16, $p < .001$), and vigor (β = .11, $p < .05$) predicted the 12-item SHRQ (R^2 = .26). When the 21-item SHRQ was used, the same variables predicted the criterion (R^2 = .28): the humor response item (β = .26, $p < .001$), optimism (β = .20, $p < .001$), extraversion (β = .19, $p < .001$), and vigor (β = .12, $p < .05$).

Sex Differences

Tests of the main effects of sex, humor (SHRQ), and their interactions in relation to each of the stress, symptom, mood, personality, and humor measures were again conducted. Despite the larger sample size, no significant differences on any of the variables were found between men and women (all $ps > .05$).

Stress Moderation

Given that previous studies suggest that the SHRQ may demonstrate stress and health effects (e.g., Martin, 1996), we next tested whether one or both versions would either directly predict (i.e., main effects) or interact with stress to impact the latter's relationship with physical symptomatology, negative mood, positive mood, and vigor. To assess this, the 56-item daily hassles scale, the 17-item Inventory of College Students Recent Life Experiences, and the Perceived Stress Scale served as the stressor predictor variables in three separate sets of moderated multiple regression analyses, respectively. As recommended by several researchers (e.g., Frazier, Tix, & Baron, 2004), each of the stress and humor variables were first centered prior to the main analyses. In each analysis, hierarchical multiple regression was used with the demographic variables (sex and age of participant) entered on step one, the stress deviation score variable entered at step two, the humor deviation scores entered at step 3, and last, the stress by humor product-term deviation scores at step four. A significant interaction term (ΔR^2) indicates a stress moderation effect.[20]

The Daily Hassles-56. When the full SHRQ scale was first analyzed, significant interaction effects were found with respect to both vigor ($\Delta R^2 = .01$, $p < .05$) and symptomatology ($\Delta R^2 = .01$, $p < .05$). Similarly, when the 12-item SHRQ was used in place of the 21-item measure, an interaction effect was found for symptomatology ($\Delta R^2 = .01$, $p < .01$) and a marginally significant interaction with vigor ($\Delta R^2 = .01$, $p < .10$). Using the procedures suggested by Cohen, Cohen, West, and Aiken (2003, p. 269), both significant and marginally significant (exploratory) interaction effects were plotted (see Figures 1a through 1d; predicted scores). As Figures 1a through 1d suggest, individuals who self-described as using humor in a wide range of situations and who also experienced high levels of stress, reported higher levels of vigor and less symptomatology than those who used less humor.[21]

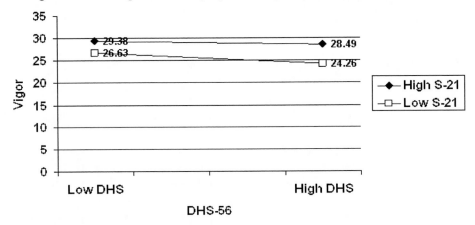

(A) SHRQ-21 by DHS-56: Vigor as the criterion ($p < .05$)

Figure 1 (Continued)

---

[20] To simplify interpretation, the main effects for the other variables (e.g., stress) are not reported here.

[21] 1 standard deviation above and below the mean.

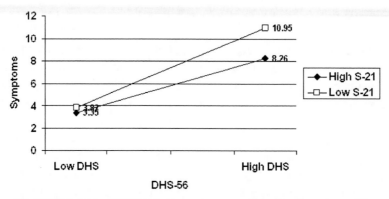

(B) SHRQ-21 by DHS-56: Symptoms as the criterion (*p* < .05)

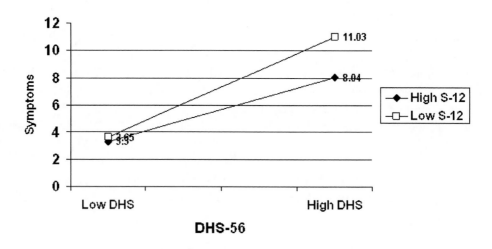

(C) SHRQ-12 by DHS-56: Symptoms as the criterion (*p* < .05)

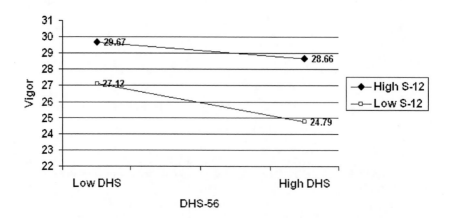

(D) SHRQ-12 by DHS-56: Vigor as the criterion (*p* < .10)

Figure 1. Interaction effects between the SHRQ-12 and SHRQ-21 and stress (DHS-56) in relation to vigor and symptomatology.

Main effects were also found for both versions of the SHRQ in relation to both positive and negative mood. When positive mood was the criterion, both the 12-item SHRQ ($\beta = .28$, $p < .001$ and the 21-item SHRQ ($\beta = .32$, $p < .001$) were statistically significant. And last, the 12-item SHRQ ($\beta = -.19$, $p < .001$) and the 21-item SHRQ ($\beta = -.21$, $p < .001$) were each significant in predicting negative mood.

The Inventory of College Students Recent Life Experiences -17. Interestingly, when the Inventory of College Students Recent Life Experiences was the stress predictor, there was a marginally significant interaction with the full SHRQ measure in relation to positive mood ($\Delta R^2 = .01$, $p < .10$). However, when the brief SHRQ was used, the interaction was significant ($\Delta R^2 = .01$, $p < .05$). Similarly, a marginally significant interaction was found between the 12-item SHRQ and the Inventory of College Students Recent Life Experiences in relation to symptomatology ($\Delta R^2 = .004$, $p < .10$). No significant or marginally significant interactions were found with respect to the 21-item version. To determine if these interactions paralleled the trends in Figures 1a through 1d, the three significant and marginally significant product-term interactions (i.e., predicted scores) were plotted. As Figures 2a through 2c suggest, under high stress, individuals who consistently reported using humor in a variety of situations, also tended to report experiencing more positive mood and less symptomatology relative to those who had low scores on the humor measures. For both the 12- and 21-item SHRQs, main effects were found in relation to vigor (12-item version: $\beta = .26$, $p < .001$; 21-item version: $\beta = .28$, $p < .001$) and negative mood (12-item version: $\beta = -.13$, $p < .001$; 21-item version: $\beta = -.13$, $p < .001$).

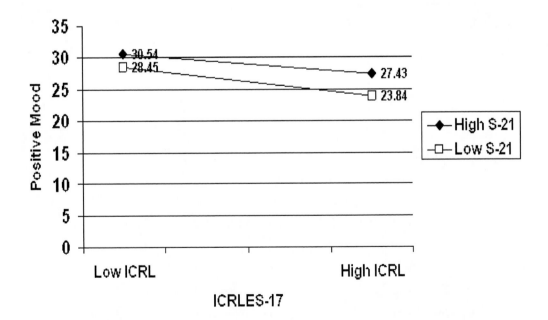

(A) SHRQ-21 by ICRLES-17: Positive mood as the criterion ($p < .10$)

Figure 2 (Continued)

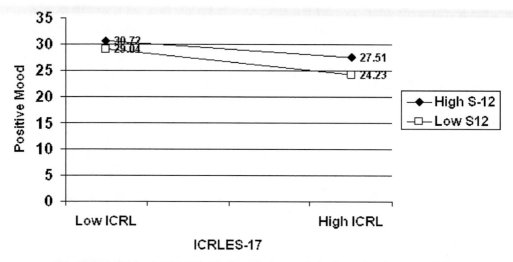

(B) SHRQ-12 by ICRLES-17: Positive mood as the criterion (*p* < .05)

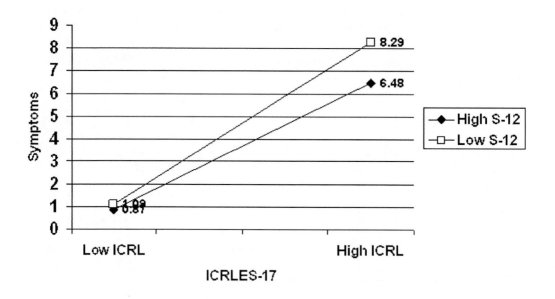

(C) SHRQ-12 by ICRLES-17: Symptomatology as the criterion (*p* < .10)

Figure 2. Interaction effects between the SHRQ-12 and SHRQ-21 and stress (ICRLES-17) in relation to positive mood and symptomatology.

The Perceived Stress Scale. No significant interaction effects were found for either version of the SHRQ when the Perceived Stress Scale was the stress predictor, although at the third step of each analysis, both versions of the SHRQ predicted the criteria, with the exception of the symptomatology scale. Specifically, the SHRQ predicted positive mood (12 items: β = .18, *p* < .001; 21 items: β = .21, *p* < .001), negative mood (12 items: β = -.08, *p* <

.05; 21 items: β = -.09, p < .05), and vigor (12 items: β = .20, p < .001; 21 items: β = .23, p < .001).

DISCUSSION

The results from study 2 further suggest that the brief SHRQ may be a useful measure for researchers when time is limited or when mass testing is involved. Generally, the results from the second study indicate that the 12-item measure possesses an acceptable level of internal consistency (albeit with some variability between men and women and between the 12- and 21-item versions) and corresponds quite highly with the 21-item measure. Further, no sex differences were found for either scale and the same personality and mood variables were found to predict both the 12- and 21-item measures. The 12-item measure was also found to moderate 2 of the 3 stress variables on health.

CONCLUSION

A bossy sort of fellow strides into a lunchroom and says to the
maître d' in a loud voice, "Is this really a first class restaurant?"
"Indeed it is, sir," the captain says. "But that's all right –
you can come in anyway."

- Allen (in Allen & Wollman, 1998)

We set out to develop a brief measure of the SHRQ, a widely used measure of the sense of humor construct. The data from our two studies suggests that the 12-item version of the SHRQ appears to be both reliable and valid as a brief version of its parent scale. Specifically, the 12-item SHRQ was found to (1) possess acceptable levels of internal consistency, (2) be void of any sex differences, (3) be correlated with a range of other humor scales, (4) be *reasonably* unrelated to a host of nonhumor variables, and (5) moderate the relationship of stress on health.

Psychometrics and the 12-item SHRQ

The 12-item SHRQ was found to hold up well to our analyses. Although the internal consistency of the short version was found to be smaller in magnitude than the 21-item measure, the overall alphas, collapsed across sex, revealed similar coefficients to those found in the literature, despite this variation. Further, in study 1 both the Coping Humor Scale and the humor response item were found to predict the 12- and 21-item measures suggesting that individuals who report using humor as a coping strategy and who respond to situations with laughter, were also more likely to smile, laugh, and display or experience amusement across different situations. Study 2 extended these findings to other humor and nonhumor related measures. As in study 1, the humor response item predicted scores on both SHRQs. In addition, optimism, extraversion, and vigor were related to our two humor criteria.

Individuals who self-described as, optimistic, extraverted, and high in vigor, also reported using humor across a range of situations (SHRQ).

The principal components analyses also bore similar results across the two humor measures. In both PCAs, the SHRQs loaded on the same components as the humor responsiveness item, as did extraversion, optimism, vigor, and positive mood. Interestingly, the trait happiness measure (MUNSH) loaded on the first component, along with the stress, mood, and symptom measures.

Overall, one interpretation of the data is that although the SHRQs are related to health outcome (see also next section), they are also somewhat independent of it. Thus, both the 12- and 21-item measures converged and diverged in expected ways with the other constructs assessed in this research.

Humor and Stress Moderation

Generally, the findings provide support for both direct effect and moderator models. The results from study 2 suggest that individuals who laughed and otherwise smiled across a range of situations and who experienced high levels of stress (DHS56, ICSRLE-17, save PSS), also tended to report less physical and behavioral symptomatology, as well as greater levels of vigor and positive mood, than those who self-described as less humorous. In addition, the pattern of the interactions was found to be similar across both measures. Generally, these findings support and extend previous studies linking the SHRQ to well-being and perceived physical health (e.g., Abel, 1998; Lefcourt & Martin, 1986; see also Kerkkänen, Kuiper, & Martin, 2004 for a different perspective). The data analyses also revealed that both versions of the SHRQ were related to and predicted a variety of stress (PSS and the ICSRLE-17) and health related criteria including increased positive mood and vigor, as well as decreased negative mood and perceived physical symptomatology (see e.g., Martin, 1996, 2001, 2007). Overall, humor appears to be beneficial during high periods of stress and cross-situationally where stress is not an issue.

Implications, Limitations, and Suggestions for Further Research

The data presented herein suggests that the brief SHRQ is a useful tool for researchers interested in examining the health enhancing effects of humor. In particular, the results suggest that the brief version may be useful in several distinct research contexts (e.g., mass testing, time sensitive conditions). Further, although the findings shed additional light on the SHRQ, and humor and laughter responsiveness in general, some caution is warranted concerning these findings. First, the usual caveats surrounding the use of correlational data should be noted. That is, although we have suggested that those who self-report as using humor across a range of situations are more likely to experience less stress and fewer health problems, it is also possible that those who report feeling good about themselves (e.g., positive mood) may also be more likely to laugh and use humor. For example, some research (e.g., Deckers, 1998) suggests that positive mood may also enhance the effectiveness of some individuals'use of humor. Theoretically, the behavioral model may help to explain such conclusions. For example, in describing the role of reinforcement that we suggested earlier, we speculate that mood (distal) may modify the direct (proximal) antecedents (e.g., humorous cue) in prompting humor use.

A second limitation is that other third variables (e.g., neuroticism) not incorporated into these studies may help to explain the moderating (or confounding) effects of humor on health (see e.g., Korotkov & Hannah, 1994). For example, in Korotkov and Hannah, when neuroticism was controlled for, the moderating effects of coping humor were no longer significant. Thus, (controlled) prospective and experimental multivariate research designs would be helpful in clarifying these relationships.

Although this study found the SHRQ to moderate the effects of stress on health, further exploration concerning the theoretical processes or mechanisms linking humor to stress and health would be useful. In general, such mechanisms may focus on the biopsychosocial variables that help to transmit the effects of an independent or predictor variable (e.g., humor) to a dependent or criterion variable (e.g., health). More complex models are also possible (e.g., moderated mediation; see e.g., MacKinnon, 2008). However, in supporting Friedman (2000) and others (e.g., Korotkov, in press-a and b; Roberts et al., 2007) who point out that empirical studies linking personality in general, to health, have failed to adequately test such intervening variables, Martin (2002) similarly indicates that despite widespread (and overblown) media reports concerning the benefits of humor, support for these processes remains tentative (see also e.g., Kuiper, Grimshaw, Leite, & Kirsh, 2004).

Further to this, the models discussed in the introduction section, reviews, extends, and reinforces the various potential mechanisms that may help to understand such processes. For example, humor use may, as suggested by those espousing the incongruity model, support a distancing function (e.g., escape or avoidance; e.g., O'Connell, 1976). The juxtaposition of two disparate ideas may influence such efforts. Alternatively, laughter or humor may allow for a significant reduction in physiological arousal (e.g., Berlyne, 1972). Superiority or disparagement theorists may further argue that humor use allows one to master a demanding situation in order to regain control and raise esteem levels (e.g., Levine, 1977; see also behavioral models re: social cognitive theory). And last, behaviorists would argue that humor use and laughter could serve multiple functions. For example, laughter may help to attract social attention as well as decrease sensory overload. Conversely, laughter may help to increase underload in those situations where, for example, boredom is significant. The stress moderating effects observed in our research requires follow-up in order to assess each of these possible functions as well as to examine the isomorphic nature of these functions with the other theories.

Just as it is important to elucidate the mechanisms linking humor to positive health, it is also valuable to determine and highlight those factors that prompt or promote (state) humor use in the first place.[22] Surprisingly, few studies have been conducted in this vein. For example, as alluded to earlier, some research suggests that being in a positive mood may have a significant impact on humor use (Deckers).[23] The literature also suggests that humor motivation and communication may be influential factors in the production of humor

---

[22] As should be evident, one limitation of trait based approaches to humor assessment is that traits tend to be static and relatively unchanging constructs. This contrasts with those paradigms (e.g., social-learning) which suggests that humor can be learned (modeled and corrected) as well as self-regulated in various social contexts.

[23] Some research also suggests that humor production can be increased through priming. For example, in Lehman et al. (2001), it was found that participants in a humor video (priming) instructional group produced more humorous narratives.

(Feingold & Mazella, 1993). Given these data, we suggest that a more complex and combined trait/affective, cognitive social learning, and biobehavioral model may be of some benefit in explaining humor use (e.g., efficacy, self-regulation) and improved health status. That is, we recommend that researchers move beyond or complement simple trait based approaches to humor use to focus additional energies on humor generation and its impact on stress and health. The model we present in Figure 3 reflects this perspective.

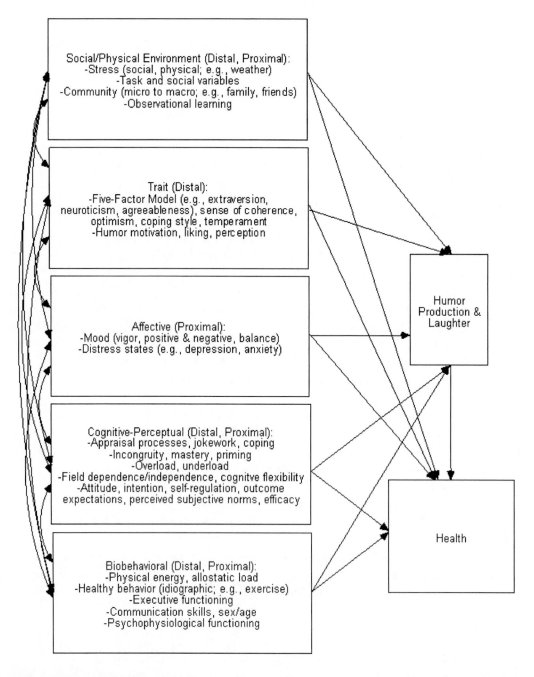

Figure 3: Humor and health model.

As can be gleaned from Figure 3, we further suggest that researchers consider both the distal and proximal antecedents (see e.g., Eysenck, 1997) to humor use, both idiographically and nomothetically, as well as dynamically (e.g., bidirectional paths), in order to incorporate such factors into their own models.[24] While admittedly not comprehensive, the model we propose combines in particular, both trait and cognitive social learning approaches. At this point in our study, we make no assumptions concerning the precise mediating influences of humor production and subsequent health impacts, given in part the often dynamic interchanges that occur with such variables (e.g., positive mood as both an antecedent and consequence of humor). However, the model itself does move beyond simple antecedent-mediator-consequence models and suggests, as many have speculated on, other person-health based processes or pathways (e.g., extraversion and health; see e.g., Friedman, 2008 and Korotkov, in press-a and b). Indeed, the web of causation we advance is ultimately, highly complex (see e.g., Figure 3, implied covariances).

Summary and Conclusions

The purpose of this chapter was to focus on the development of a brief version of the Situational Humor Response Questionnaire. In doing so, we briefly discussed the current state of the literature and suggested that researchers may benefit from a pared down version of the SHRQ. Using data from two studies, the results suggest that the brief SHRQ we described herein represents a reliable and valid measure for use in situations where mass testing takes place, where time may be an issue, and in other situations the researcher or clinician deems appropriate.

AUTHOR NOTE

The authors would like to thank Kimberly Korotkov for reviewing this manuscript.

REFERENCES

Abel, M. H. (1998). Interaction of humor and gender in moderating relationships between stress and outcomes. *The Journal of Psychology, 132*(3), 267 – 276.

Abel, M. H. (2002). Humor, stress, and coping strategies. *Humor: International Journal of Humor Research, 15*(4), 365 – 381.

Allen, S., & Wollman, J. (1998). *How to be funny: Discovering the comic in you.* Amherst, NY: Prometheus Books.

Apte, M. L. (1985). *Humor and laughter: An anthropological approach.* Ithaca, NY: Cornell University Press.

Apter, M. J., & Smith, K. C. P. (1977). Humour and the theory of psychological reversals. In A. J. Chapman & H. Foot (Eds.), *It's a funny thing, humour.* Oxford: Pergamon.

---

[24] Some of the unidirectional paths presented in Figure 3 are in actuality bidirectional. The use of one way arrows was meant to simplify the model.

Bandura, A. (1997). *Self-efficacy: The exercise of control*. New York: W.H. Freeman.

Bell, N. J., McGhee, P. E., & Duffey, N. S. (1986). Interpersonal competence, social assertiveness and the development of humour. *British Journal of Developmental Psychology, 4*(1), 51-55.

Berger, A. (2010). What's so funny about that? *Society, 47*(1), 6-10.

Berlyne, D. E. (1972). Humor and its kin. In J. H. Goldstein & P. E. McGhee (Eds.), *The psychology of humor* (pp. 43-60). New York: Academic.

Bonanno, G. A., & Jost, J. T. (2006). Conservative shift among high-exposure survivors of the September 11th terrorist attacks. *Basic and Applied Social Psychology, 28*(4), 311 – 323.

Boyle, G. J., & Joss-Reid, J. M. (2004). Relationship of humour to health: A psychometric investigation. *British Journal of Health Psychology, 9*, 51-66.

Brock, A. (2004). Analyzing scripts in humorous communication. *Humor: International Journal of Humor Research, 17* (4), pp. 353–360.

Burridge, R. T. (1978). The nature and potential of therapeutic humor (Doctoral dissertation, California Institue of Asian Studies, 1978). *Dissertation Abstracts International, 39*, 2974.

Butovskaya, M., & Kozintsev, A. (1996). A neglected form of quasi-aggression in apes: possible relevance for the origins of humor. *Current Anthropology, 37*(4), 716-717.

Caldwell, T. L., Cervone, D., & Rubin, L. H. (2008). Explaining intra-individual variability in social behavior through idiographic assessment: The case of humor. *Journal of Research in Personality, 42*, 1229-1242.

Cann, A., & Etzel, K. C. (2008). Remembering and anticipating stressors: Positive personality mediates the relationship with sense of humor. *Humor: International Journal of Humor Research, 21*(2), 157 – 178.

Cann, A., Holt, K., Calhoun, L. G. (1999). The roles of humor and sense of humor in response to stressors. *Humor: International Journal of Humor Research, 12*(2), 177 – 193.

Carver, C. S., Scheier, M. F., & Weintraub, J. K. (1989). Assessing coping strategies: A theoretical based approach. *Journal of Personality and Social Psychology, 56*(2), 267-283.

Cassell, J. L. (1974). The function of humor in the counseling process. *Rehabilitation Counseling Bulletin,* 240-245.

Cohen, J., Cohen, P., West, S. G., & Aiken, L. S. (2003). *Applied multiple regression/ correlational analysis for the behavioral sciences* (third edition). Mahwah, NJ: Lawrence Erlbaum Associates, Publishers.

Cohen, S., & Williamson, G. (1988). Perceived stress in a probability sample in the United States. In S. Spacapan & S. Oskamp (Eds.), *The social psychology of health* (pp. 31 – 67). Newbury Park, CA: Sage.

Comisky, P., Crane, J., & Zillmann, D. (1980). Relationship between college teachers' use of humor in the classroom and students' evaluations of their teachers. *Journal of Educational Psychology, 72*(4), 511-519.

Cook, T. D., & Campbell, D. T. (1970). *Quasi-experimentation: Design & analysis issues for field settings.* Boston, MA: Houghton Mifflin Company.

Cousins, N. (1976). Anatomy of an illness: As perceived by the patient. *The New England Journal of Medicine, 295*(26), 1458-1463.

Cousins, N. (1979). *Anatomy of an illness as perceived by the patient: Reflections on healing and regeneration.* New York: Bantom Books.

Dean, R. A. (1997). Humor and laughter in palliative care. *Journal of Palliative Care, 13*(1), 34-39.

Deckers, L. (1998). Influence of mood on humor. In W. Ruch (ed.), *The sense of humor: Explorations of a personality characteristic.* Berlin, Germany: Mouton de Gruyter.

Delongis, A., Folkman, S., & Lazarus, R. S. (1988). The impact of daily stress on health and mood: Psychological and social resources as mediators. *Journal of Personality and Social Psychology, 54*(3), 486 – 495.

Dixon, N. F. (1980). Humor: A cognitive alternative to stress? In I.G. Sarason & C.D. Spielberger (Eds.), *Stress and anxiety* (Vol. 7, pp. 281-289). Washington, DC: Hemisphere.

Dormann, C., & Biddle, R. (2006). Humor in game-based learning. *Learning, Media & Technology, 31*(4), 411-424.

Dunkelblau, E. (1987). "That'll be five cents, please!": Perceptions of psychotherapy in jokes and humor. In W.H. Fry and W.A. Fry, Jr. (Eds.), *Handbook of humor and psychotherapy: Advances in the clinical use of humor.* Sarasota, Florida: Professional Resource Exchange, Inc.

Durand, V. M. (1990). *Severe behavior problems: A functional communication training approach.* New York: Guilford Press.

Ellis, A. (1977). Fun as psychotherapy. *Rational Living, 12*, 2-6.

Epstein, R., & Joker, V. R. (2007). A threshold theory of the humor response. *The Behavior Analyst, 30*(1), 49-58.

Eysenck, H. J. (1942). The appreciation of humor: An experimental and theoretical study. *British Journal of Psychology, 32*, 295-309.

Eysenck, H. J. (1972). Forward. In J. H. Goldstein & P. E. McGhee (Eds.), *The psychology of humor.* New York: Academic Press.

Eysenck, H. J. (1997). Personality and experimental psychology: The unification of psychology and the possibility of a paradigm. *Journal of Personality and Social Psychology, 73*(6), 1224-1237.

Feingold, A., & Mazzella, R. (1993). Preliminary validation of a multidimensional model of wittiness. *Journal of Personality, 61*(3), 439-456.

Ferguson, M. A., & Ford, T. E. (2008). Disparagement humor: A theoretical and empirical review of psychoanalytic, superiority, and social identity theories. *Humor: International Journal of Humor Research, 21*(3), 283-312.

Frazier, P. A., Tix, A. P., & Barron, K. E. (2004). Testing moderator and mediator effects in counseling psychology research. *Journal of Counseling Psychology, 51*(1), 115 – 134.

Freud, S. (1928). Humour. *International Journal of Psychoanalysis, 9*, 1-6.

Freud, S. (1936). *The problem of anxiety.* New York: The Psychoanalytic Quarterly Press and W.W. Norton and Company.

Freud, S. (1960[1905]). Jokes and their relation to the unconscious. New York: Norton.

Friedman, H. S. (2008). The multiple linkages of personality and disease. *Brain, Behavior, and Immunity, 22*(5), 668-675.

Fry, P. S. (1995). Perfectionism, humor, and optimism as moderators of health outcomes and determinants of coping styles of women executives. *Genetic, Social, and General Psychology Monographs, 121*(2), 211-245.

Fry, W. F. (1994). The biology of humor. *Humor: International Journal of Humor Research,* *7*(2), 111-126.

Giuliani, N. R., McRae, K., & Gross, J. J. (2008). The up- and down-regulation of amusement: Experiential, behavioral, and autonomic consequences. *Emotion, 8*(5), 714 – 719.

Goldstein, J. H. (1987). Therapeutic effects of laughter. In W. H. Fry and W. A. Salameh (Eds.), *Handbook of humor and psychotherapy: Advances in the clinical use of humor.* Sarasota, Florida: Professional Resource Exchange, Inc.

Gollob, H. F., & Levine, J. (1967). Distraction as a factor in the enjoyment of aggressive humor. *Journal of Personality and Social Psychology, 5*, 368-372.

Grieg, J. Y. T. (1969). *The psychology of laughter and comedy.* New York: Cooper Square Publishers, Inc.

Grossman, S. A. (1977). The use of jokes in psychotherapy. In A. J. Chapman and H. C. Foot (Eds.), *Its' a funny thing, humour.* New York: Pergamon Press.

Gruner, C. R. (1997). *The game of humor: A comprehensive theory of why we laugh.* New Brunswick, NJ: Transaction Publishers.

Haig, R. A. (1988). *The anatomy of humor: Biopsychosocial and therapeutic perspectives.* Springfield, IL: Thomas.

Hehl, F. J., & Ruch, W. (1985). The location of sense of humor within comprehensive personality spaces: An exploratory study. *Personality and Individual Differences, 6*(6), 703 – 715.

Herzog, T. R., & Strevey, S. J. (2008). Contact with nature, sense of humor, and psychological well-being. *Environment and Behavior, 40*(6), 747-776.

Hulse, J. R. (1994). Humor: a nursing intervention for the elderly. *Geriatric Nursing, 15*(2), 88-90.

Kanner, A. D., Coyne, J. C., Schaefer, C., & Lazarus, R. S. (1981). Comparison of two modes of stress measurement: Daily hassles and uplifts versus major life events. *Journal of Behavioral Medicine, 4*(1), 1 – 39.

Kant, I. (1952 [1790]). *The critique of judgement.* Oxford: Clarendon Press.

Kerkkänen, P., Kuiper, N. A., & Martin, R. A. (2004). Sense of humor, physical health, and well-being at work: A three-year longitudinal study of Finnish police officers. *Humor: International Journal of Humor Research, 17*(1/2), 21 – 35.

Klein, A. (1989). *The healing power of humor.* Los Angeles: Jeremy P. Tarcher, Inc.

Kline, P. (1977). The psychoanalytic theory of humour and laughter. In A. J. Chapman & H. C. Foot (Eds.), *It's a funny thing, humour.* Oxford: Pergamon Press.

Koestler, A. (1964). *The act of creation.* London: Hutchinson.

Kohn, P. M., Lafreniere, K., & Gurevich, M. (1990). The Inventory of College Students' Recent Life Experiences: A decontaminated hassles scale for a special population. *Journal of Behavioral Medicine, 13*(6), 616 – 630.

Korotkov, D. (1991). An exploratory factor analysis of the sense of humour personality construct: A pilot project. *Personality and Individual Differences, 12*, 395-397.

Korotkov, D. (2000). *Measuring hassles and physical symptomatology.* Unpublished manuscript.

Korotkov, D., & Hannah, T. E. (1994). Extraversion and emotionality as proposed superordinate stress moderators: A prospective analysis. *Personality and Individual Differences, 16*(5), 787-792.

Korotkov, D. (in press-a). *Extraverted and energized: A review and tests of stress moderation and mediation.* New York: Nova Science Publishers.

Korotkov, D. (in press-b). Extraversion, daily life stress, perceived energy, and health: A review and tests of stress moderation and mediation. In A.M. Columbus (ed.), *Advances in psychology research* (Vol. 70). New York: Nova Science Publishers.

Kozma, A., Stones, M.J., & McNeil, K. (1991). *Psychological well-being in later life.* Toronto: Butterworth.

Kuiper, N. A., & Borowicz-Sibenik, M. (2005). A good sense of humor doesn't always help: Agency and communion as moderators of psychological well-being. *Personality and Individual Differences, 38*, 365-377.

Kuiper, N. A., Grimshaw, M., Leite, C., & Kirsh, G. (2004). Humor is not always the best medicine: Specific components of sense of humor and psychological well-being. *Humor: International Journal of Humor Research, 17*(1/2), 135-168.

Kuiper, N. A., & Nicholl, S. (2004). Thoughts of feeling better? Sense of humor and physical health. *Humor: International Journal of HumorResearch, 17*(1-2), 37 – 66.

Kulpers, G. (2006). *Good humor, bad taste: A sociology of the joke.* Berlin–New York: Mouton de Gruyter.

Lazarus, R. S., & Folkman, S. (1984). *Stress, appraisal, and coping.* New York: Springer Publishing Company.

Lee, Y. H., & Lim, E. A. C. (2008). What's funny and what's not: The moderating role of cultural orientation in ad humor. *Journal of Advertising, 37*(2), 71-84.

Lefcourt, H. M., & Martin, R. A. (1986). *Humor and life stress: Antidote to adversity.* New York: Springer-Verlag.

Lehman, K. M., Burke, K. L., Martin, R., Sultan, J., & Czech, D. R. (2001). A reformulation of the moderating effects of productive humor. *Humor: International Journal of Humor Research, 14*(2), 131-161.

Levine, J. (1969). *Motivation in humor.* New York: Atherton Press.

Levine, J., & Rakusin, J. (1959). The sense of humor of college students and psychiatric patients. *The Journal of General Psychology, 60*, 183 – 190.

Lewis, P. (2006). *Cracking up: American humor in a time of conflict.* Chicago, IL: Unversity of Chicago Press.

Luiselli, J. K., & Cameron, M. J. (1998). *Antecedent control: Innovative approaches to behavioral support.* Baltimore, Maryland: Paul H. Brookes Publishing Co.

MacKinnon, D. P. (2008). *Introduction to statistical mediation analysis.* New York: Lawrence Erlbaum Associates.

MacMillan, A. M. (1957). The Health Opinion Survey: Technique for estimating prevalence of psychoneurotic and related types of disorder in communities. *Psychological Reports, 3*, 325-339.

Marshall, G. N., Wortman, C. B., Vickers, Jr., Kusulas, J. W., & Hervig, L. K. (1994). The Five-Factor Model of Personality as a framework for personality-health research. *Journal of Personality and Social Psychology, 67*(2), 278-286.

Martin, R. A. (1996). The Situational Humor Response Questionnaire (SHRQ) and Coping Humor Scale (CHS): A decade of research findings. *Humor: International Journal of Humor Research, 9*(3-4), 251 – 272.

Martin, R. A. (2001). Humor, laughter, and physical health: Methodological issues and research findings. *Psychological Bulletin, 127*(4), 504 – 519.

Martin, R. A. (2002). Is laughter the best medicine? Humor, laughter, and physical health. *Current Directions in Psychological Science, 11*(6), 216-220.

Martin, R. A. (2007). *The psychology of humor: An integrative approach.* London, UK: Elsevier Academic Press.

Martin, R. A., & Dobbin, J. P. (1988). Sense of humor, hassles, and immunoglobulin A: Evidence for a stress-moderating effect of humor. *International Journal of Psychiatry in Medicine, 18*(2), 93 – 105.

Martin, R. A., & Lefcourt, H. M. (1984). Situational Humor Response Questionnaire: Quantitative measure of sense of humor. *Journal of Personality and Social Psychology, 47*(1), 145 – 155.

Martin, R. A., & Lefcourt, H. M. (1983). The sense of humor as a moderator of the relationship between stressors and moods. *Journal of Personality and Social Psychology, 45,* 1313 – 1324.

Martin, G., & Pear, J. (2007). *Behavior modification: What it is and how to do it.* Upper Saddle River, New Jersey: Pearson – Prentice Hall.

Martin, R. A., Puhlik-Doris, P., Larsen, G., Gray, J., & Weir, K. (2003). Individual differences in uses of humor and their relation to psychological well-being: Development of the Humor Styles Questionnaire. *Journal of Research in Personality, 37,* 48 – 75.

McCrae, R. R., & Costa Jr., P. T. (1985). Updating Norman's 'adequate taxonomy': Intelligence and personality dimensions in natural language and in questionnaires. *Journal of Personality and Social Psychology, 49*(3), 710 – 721.

McGhee, P. E. (1979). *Humor: Its origin and development.* San Francisco: Freeman.

McNeil, J. K. (1987). *Mood: Measurement, diurnal variation and age effects.* Unpublished doctoral dissertation, Memorial University of Newfoundland, St. John's, Newfoundland.

Meyer, J. C. (1997), Humor in member narratives: Uniting and dividing the work. *Western Journal of Communication, 61,* 188-208.

Mihalcea, R., & Strapparava, C. (2006). Learning to laugh (automatically): Computational models for humor recognition. *Computational Intelligence, 22*(2), 126-142.

Mik-Meyer, N. (2007). Interpersonal relations or jokes of social structure? Laughter in social work. *Qualitative Social Work: Research and Practice, 6*(1), 9-26.

Mindess, H., Miller, C., Turek, J., Bender, A., & Corbin, S. (1985). *The Antioch Humor Test: Making sense of humor.* New York: Avon.

Moody, R. (1978). *Laugh after laugh: The healing power of humor.* Jacksonville, FL: Headwaters Press.

Moran, C. C., & Hughes, L. P. (2006). Coping with stress: Social work students and humour. *Social Work Education, 25*(5), 501 – 517.

Morris, J. S. (2009). The Daily Show with Jon Stewart and audience attitude change during the 2004 party conventions. *Political Behavior, 31*(1), 79-102.

Nahemow, L., McCluskey-Fawcett, K. A., & McGhee, P. A. (1986). *Humor and aging.* Orlando, Florida: Academic Press.

Nerhardt, G. (1976). Incongruity and funniness: Towards a new descriptive model. In A.J. Chapman & H.C. Foot (Eds.), *Humour and laughter: Theory, research, and applications.* (pp. 55-62) London: Wiley.

Nevo, O., Aharonson, H., & Klingman, A. (1998). The development and evaluation of a systematic program for improving sense of humor. In W. Ruch (ed.), *The sense of humor: Explorations of a personality characteristic.* New York: Mouton de Gruyter.

O'Connell, W. E. (1976). Freudian humour: The eupsychia of everyday life. In A. J. Chapman & H. C. Foot (Eds.), *Humour and laughter: Theory, research, and applications.* London: Wiley.

O'Neill, R. E., Horner, R. H., Albin, R. W., Sprague, J. R., Storey, K., & Newton, J. S. (1997). *Functional assessment and program development for problem behavior: A practical handbook.* Pacific Grove, CA: Brooks/Cole Publishing Company.

Oring, E. (1992). *Jokes and their relations.* Lexington: The University Press of Kentucky.

Peter, L. J., & Dana, B. (1982). *The laughter prescription.* New York: Ballantine Books.

Peterson, C., & Seligman, M. E. P. (2004). *Character strengths and virtues: A handbook and classification.* Washington, DC: American Psychological Association.

Richman, J. (1996). Points of correspondence between humor and psychotherapy. *Psychotherapy: Theory, Research, Practice, Training, 33*(4), 560-566.

Roberts, B. W., Kuncel, N. R., Shiner, R., Caspi, A., & Goldberg, L. R. (2007). The power of personality: The comparative validity of personality traits, socioeconomic status, and cognitive ability for predicting important life outcomes. *Perspectives on Psychological Science, 2*(4), 313-345.

Rogerson-Revell, P. (2007). Humour in business: A double-edged sword. A study of humour and style shifting in intercultural business meetings. *Journal of Pragmatics, 39*(1), 4-28.

Ruch, W. (1992). Assessment of appreciation of humor: Studies with the 3 WD Humor Test, in C. D. Spielberger & J. Butcher (eds.), *Advances in personality assessment* (Vol. 9). Hillsdale, NJ: Erlbaum.

Ruch, W. (1998a). *The sense of humor: Explorations of a personality characteristic.* Berlin, Germany: Mouton de Gruyter.

Ruch, W. (1998b). Sense of humor: A new look at an old concept. In W. Ruch (ed.), *The sense of humor: Explorations of a personality characteristic.* Berlin, Germany: Mouton de Gruyter.

Ruch, W., & Deckers, L. (1993). Do extraverts "like to laugh"? An analysis of the Situational Humor Response Questionnaire (SHRQ). *European Journal of Personality, 7*(4), 211-220.

Ruch, W., Kohler, G., & van Thriel, L. (1997).To be in good or bad humor: Construction of the State-Trait-Cheerfulness-Inventory-STCI. *Personality and Individual Differences, 22*(4), 477-491.

Salvatore, A. (1994). *Linguistic theories of humor.* Berlin–New York: Mouton deGruyter.

Saroglou, V., & Scariot, C. (2002). Humor Styles Questionnaire: Personality and educational correlates in Belgian high school and college students. *European Journal of Personality, 16*, 43 – 54.

Scheier, M. F., & Carver, C. S. (1985). Optimism, coping, and health: Assessment and implications of generalized outcome expectancies. *Health Psychology, 4*, 219 – 247.

Semrud-Clikeman, M., & Glass, K. (2008). Comprehension of humor in children with nonverbal learning disabilities, reading disabilities, and without learning disabilities. *Annals of Dyslexia, 58*(2), 163-180.

Simon, J. M. (1988). Humour and the older adult: Implications for nursing. *Journal of Advanced Nursing, 13*, 441 – 446.

Simon, R. K. (1977). Freud's concepts of comedy and suffering. *Psychoanalytic Review, 64*(3), 391-407.

Sulloway, F. J. (1979). *Freud, biologist of the mind: Beyond the psychoanalytic legend*. New York: Basic Books.

Suls, J. M. (1983). Cognitive processes in humor appreciation. In P.E. McGhee & J.H. Goldstein (Eds.), *Handbook of humor research* (Vol. 1, pp. 39-58). New York: Springer Verlag.

Svebak, S. (1974). Revised questionnaire on the sense of humor. *Scandinavian Journal of Psychology, 15*, 328 – 331.

Svebak, S. (1996). The development of the Sense of Humor Questionnaire: From SHQ to SHQ-6. *Humor: International Journal of Humor Research, 9*(3-4), 341 – 361.

Svebak, S., Götestam, K. G., & Jensen, E. N. (2004). The significance of humor, life regard, and stressors for bodily complaints among high school students. *Humor: International Journal of Humor Research, 17*(1/2), 67 – 83.

Svebak, S., Jensen, E. N., & Götestam, K. G. (2008). Some health effects of implementing school nursing in a Norwegian high school: A controlled study. *The Journal of School Nursing, 24*(1), 49 – 54.

Svebak, S., Martin, R. A., & Holmen, J. (2004). The prevalence of sense of humor in a large, unselected county population in Norway: Relations with age, sex, and some health indicators. *Humor: International Journal of HumorResearch, 17*(1 – 2), 121 – 134.

Thorson, J. A., & Powell, F. C. (1993). Development and validation of a multidimensional sense of humor scale. *Journal of Clinical Psychology, 49*(1), 13 – 23.

Tŭmkaya, S. (2007). Burnout and humor relationship among university lecturers. *Humor: International Journal of Humor Research, 20*(1), 73 – 92.

Turner, R. G. (1980). Self-monitoring and humor production. *Journal of Personality, 48*, 163-172.

Vaillant, G. E. (2000). Adaptive mental mechanisms: Their role in positive psychology. *American Psychologist, 55*(1), 89-98.

Ventis, W. L., Higbee, G., & Murdock, S. A. (2001). Using humor in systematic desensitization to reduce fear. *Journal of General Psychology, 128*(2), 241-253.

Vollrath, M. (2001). Personality and stress. *Scandinavian Journal of Psychology, 42*, 335-347.

Watson, K. K., Matthews, B. J., & Allman, J. M. (2007). Brain activation during sight gags and language-dependent humor. *Cerebral Cortex, 17*(2), 314-324.

Wyer, R. S., & Collins, J. E. (1992). A theory of humor elicitation. *Psychological Review, 99*(4), 663-688.

Zigler, E., Levine, J., & Gould, L. (1966). Cognitive processes in the development of children's appreciation of humor. *Child Development, 37*(3), 507-518.

Zijderveld, A. C. (1995). Humor, laughter, and sociological theory. *Sociological Forum, 10*(2), 341-345.

Ziv, A (1979). The teacher's sense of humour and the atmosphere in the classroom. *School Psychology International, 1*(2), 21-23.

Ziv, A. (1984). *Personality and sense of humor*. New York: Springer.

Zweyer, K., Velker, B., & Ruch, W. (2004). Do cheerfulness, exhilaration, and humor production moderate pain tolerance? A FACS study. *Humor: International Journal of Humor Research, 17*(1-2), 85-119.

In: Health Psychology
Editor: Ryan E. Murphy, pp. 37-58

ISBN 978-1-61728-981-1
© 2010 Nova Science Publishers, Inc.

Chapter 2

DEVELOPMENTS IN CULTURAL COMPETENCY RESEARCH

Georgia Michalopoulou, Pamela Falzarano, Cynthia Arfken, and David Rosenberg

Wayne State University School of Medicine
Department of Psychiatry and Behavioral Neurosciences

ABSTRACT

Racial and ethnic minority groups are known to experience poor health status and increased health risks, which are remarkably consistent across a range of illnesses and health care services, even when social determinants are controlled. These disparities occur in the context of cultural differences between physicians and patients. A considerable body of research indicates cultural barriers and biases on the part of physicians affect clinical recommendations resulting in lower quality of services and thus contributing to health disparities. The response has been an emphasis on cultural competency training for physicians. Unfortunately, that response, while needed, does not adequately address the cultural gap between physicians and patients and does not necessarily result in culturally competent care. Studies conducted with an eye towards addressing health disparities and formulating an evidence based cultural competency intervention are described in this chapter. It is suggested that cultural competency judgments may be quantified using patient rather than physician reports, and that this largely overlooked measurement strategy may enhance research within this area of inquiry. The relationship of the cultural competency construct and variables such as satisfaction with the medical encounter has been proven to be important to health care behaviors and is examined in this chapter. Finally, as a strategy to address health disparities by empowering patients, the implementation of a simple intervention which would address communication barriers between African American patients and their physicians is reviewed.

PATIENT CENTERED APPROACH TO HEALTH DISPARITIES

Disparities in Health Status, Care, and Outcomes

Health disparities persist between men and women (Gregg, Gu, Cheng, Venkat Narayan, & Cowie, 2007; Heo, Allison, & Fontaine, 2004); across age groups (Jazieh & Buncher, 2002; Jerant, Franks, Jackson, & Doescher, 2004); among people who vary in terms of their educational level and economic resources (Meara, Richards, & Cutler, 2008) as well as across geographic regions (Chandra & Skinner, 2003; Groeneveld, Heidenreich, & Garber, 2005). The direction and the magnitude of these differences varies and depends upon the specific population or health issue studied (Bach, Pham, Schrag, Tate, & Hargraves, 2004). Yet, in general, it is racial and ethnic minority groups that are known to experience poor health status and increased health risks (Karlsen & Nazroo, 2002). At no time in U.S. history has the overall health status of racial and ethnic minority populations equaled or even approximated that of the majority (European American) (Liao et al., 2004; Ulmer, McFadden, & Nerenz, 2009). (In this chapter, European American is the term used to describe the majority population in the U.S.)

In 2002, the Institute of Medicine concluded that racial disparities in *health status, health care,* and *outcomes* are pervasive. Its report, *Unequal Treatment: Confronting Racial and Ethnic Disparities in Healthcare* called attention to poorer access to health care and worse health outcomes among certain racial and ethnic groups (Smedley, Stith, & Nelson, 2002). Since the release of *Unequal Treatment,* evidence of health and health care disparities among racial and ethnic minorities has continued to be documented (Ulmer et al., 2009).

Before we begin, certain terms need to be defined. *Health* is defined as it was by the World Health Organization in 1948, as a state of complete physical, mental, and social well-being and not merely the absence of disease or infirmity (Jadad & O'Grady, 2008; World Health Organization [WHO], 1979). *Health care* is the prevention, treatment, and management of illness and the preservation of mental and physical well being. *Health care disparities* are the differences or gaps in care experienced by one population compared with another population (Agency for Healthcare Research and Quality [AHRQ], 2008). *Quality of care* is the degree to which health services for individuals and populations increase the likelihood of desired *health outcomes* and are consistent with current professional knowledge (Thom et al., 2006). *Culture* refers to an integrated pattern of learned beliefs and behaviors shared among a group and include: thoughts, styles of communicating, ways of interacting, views on roles and relationships, values, practices, and customs (U.S. Department of Health and Human Services [DHHS], 2001b).

Disparities in Rates of Illness, Mortality, and Care

Racial and ethnic disparities in health are, with few exceptions, remarkably consistent across a range of illnesses and health care services and evidence of such disparities may be found in a review of studies of health areas such as cardiovascular, diabetes, cancer, mental health, obesity, asthma, HIV, cerebra-vascular disease, etc. (Smedley et al., 2002). A few conditions have been selected to illustrate these differences:

Cardiovascular Disease

Cardiovascular disease provides, perhaps, the most convincing evidence of health and health care disparities among minority groups (Mensah, Mokdad, Ford, Greenlund, & Croft, 2005). Much literature indicates that African Americans have higher rates of cardiovascular disease than European Americans (Hozawa, Folsom, Sharrett, & Chambless, 2007; Mensah et al., 2005; Watkins, 2004). African American and Hispanic American patients are more likely to undergo cardiovascular procedures in hospitals that perform a low-volume of such procedures, and these hospitals usually have poorer outcomes than high-volume hospitals with more expertise (Trivedi, Sequist, & Ayanian, 2006); African Americans are more likely than European Americans and Hispanic Americans to die following cardiovascular procedures, despite hospital experience (Trivedi et al., 2006); African Americans are less likely to be catheterized; and, if catheterized, they are 20-50 percent less likely than European Americans to undergo procedures such as angioplasty (Ashton et al., 2003; LaVeist, Nickerson, & Bowie, 2000; Smedley et al., 2002); and, African Americans are less likely to receive such recommended medications as beta blockers, blood clot drugs or aspirin. Similar but less consistent disparities are found for Hispanic American patients (Ashton et al., 2003; LaVeist et al., 2000; Smedley et al., 2002). The summary in *Unequal Treatment* and recent reviews on cardiac care have concluded, after examining the most rigorous studies investigating racial and ethnic differences in angiography, angioplasty, and cardiovascular surgery, that disparities in the quality of medical care are pervasive and that they persist even after adjustment for potentially confounding factors (Mensah et al., 2005; Smedley et al., 2002).

Diabetes

Another area where health disparities are striking is diabetes (Fisher, Goodman, & Chandra, 2008). Diabetes incidence is about 2.4-fold greater in African American women and about 1.5-fold greater in African American men than in their European American counterparts (Brancati, Kao, Folsom, Watson, & Szklo, 2000). African Americans with diabetes are more likely to develop diabetes complications and experience greater disability from the complications than European Americans with diabetes (Black, 2002; Smedley et al., 2002). Racial disparities in diabetes care have been documented in multiple health care settings, with African Americans being less likely than European Americans to achieve adequate glycemic control (Bonds et al., 2003; Harris, Eastman, Cowie, Flegal, & Eberhardt, 1999; McBean, Huang, Virnig, Lurie, & Musgrave, 2003); to receive appropriate eye examinations (Schneider, Zaslavsky, & Epstein, 2002; Virnig et al., 2002); and cholesterol examinations (Heisler, Smith, Hayward, Krein, & Kerr, 2003; Virnig et al., 2002). African Americans are four times as likely as European Americans to undergo a leg amputation, a devastating complication of diabetes and disease of the blood vessels (Fisher et al., 2008). Death rates for people with diabetes are 27% higher for African Americans compared with European Americans (Sequist, Adams, Zhang, Ross-Degnan, & Ayanian, 2006; Smedley et al., 2002; Thom et al., 2006).

Cancer

Cancer incidence and death rates also vary considerably among racial and ethnic groups. The National Cancer Institute reports African American men have a 19% higher cancer incidence rate with a 37% higher death rate than European American men, whereas African American women have a 6% lower cancer incidence rate but a 17% higher death rate than European American women (National Cancer Institute, 2001; Farrow & Vaughan, 1996; Jemal et al., 2008; Shavers & Brown, 2002). Racial/ethnic disparities in cancer outcomes are often attributed to a more advanced stage of disease at diagnosis among minorities (Liu, Kasl, Flannery, Lindo, & Dubrow, 1995; Mayberry et al., 1995; Optenberg et al., 1995; Shavers & Brown, 2002). Yet, even after adjusting for the stage of the cancer at diagnosis, several investigators have reported disparities in cancer survival and mortality by race/ethnic group (Aziz et al.,1996; Bain, Greenberg, & Whitaker, 1986; Boyer-Chammard, Taylor, & Anton-Culver, 1999; Cooper, Yuan, & Rimm, 1997; Fisher, Anderson, Redmond, & Fisher, 1993; Jones et al., 1995; Kimmick, Muss, Case, & Stanley, 1991; McWhorter & Mayer, 1987; Shavers & Brown, 2002; Vernon, Tilley, Neale, & Steinfeldt, 1985). This suggests that factors other than the stage at diagnosis contribute to the disparate cancer mortality observed among racial/ethnic minority populations.

Mental Health

According to the U.S. Surgeon General's report on racial and ethnic disparities in mental health and mental health care, the prevalence of mental disorders is believed to be higher among African Americans than among European Americans, and African Americans are more likely than European Americans to use the emergency room for mental health problems (DHHS, 2001a). The report also found that more so than in other areas of health and medicine, mental health services are "plagued by disparities in the availability of and access to its services," and that "these disparities are viewed readily through the lenses of racial and cultural diversity, age, and gender"(DHHS, 2003; Smedley et al., 2002). Racial and ethnic minorities are less likely to use mental health services due to cultural beliefs related to mental health and the stigma of getting care for mental illnesses. Thus, few racial and ethnic minorities in need of mental health treatment receive treatment (Atdjian & Vega, 2005; AHRQ, 2008). And of those who do, services are often not appropriate to their needs (Borowsky et al., 2000; Cooper et al., 2003; Wang et al., 2005). Documented mental health care disparities include misdiagnosis, over diagnosis of schizophrenia and depression (Kuno & Rothbard, 2005; Minsky, Vega, Miskimen, Gara, & Escobar, 2003), inappropriate use of anti-psychotic medications, the use of these medications at higher dosages, and under-representation in research studies among racial and ethnic minorities (Atdjian & Vega, 2005; Minsky et al., 2003; Miskimen, Marin, & Escobar, 2003; Segal, Bola, & Watson, 1996; Smedley et al., 2002; Snowden, 2001; Strakowski et al., 1996; Takeuchi, Sue, & Yeh, 1995; Vega & Rumbaut, 1991).

Factors Influencing Health Care Disparities

Social Determinants

With universal recognition of these well-documented health and health care disparities, a major focus of health services researchers has been to understand the association between observed differences in health status and risks to health with an emphasis on understanding the role of social determinants of care. Social determinants of care, such as socioeconomic status, education, health insurance, language, employment, transportation, child care, housing and geographic location of the institution where care is to be received have been considered the root causes of health disparities (see Figure 1). It is difficult to disentangle the complex interaction between race/ethnicity and social determinants of care in order to understand direct determinants of treatment and how they may influence the receipt of optimal care (Guidry, Aday, Zhang, & Winn, 1997, 1998; Shavers & Brown, 2002). In a study of cost barriers to treatment, African Americans more frequently than both Hispanic Americans and European Americans reported that they lost their medical insurance coverage after their diagnosis, were denied coverage after changing jobs, and reached their insurance spending limits (Guidry et al., 1998; Shavers & Brown, 2002). However, social determinants only partially explain observed racial differences in health outcomes. African Americans receive a lower quality of health care than European Americans even when social determinants, such as patients' insurance status and income are controlled (Saha, Arbelaez, & Cooper, 2003).

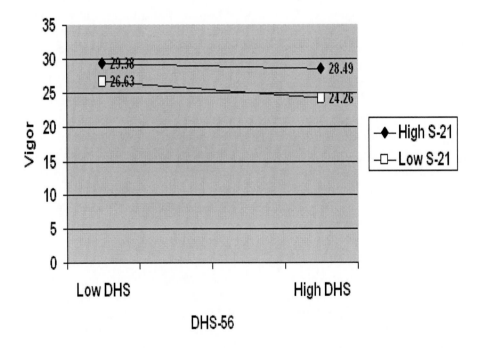

Figure 1. Root Causes of Halth Disparities.

Cultural Barriers

A considerable body of research in this area has documented that **cultural barriers** contribute to lower quality of services. Racial and ethnic disparities in health care occur in the context of cultural differences between physicians and patients. Findings from several studies suggest that a physician's perception of patients may be influenced by cultural characteristics such as race, ethnicity, gender, preferences, and personal biases (Einbinder & Schulman, 2000; Rathore et al., 2000; Shavers & Brown, 2002; van Ryn & Burke, 2000), which may be manifested in differences in patient referral patterns and treatment recommendations (Einbinder & Schulman, 2000; Rathore et al., 2000; Schulman et al., 1999; Shavers & Brown, 2002). A study published by the New England Journal of Medicine (Schulman) examined how race and gender influenced physicians' clinical decisions and recommendations. They utilized actors as patients to present descriptions of chest pain. Their findings suggested that a patient's race and gender influence a physician's recommendation with respect to cardiac catheterization regardless of the patient's clinical characteristics (Schulman et al., 1999). Weisse et al. (2001), using a similar methodology as that of Schulman, found that male physicians prescribed twice the level of analgesic medication for European American patients than for African American patients, and female physicians, in contrast, prescribed higher doses of analgesics for African American than for European American patients. Their findings suggest that male and female physicians may respond differently to gender and/or racial cues (Weisse, Sorum, Sanders, & Syat, 2001). In a survey of eight New York State hospitals, physicians were found to more frequently have negative perceptions of African Americans and persons of low or middle socioeconomic status on a number of dimensions including level of intelligence, personality characteristics, the likelihood of high risk behaviors, and non-compliance as compared to European Americans and persons of high socioeconomic status (Shavers & Brown, 2002; van Ryn & Burke, 2000).

Patient and physician interactions encompass various aspects of care, including whether patients can get appointments in a timely manner, whether they feel respected and listened to, and whether they understand their care. Poor patient-physician communication can result from a number of complex factors including a physician's lack of familiarity with cultural norms, language barriers, a patient's low health literacy, a chaotic work environment, and a lack of time during a visit. Poor patient-physician communication can lead to inefficient care and medical errors. Addressing these health care disparities requires special attention to cultural attitudes and perceptions that affect health behaviors and patterns of health care access and utilization (NHQR, 2008).

Cultural Competency

Culture shapes how we explain and value our world and provides us with the lens through which we find and interpret meaning. The dominant culture for much of United States history stems from the beliefs, norms, and values of European Americans. But today's America is unmistakably multicultural (DHHS, 2001b). And because there are a variety of ways to define a cultural group (e.g., by ethnicity, religion, geographic region, age group, sexual orientation, or profession), many people consider themselves as having multiple cultural identities.

Generally, interpersonal theories of cultural competency assert that communication between patients and physicians may be affected by their cultural differences, and that the resulting miscommunications may negatively affect the quality of care that a patient receives (Perloff, Bonder, Ray, Ray, & Siminoff, 2006; Sue, 2006). These deficits can occur through *instrumental* communication routes, as when language barriers prevent patients from understanding an important diagnosis or prescribed treatment regimen; or, conversely, when they prevent physicians from understanding patient questions or reports of physical symptoms (Ashton et al., 2003). More often however, miscommunications are construed in terms of the *interpersonal* deficits that they can create. For instance, sub par clinical interactions may impact patients' trust of their medical care provider, which contributes to health deficiencies by altering important patient behaviors such as adherence or utilization (Lucas, Michalopoulou, Falzarano, Menon, & Cunningham, 2008).

Culture is important because it bears upon whether people seek help, what types of help they seek, how they approach the clinical setting, how much stigma they attach to an illness, how they communicate their symptoms and which ones they report, and what coping styles and social supports they have (DHHS, 2001b). Some cultures may exhibit sets of symptoms more common in some societies than in others. All cultures also feature strengths, such as resilience and adaptive ways of coping, which may buffer some people from developing certain disorders (DHHS, 2001b; Lightsey, 2006). Correspondingly, medical researchers and health care professionals are increasingly aware that a provider's understanding of culture may play an important role in minority healthcare. Cultural competency is particularly appealing in suggesting that it may be possible to reduce health disparities by recognizing and adjusting qualities of healthcare delivery that reflect patient culture (Lucas, 2008). The multitude of cultures we belong to, and are influenced by, make the term cultural competency a difficult construct in terms of definition, attainment, as well as measurement.

Cultural Competency Theory and Measurement

Researchers have postulated numerous theories of physician cultural competency. For instance, some theories emphasize outcomes in proposing that physicians may attain a cultural competency 'end state' with sufficient training and experience (Betancourt, Green, Carrillo, & Ananeh-Firempong, 2003; Sue, 2001). Other theories emphasize process, with the constantly evolving interplay of culture and medicine mandating that physicians perpetually monitor and revise their cultural competency skill sets (Schim, Doorenbos, Benkert, & Miller, 2007). In addition to these theoretical considerations, researchers have approached cultural competency from many sustainable levels (Perloff et al., 2006; Sue, 2006). For example, some theories of cultural competency have been developed solely to consider characteristics of institutions or particular medical specialties. Although many levels of analysis are viable, the most widely utilized are those that encompass the dyadic or clinical (i.e. physician-patient) interaction. In general, this interpersonal perspective has proposed that physicians' understanding of particular cultural characteristics, values, and traditions may contribute to the quality of treatment that a patient receives. Thus, physician cultural competency may be relevant in ambulatory clinics, emergency rooms, or other settings where individuals receive medical care through face to face interactions with physicians or other health care providers.

Critics of cultural competency research have argued that proposed theories are not well articulated in attempts to alter judgments of physician cultural competency, and there have been few attempts to develop measures that formally map onto them (Fortier & Bishop, 2004; Perloff et al., 2006). Foremost, existing measures predominantly assess physician rather than patient perceptions of cultural competency (Campinha-Bacote, 1999; Culhane-Pera, Reif, Egli, Baker, & Kassekert, 1997; Doorenbos, Schim, Benkert, & Borse, 2005; Weissman et al., 2005). This is problematic not only because physicians may inaccurately perceive or report their own characteristics (van Ryn & Burke, 2000; van Ryn & Fu, 2003), but more importantly because physician judgments may predict minority health and behavior less robustly than patient judgments. Researchers have therefore articulated a need to develop patient report measures of physician cultural competency (Fortier & Bishop, 2004; Perloff et al., 2006).

It is also limiting that many prior attempts to measure cultural competency have been directed only at measuring physicians' objective knowledge of particular subgroups. For instance, cultural competency schemas have been developed to assess physicians' knowledge of characteristics that are associated with African Americans, Hispanic Americans, Asian Americans, and others (for examples see DHHS, 2006). Although appropriate in some contexts or for some training objectives, culture specific 'knowledge quizzes' are problematic in that they may exclude other equally meaningful physician competencies (Sue, Ivey, & Pederson, 1996). In addition, they do not consider that a physician's knowledge of objective cultural characteristics may vastly differ from a patient perceiving him or her to be culturally competent. Finally, because of their varied composition, 'knowledge quizzes' do not generally lend themselves to cross-cultural use. This is usually because different sets of items are required to measure competencies that are associated with specific cultures, which impedes standardized comparison. In sum, researchers have been unable to formulate generally meaningful and standardized comparisons of cultural competency judgments. This is especially troubling not only because it has prevented descriptive research, but also because it has limited attempts to design and evaluate many forms of cultural competency intervention.

Studies that were conducted with an eye towards addressing the limitations and formulating an evidence based cultural competency intervention, are described in this chapter. We developed a theoretically grounded and generally applicable method for measuring cultural competency. This measure is 1) patient rather than physician report, 2) general rather than culture specific, and 3) derived from an established theory of cultural competency. The theoretical model adopted for the development of this measure is based on a well known tripartite model of cultural competency (Sue et al., 1996), in which medical patients consider their physician's knowledge of cultural characteristics, awareness of cultural differences, and skill in incorporating cultural factors while providing health care. In general, we suggest that cultural competency judgments may be quantified using patient rather than physician reports, and that this largely overlooked measurement strategy may enhance research within this area of inquiry.

Following the development of our *Perceived Cultural Competency Scale*, the cultural competency construct and its relationship with other variables that have been proven to be important to health care outcomes was examined. These variables included satisfaction with the visit, having a physician of the same race, having a regular physician, having a physician of the same gender, patient-physician communication, patient participation during the visit, and wait-time for visit and test results. Finally, as a strategy to address health disparities by empowering patients, the implementation of a simple intervention which would address communication barriers between African American patients and their physicians was studied.

As an initial starting point, we opted to administer our measure to a low-income and predominantly African American urban sample. Issues of cultural competency in health care delivery are relevant to a range of cultural and ethnic subgroups, they are historically linked most readily to African American health and illness (Juckett, 2005). Participants were recruited from a diverse group of clinical contexts in the greater Detroit (Michigan) metropolitan area. Our recruitment sites included an ambulatory general medicine clinic, a child and adolescent asthma clinic, a mental health clinic, and a domestic violence medical clinic. Because the asthma clinic was predominantly responsible for treating child and adolescent patients, our recruitment efforts at this site targeted the parents of children who presumably had regular interactions with their child's physician. Participants were approached by one of two female research assistants in the waiting room of their respective clinic prior to their health care visit. They were instructed to think of their latest interaction with the physician as they completed the survey. The content of the survey was adjusted to be 4th grade reading level and patients were given the option to have the survey read to them.

PATIENT CENTERED CULTURAL COMPETENCY RESEARCH

Development of a Patient Report Measure

Based on a priori theoretical considerations of perceived cultural competency (Sue et al., 1996), we designed our measure to assess three specific domains. The domain of cultural knowledge was defined as the extent to which patients believed that their physician was familiar with the culture's specific characteristics. ("How informed does your doctor seem to be about your culture?") The second domain, cultural awareness, was defined as the extent to which patients believed that their physician was aware of differences between cultures. ("Do you feel as though your doctor makes an effort to understand cultural differences?") Finally, the third domain, cultural skill, was defined as the extent to which patients believed that their physician was equipped to treat individuals of the patients' culture. ("Do you think that your doctor is well equipped to treat patients of your ethnic or cultural background?") All questions were answered using appropriately labeled seven-point scales, and a combined cultural competency score was calculated by summing together scores for all nine items. Total scores for the nine item measure could thus range from 9 to 63.

Internal consistencies for our nine item measure and a complete analysis of the psychometric properties of this scale, using both European and African American participants, are described in Lucas, Michalopoulou et al., 2008. Our proposed patient report measure confirmed an a priori hypothesized three factor model that included unique judgments of physicians' cultural knowledge, awareness, and skill (Sue et al., 1996). In addition, these factors indicated a higher order cultural competency construct that was replicated across multiple clinical contexts, and that generally demonstrated convergent and incremental validity when correlated with other related measures. Finally, cultural competency was unrelated to perceived stress, which suggested that these judgments are distinct from at least some aspects of negative affectivity.

Perhaps most importantly, our results suggest that it is possible to measure physician cultural competency not only from the perspective of health care recipients, but also using a general rather than culture specific measure. There are several important advantages to this approach, including the potential to standardize cultural competency research across multiple clinical and cultural contexts. Ultimately, this may afford several new directions for research in this domain. For example, researchers could employ the use of multilevel modeling to examine general versus culture specific elements of physician competency judgments. A related and important direction might be to systematically investigate both antecedent conditions, and the behavioral or health consequences of physician competency judgments. For example, advocates of participatory medicine have suggested that better health outcomes result from patients perceiving 'voice' or involvement in their medical treatment (Haidt, Kroll, & Sharf, 2006). It could be that the effect of participatory medicine on patient outcomes and behavior is mediated in part by its relationship to perceived cultural competency. These results address several important needs in cultural competency research in the way of measurement standardization, and this suggests many possibilities for future research.

Perceptions of Physician's Cultural Competency and Satisfaction with the Visit

The development of the patient report measure described above confirmed the construct validity and reliability of the instrument in an urban sample (Lucas et al., 2008). However, it did not examine if the patient's perception of physician's cultural competency was associated with satisfaction with the visit. Satisfaction with the visit, while not measuring all components of quality of a visit, is a frequently used measure of quality (Smedley et al., 2002). Moreover, collecting satisfaction data and having high satisfaction rates with visits are required by accreditation bodies as a performance indicator (Pellegrin, Stuart, Maree, Frueh, & Ballenger, 2001).

Any examination of the association between patients' perception of physicians' cultural competency and satisfaction has to consider the race of the patient and physician and the consistency of their contact (e.g., regular physician) (Baker, Mainous, Gray, & Love, 2003; Cooper-Patrick et al., 1999). While it is possible that cultural competency mediates the association between race-concordance of patient and physician and the patients' satisfaction, it may be independent. In this case, the different social status may affect the perception of cultural competence. Likewise, the interaction with a regular physician may reflect the selection and continued interaction with a physician who is culturally competent although it is also possible that the interactions occur independent of shared cultural perspective. If cultural competency is associated with satisfaction with the visit in both race-concordant and race-discordant visits, then cultural competency is relevant to the patients as well as to the medical institution; this would provide a target for enhancing satisfaction, improving health outcomes, and thus reducing disparities. To examine this issue, *Perceptions of Physician's Cultural Competency and Satisfaction*, data from a sample of 322 African-American patients were analyzed. (For a detailed analysis see Michalopoulou et al., 2009).

Our results confirmed that patients' perceptions of physicians' cultural competency were positively associated with satisfaction with the visit (Figure 2). This association remained significant even when controlling for patient-physician communication, patient participation in the visit, patient-physician race concordance, regular doctor, clinic, and wait time of visits and test results. Cultural competency scores were higher in visits with the regular physician. These participants who reported on physicians with whom they had an established relationship were also more likely to rate the visit as perfectly satisfied. These findings may be due to feelings of trust and credibility with the physician as tested over time. To have a regular physician involves both initial selection and active maintenance of the relationship. Although cultural competency scores were higher in patient-physician race concordant visits, patient-physician race concordance was not significantly associated with being perfectly satisfied with the visit. Race concordance did not guarantee participants' satisfaction with the visit.

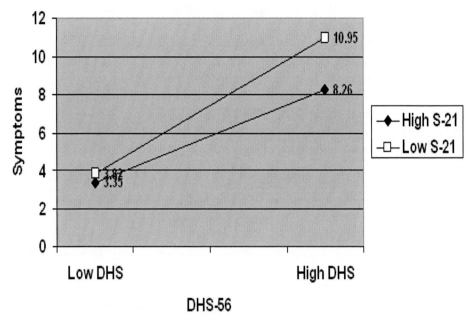

p<**.009**

Figure 2. Patient's Perception of Physician's Cultural Competency.

These results highlight the important role that patients' perceptions of interpersonal processes – in this case, cultural competency – play in the provision of health care to urban African Americans. The measures of cultural awareness, cultural knowledge, cultural skill, and a combined total can be used to help predict satisfaction with the visit. This finding suggests interventions that enhance qualities of health care delivery that reflect patient culture may increase satisfaction, improve clinical outcomes, and reduce health disparities.

Implementing Ask Me 3™ to Improve African American Patient Satisfaction and Perceptions of Physician Cultural Competency

Recent studies have shown that culturally sensitive care is not only dependent on the "sensitivity" of physicians, but also hinges on the development of congruence between the patient's need to relate information regarding his/her illness and the physician's need to listen, diagnose the problem, and prescribe appropriate treatment options (Ashton et al., 2003; Perloff et al., 2006). Patients' communicative behaviors such as, providing a health narrative, asking questions, expressing concerns, and being assertive, influence the physician's behavior and the events of the visit (Ashton et al., 2003; Street, 2001). Patients who ask more questions and express more concerns receive more information from physicians. (Ashton et al., 2003;

Greenfield, Kaplan, & Ware, 1985; Street, 1991, 1992). Similarly, patients who participate actively in the medical interaction are better able to recall what the physician recommended and what health issues were discussed (Ashton et al., 2003; Carter, Inui, Kukull, & Haigh, 1982; Heszen-Klemens & Lapinska, 1984). Physicians perceive patients who state their concerns and ask questions as better communicators and believe they have a better idea what patients need and the extent to which they are satisfying those needs when patients are actively engaged in the interaction (Ashton et al., 2003; Merkel, 1984)

Ethnic and cultural norms influence a patient's propensity to engage in a congruent communicative style during the medical interaction (Ashton et al., 2003). For example, African American patients ask fewer questions, refrain from making inquiries they think the doctor will find objectionable, and feeling the doctor does not respect them, shy away from talking very much about their illness (Perloff et al., 2006). In this way, they confirm physicians' bias that they are less concerned with their health (Perloff et al., 2006).

By focusing on the cultural barriers African American patients experience in communicating with their physicians, we attempted to facilitate congruence in the patient-physician interaction by assigning African American patients the responsibility to participate in the visit. We identified the *Ask Me 3*™ pamphlet (Partnership for Clear Health Communication [PCHC], 2002), a simple patient-centered approach that facilitates clear communication between patients and physicians, to improve health outcomes, by encouraging patients to understand the answers to three simple but essential questions in every health care interaction: What is my main problem? What do I need to do? Why is it important for me to do this? It was developed and is supported by the Partnership for Clear Health Communication, a large coalition of national health care organizations.

Although to our knowledge very little research has been conducted to test the *Ask Me 3*™ pamphlet's efficacy when implemented in clinical practice, existing evidence shows that *Ask Me 3*™ questions serve as an activation tool that encourages patient participation in the health care visit, decision making, establishing good interpersonal relations, and facilitating information exchange and is an important strategy for reducing health disparities. The *Ask Me 3*™ is supported by and cited as a communication resource by numerous professional organizations as well as included in the AMA Manual for Clinicians (Weiss, 2007). Even long after *Ask Me 3*™ is implemented in a practice, many patients continue to ask questions and find them a useful framework for engaging in conversation with their physicians (Mika, Wood, Weiss, & Treviño, 2007). We hypothesized that when African American patients asked those questions, the patient involvement in the clinical process would be promoted, patient satisfaction with the visit would increase, and patients' perceptions of physician cultural competency would improve (Michalopoulou, Falzarano, Arfken, & Rosenberg, 2010).

An intervention group (n=32) received the *Ask Me 3*™ pamphlet as part of their registration process. A control group (n=32) was obtained and included patients that did not receive the *Ask Me 3*™ pamphlet. All research participants were asked to complete the *Perceived Cultural Competency Measure* after the physician consultation. The intervention group was also interviewed regarding the use of the pamphlet following their visit with the physician.

Although the group that received the *Ask Me 3*™ pamphlet consistently reported higher scores for the specific physician encounter variables, there were no statistically significant differences in satisfaction (the primary outcome), cultural competency, fair procedures, nor participation for use of pamphlet versus not. When controlling for regular doctor, satisfaction was significantly different between the two groups (Figure 3). Having a regular doctor drove satisfaction significantly higher. 97% of patients reported finding the brochure helpful. 91% reported knowing more about their medical condition or illness after the visit.

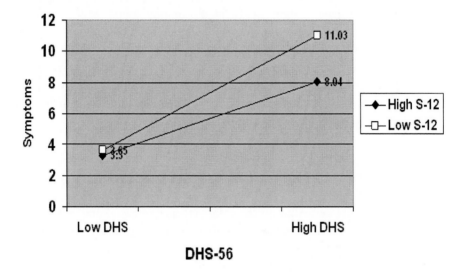

Having a regular doctor drives satisfaction significantly higher $p<.04$

Figure 3. Patient Ratings of the Specific Physician Encounter.

We found a consistent pattern of increased scores on specific physician encounter variables when the *Ask Me 3*™ pamphlet is used. Ratings of satisfaction and cultural competency as well as fair procedures and participation are higher with use of the pamphlet, but not significant.

In this study, having a regular doctor drives satisfaction "significantly" higher. This finding suggests that having a regular doctor has a significant role in patient's satisfaction and is consistent with findings from our previous work wherein perceptions of cultural competency and satisfaction were higher when patients were reporting on their regular physician. These findings suggest that establishing good interpersonal relations, facilitating information exchange and patient involvement in decision making, are important communication goals for physicians to accomplish during interactions with patients. This may improve the selection and retention of a "regular physician," improving patients' perceptions of their physicians' cultural competence, improving health behaviors and health outcomes, thus resulting in reduction of health care disparities (APA, 2003; Lucas et al., 2008).

A short interview following the patient-physician encounter indicated the pamphlet was positively received with the majority of patients asking the questions, writing in the brochure, and reporting on its usefulness. Patients also reported knowing more about their condition or illness following the visit. Patient responses from our interview were similar to those previously documented (Mika et al., 2007). To the question, "Do you feel you know more about your medical condition or illness after the visit?" One respondent said, "Yes, some symptoms I was a bit concerned about may not be as serious as I had believed them to be." Another respondent stated, "Yes, I was more assertive".

This study found the *Ask Me 3*™ pamphlet is an easily implemented, low-cost method to help African American patients increase their participation in the patient-physician interaction. Low-income and minority-group members often lack a sense of self-empowerment in health care settings and cultural norms argue against questioning of authority, but research shows that improving empowerment through a variety of approaches can improve health care and health outcomes (Findley et al., 2004; May, Mendelson, & Ferketich, 1995; Mika et al., 2007; Sarkisian et al., 2005; Valdez, Banerjee, Ackerson, & Fernandez, 2002). It is a low cost and logistically feasible tactic that is readily implemented in primary care settings to facilitate patient–physician interaction, improve satisfaction with the visit and patient perceptions of physician cultural competency.

CONCLUSIONS AND FUTURE RESEARCH

In this chapter we have reviewed much of the evidence of racial and ethnic disparities in health and health care and have discussed contributing factors of these disparities as well as promising strategies to improve health outcomes for racial and ethnic minorities. Racial and ethnic disparities in health care pose ethical and economic dilemmas (Smedley et al., 2002). The productivity and prosperity of a nation is closely linked with its health status, yet if racial and ethnic minorities receive a lower quality of health care, then these groups are further hindered in the efforts to advance economically and professionally (Smedley et al., 2002). As the United States is becoming increasingly diverse, it is likely that excess disease burden will result in a less healthy nation and compromise the nation's future productivity (Bovbjerg, Hatry, & Morley, 2009; Smedley et al., 2002; Waidmann, 2009).

According to projections released by the U.S. Census Bureau, the nation will be more racially and ethnically diverse by midcentury (see Figure 4). Minorities, now roughly one-third of the U.S. population, are expected to become the majority in 2042, with the nation projected to be 54% minority in 2050 (U.S. Census Bureau, 2008).

Over the 10-year period from 2009 through 2018, the total cost of health disparities has been estimated at approximately $337 billion (Waidmann, 2009). With the dramatic changes in the demographic profiles of racial and ethnic minorities that have been projected over the coming decades, these annual costs will more than double (Waidmann, 2009).

Recognizing the complexity of health status and health care disparities, it is imperative for health care researchers to increase awareness through research efforts and the implementation of interventions to create an equal health care environment, unburdened by biases and cultural barriers. More specifically, prospective studies are needed to focus on patient-physician interactions, increasing minority patients' ability to participate in treatment decisions and empower them as self-advocates within health care systems (Smedley et al., 2002). Further, examining the relationship between physician self assessment, patient perspectives and clinical outcomes measures will lead to understanding the specific cultural factors that contribute to disparities and health outcomes.

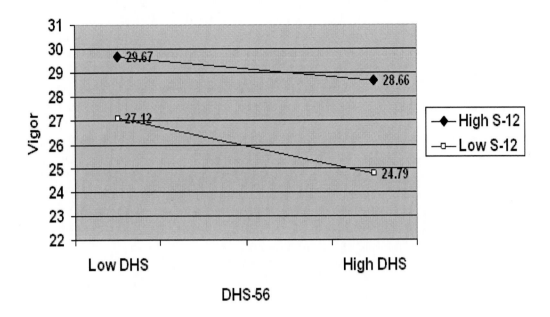

Figure 4.

REFERENCES

Agency for Healthcare Research and Quality [AHRQ]. (2008). *National Healthcare Disparities Report 2008* (Publication No. 09-0002). Rockville, MD: U.S. Department of Health and Human Services AHRQ. Retrieved from www.ahrq.gov/qual/qrdr08.htm

APA. (2003). Guidelines on Multicultural Education, Training, Research, Practice, and Organizational Change for Psychologists. *Am Psychol, 58*(5), 377-402. Retrieved from http://www.apapracticecentral.org/ce/guidelines/multicultural.pdf.

Ashton, C. M., Haidet, P., Paterniti, D. A., Collins, T. C., Gordon, H. S., O'Malley, K., Petersen, L. A., Sharf, B. F., Suarez-Almazor, M. E., Wray, N. P., & Street, R. L.. (2003). Racial and ethnic disparities in the use of health services: Bias, preferences, or poor communication? *Journal of General Internal Medicine, 18*(2), 146-152.

Atdjian, S., & Vega, W. A. (2005). Disparities in Mental Health Treatment in U.S. Racial and Ethnic Minority Groups: Implications for Psychiatrists. *Psychiatr Serv, 56*(12), 1600-1602.

Aziz, H., Hussain, F., Edelman, S., Cirrone, J., Aral, I., Fruchter, R., Homel, P., & Rotman, M. (1996). Age and race as prognostic factors in endometrial carcinoma. *American Journal of Clinical Oncology-Cancer Clinical Trials, 19*(6), 595-600.

Bach, P. B., Pham, H. H., Schrag, D., Tate, R. C., & Hargraves, J. L. (2004). Primary Care Physicians Who Treat Blacks and Whites. *N Engl J Med, 351*(6), 575-584.

Bain, R. P., Greenberg, R. S., & Whitaker, J. P. (1986). Racial differences in survival of women with breast cancer. *Journal of Chronic Diseases, 39*(8), 631-642.

Baker, R., Mainous, A. G., Gray, D. P., & Love, M. M. (2003). Exploration of the relationship between continuity, trust in regular doctors and patient satisfaction with consultations with family doctors. *Scandinavian Journal of Primary Health Care, 21*(1), 27 - 32.

Betancourt, J. R., Green, A. R., Carrillo, J. E., & Ananeh-Firempong, O. (2003). Defining cultural competence: a practical framework for addressing racial/ethnic disparities in health and health care. *Public Health Reports, 118*(4), 293-302.

Black, S. A. (2002). Diabetes, Diversity, and Disparity: What Do We Do With the Evidence? *American Journal of Public Health, 92*(4), 543-548.

Bonds, D. E., Zaccaro, D. J., Karter, A. J., Selby, J. V., Saad, M., & Goff, D. C. (2003). Ethnic and Racial Differences in Diabetes Care. *Diabetes Care, 26*(4), 1040-1046.

Borowsky, S., Rubenstein, L., Meredith, L., Camp, P., Jackson-Triche, M., & Wells, K. (2000). Who is at risk of nondetection of mental health problems in primary care? *Journal of General Internal Medicine, 15*(6), 381-388.

Bovbjerg, R. R., Hatry, H. P., & Morley, E. (2009). Making a Business Case for Reducing Racial and Ethnic Disparities in Health Care: Key Issues and Observations. *The Urban Institute.*

Boyer-Chammard, A., Taylor, T. H., & Anton-Culver, H. (1999). Survival differences in breast cancer among racial/ethnic groups: A population-based study. *Cancer Detection and Prevention, 23*(6), 463-473.

Brancati, F. L., Kao, W. H. L., Folsom, A. R., Watson, R. L., & Szklo, M. (2000). Incident Type 2 Diabetes Mellitus in African American and White Adults: The Atherosclerosis Risk in Communities Study. *JAMA, 283*(17), 2253-2259.

Campinha-Bacote, J. (1999). A model and instrument for addressing cultural competence in health care. *The Journal of Nursing Education, 38*(5), 203-207.

Carter, W. B., Inui, T. S., Kukull, W. A., & Haigh, V. H. (1982). Outcome-based doctor-patient interaction analysis: II. Identifying effective provider and patient behavior. *Med Care, 20*(6), 550-566.

Chandra, A., & Skinner, J. (2003). Geography and Racial Health Disparities (Vol. Working Paper 9513, pp. 1-46). Cambridge, MA: National Bureau of Economic Research.

Cooper-Patrick, L., Gallo, J. J., Gonzales, J. J., Vu, H. T., Powe, N. R., Nelson, C., et al. (1999). Race, Gender, and Partnership in the Patient-Physician Relationship. *JAMA, 282*(6), 583-589.

Cooper, G. S., Yuan, Z., & Rimm, A. A. (1997). Racial disparity in the incidence and case-fatality of colorectal cancer: analysis of 329 United States counties. *Cancer Epidemiology Biomarkers & Prevention, 6*(4), 283-285.

Cooper, L. A., Gonzales, J. J., Gallo, J. J., Rost, K. M., Meredith, L. S., Rubenstein, L. V., Wang, N., & Ford, D. E. (2003). The Acceptability of Treatment for Depression among African-American, Hispanic, and White Primary Care Patients. *Medical Care, 41*(4), 479-489.

Culhane-Pera, K. A., Reif, C., Egli, E., Baker, N. J., & Kassekert, R. (1997). A curriculum for multicultural education in family medicine. *Family Medicine, 29*(10), 719-723.

Doorenbos, A. Z., Schim, S. M., Benkert, R., & Borse, N. N. (2005). Psychometric Evaluation of the Cultural Competence Assessment Instrument Among Healthcare Providers. *Nursing Research, 54*(5), 324-331.

Einbinder, L. C., & Schulman, K. A. (2000). The Effect of Race on the Referral Process for Invasive Cardiac Procedures. *Med Care Res Rev, 57*(suppl. 1), 162-180.

Farrow, D. C., & Vaughan, T. L. (1996). Determinants of survival following the diagnosis of esophageal adenocarcinoma (United States). *Cancer Causes and Control, 7*(3), 322-327.

Findley, S., Irigoyen, M., Sanchez, M., Guzman, L., Mejia, M., Sajous, M., Levine, D., Chimkin, F., Chen, S. (2004). Community empowerment to reduce childhood immunization disparities in New York City. *Ethnicity & Disease, 14*(3 Suppl 1), S134-S141.

Fisher, E., R., Anderson, S., Redmond, C., & Fisher, B. (1993). Pathologic findings from the national surgical adjuvant breast project protocol B-06 10-year pathologic and clinical prognostic discriminants. *Cancer, 71*(8), 2507-2514.

Fisher, E. S., Goodman, D. C., & Chandra, A. (2008). *Disparities in health and health care among Medicare Beneficiaries: A Brief report of the Dartmouth Atlas Project*. Princeton, NJ: Robert Wood Johnson Foundationo. Document Number)

Fortier, J. P., & Bishop, D. (2004). *Setting the agenda for research on cultural competence in health care: Final report*: U.S. Department of Health and Human Serivces, Office of Minority Health and Agency for Health Care Research and Quality.

Greenfield, S., Kaplan, S., & Ware, J. E. (1985). Expanding patient involvement in care. Effects of patient outcomes. *Ann Intern Med, 102*(4), 520-528.

Gregg, E. W., Gu, Q., Cheng, Y. J., Venkat Narayan, K. M., & Cowie, C. C. (2007). Mortality Trends in Men and Women with Diabetes, 1971 to 2000. *Annals of Internal Medicine, 147*(3), 149-155.

Groeneveld, P. W., Heidenreich, P. A., & Garber, A. M. (2005). Trends in implantable cardioverter-defibrillator racial disparity: The importance of geography. *Journal of the American College of Cardiology, 45*(1), 72-78.

Guidry, J. J., Aday, L. A., Zhang, D., & Winn, R. J. (1997). Transportation as a barrier to cancer treatment. *Cancer Practice, 5*(6), 361-366.

Guidry, J. J., Aday, L. A., Zhang, D., & Winn, R. J. (1998). Cost considerations as potential barriers to cancer treatment. *Cancer Practice, 6*(3), 182-187.

Haidt, P., Kroll, T. L., & Sharf, B. F. (2006). The complexity of patient participation: Lessons learned from patients' illness narratives. *Patient Education and Counseling, 62*, 323-329.

Harris, M. I., Eastman, R. C., Cowie, C. C., Flegal, K. M., & Eberhardt, M. S. (1999). Racial and ethnic differences in glycemic control of adults with type 2 diabetes. *Diabetes Care, 22*(3), 403-408.

Heisler, M., Smith, D. M., Hayward, R. A., Krein, S. L., & Kerr, E. A. (2003). Racial Disparities in Diabetes Care Processes, Outcomes, and Treatment Intensity *Medical Care, 41*(11), 1221-1232.

Heo, M., Allison, D., & Fontaine, K. (2004). Overweight, obesity, and colorectal cancer screening: Disparity between men and women. *BMC Public Health, 4*(1), 53.

Heszen-Klemens, I., & Lapinska, E. (1984). Doctor-patient interaction, patients' health behavior and effects of treatment. *Soc Sci Med, 19*(1), 9-18.

Hozawa, A., Folsom, A. R., Sharrett, A. R., & Chambless, L. E. (2007). Absolute and Attributable Risks of Cardiovascular Disease Incidence in Relation to Optimal and Borderline Risk Factors: Comparison of African American With White Subjects--Atherosclerosis Risk in Communities Study. *Arch Intern Med, 167*(6), 573-579.

Jadad, A. R., & O'Grady, L. (2008). How should health be defined? *BMJ, 337*, 1363-1364.

Jazieh, A. R., & Buncher, C. R. (2002). Racial and Age-Related Disparities in Obtaining Screening Mammography: Results of a Statewide Database. *Southern Medical Journal, 95*(10), 1145-1148.

Jemal, A., Siegel, R., Ward, E., Hao, Y., Xu, J., Murray, T., & Thun, M. J. (2008). Cancer Statistics, 2008. *CA Cancer J Clin, 58*(2), 71-96.

Jerant, A. F., Franks, P., Jackson, J. E., & Doescher, M. P. (2004). Age-Related Disparities in Cancer Screening: Analysis of 2001 Behavioral Risk Factor Surveillance System Data. *Ann Fam Med, 2*(5), 481-487.

Jones, G. W., Mettlin, C., Murphy, G. P., Guinan, P., Herr, H. W., Hussey, D. H., Chmiel, J. S., Fremgen, A. M., Clive, R. E., Zuber-Ocwieja, E. E., & Winchester, D. P, (1995). Patterns of Care for Carcinoma of the Prostate Gland: Results of a National Survey of 1984 and 1990. *Journal of the American College of Surgeons, 180*(5), 545-554.

Juckett, G. (2005). Cross-cultural medicine. *American Family Physician, 72*(11), 2267-2274.

Karlsen, S., & Nazroo, J. Y. (2002). Relation Between Racial Discrimination, Social Class, and Health Among Ethnic Minority Groups. *Am J Public Health, 92*(4), 624-631.

Kimmick, G., Muss, H. B., Case, L. D., & Stanley, V. (1991). A comparison of treatment outcomes for black patients and white patients with metastatic breast cancer. The piedmont oncology association experience. *Cancer, 67*(11), 2850-2854.

Kuno, E., & Rothbard, A. B. (2005). The Effect of Income and Race on Quality of Psychiatric Care in Community Mental Health Centers. *Community Mental Health Journal, 41*(5), 613-622.

LaVeist, T. A., Nickerson, K. J., & Bowie, J. V. (2000). Attitudes about Racism, Medical Mistrust, and Satisfaction with Care among African American and White Cardiac Patients. *Medical Care Research and Review, 57,* 146-161.

Liao, Y., Tucker, P., Okoro, C. A., Giles, W. H., Mokdad, A. H., & Harris, V. B. (2004). REACH 2010 Surveillance for Health Status in Minority Communities: United States, 2001-2002 *Morbidity and Mortality Weekly Report: Surveillance Summaries, 53*(SS06), 1-36.

Lightsey, O. R., Jr. (2006). Resilience, Meaning, and Well-Being. *The Counseling Psychologist, 34*(1), 96-107.

Liu, W. L., Kasl, S., Flannery, J. T., Lindo, A., & Dubrow, R. (1995). The accuracy of prostate cancer staging in a population-based tumor registry and its impact on the black-white stage difference. *Cancer Causes & Control, 6*(5), 425-430.

Lucas, T., Michalopoulou, G., Falzarano, P., Menon, S., & Cunningham, W. (2008). Healthcare Provider Cultural Competency: Development and Initial Validation of a Patient Report Measure. *Health Psychology 27*(2), 185-193.

May, K. M., Mendelson, C., & Ferketich, S. (1995). Community Empowerment in Rural Health Care. *Public Health Nursing, 12*(1), 25-30.

Mayberry, R. M., Coates, R. J., Hill, H. A., Click, L. A., Chen, V. W., Austin, D. F., Redmond, C. K., Fenoglio-Preiser, C. M., Hunter, C. P., Haynes, M. A., Muss, H. B., Welsey, M. N., Greenberg, R. S., & Edwards, B. K. (1995). Determinants of Black/White Differences in Colon Cancer Survival. *J. Natl. Cancer Inst., 87*(22), 1686-1693.

McBean, A. M., Huang, Z., Virnig, B. A., Lurie, N., & Musgrave, D. (2003). Racial Variation in the Control of Diabetes Among Elderly Medicare Managed Care Beneficiaries. *Diabetes Care, 26*(12), 3250-3256.

McWhorter, W. P., & Mayer, W. J. (1987). Black/white differences in type of initial breast cancer treatment and implications for survival. *Am J Public Health, 77*(12), 1515-1517.

Meara, E. R., Richards, S., & Cutler, D. M. (2008). The Gap Gets Bigger: Changes In Mortality And Life Expectancy, By Education, 1981-2000. *Health Aff, 27*(2), 350-360.

Mensah, G. A., Mokdad, A. H., Ford, E. S., Greenlund, K. J., & Croft, J. B. (2005). State of Disparities in Cardiovascular Health in the United States. *Circulation, 111*(10), 1233-1241.

Merkel, W. T. (1984). Physician perception of patient satisfaction. Do doctors know which patients are satisfied? *Med Care, 22*(5), 453-459.

Michalopoulou, G., Falzarano, P., Arfken, C., Rosenberg, D. (2009). Physicians' Cultural Competency as Perceived by African American Patients. *JNMA, 101*(9), 893-899

Michalopoulou, G., Falzarano, P., Arfken, C., Rosenberg, D. (2010). Implementing Ask Me 3™ to Improve African American Patient Satisfaction and Perceptions of Physician Cultural Competency. *Journal of Cultural Diversity, 17*(2), 62-68.

Mika, V. S., Wood, P. R., Weiss, B. D., & Treviño, L. (2007). Ask Me 3: Improving Communication in a Hispanic Pediatric Outpatient Practice. *American Journal of Health Behavior, 31*(supp), S115-S121

Minsky, S., Vega, W., Miskimen, T., Gara, M., & Escobar, J. (2003). Diagnostic Patterns in Latino, African American, and European American Psychiatric Patients. *Arch Gen Psychiatry, 60*(6), 637-644.

Miskimen, T., Marin, H., & Escobar, J. (2003). Psychopharmacological research ethics: special issues affecting US ethnic minorities. *Psychopharmacology, 171*(1), 98-104.

National Cancer Institute. (2001). *SEER cancer statistics review, 1973-1998*. Bethesda, MD: National Cancer Institute, US National Institutes of Health. Surveillance, Epidemiology, and End Results (SEER) Program (www.seer.cancer.gov).

Optenberg, S. A., Thompson, I. M., Friedrichs, P., Wojcik, B., Stein, C. R., & Kramer, B. (1995). Race, Treatment, and Long-term Survival From Prostate Cancer in an Equal-Access Medical Care Delivery System. *JAMA, 274*(20), 1599-1605.

Partnership for Clear Health Communication. (2002). Ask Me 3. Retrieved from www.pfizerhealthliteracy.com/physicians-providers/pchc-askme3.html.

Pellegrin, K. L., Stuart, G. W., Maree, B., Frueh, B. C., & Ballenger, J. C. (2001). A Brief Scale for Assessing Patients' Satisfaction With Care in Outpatient Psychiatric Services. *Psychiatr Serv, 52*(6), 816-819.

Perloff, R. M., Bonder, B., Ray, G. B., Ray, E. B., & Siminoff, L. A. (2006). Doctor-Patient Communication, Cultural Competence, and Minority Health: Theoretical and Empirical Perspectives. *American Behavioral Scientist, 49*(6), 835-852.

Rathore, S. S., Lenert, L. A., Weinfurt, K. P., Tinoco, A., Taleghani, C. K., Harless, W., & Schulman, K. A. (2000). The effects of patient sex and race on medical students' ratings of quality of life. *American Journal of Medicine, 108*(7), 561-566.

Saha, S., Arbelaez, J. J., & Cooper, L. A. (2003). Patient-Physician Relationships and Racial Disparities in the Quality of Health Care. *Am J Public Health, 93*(10), 1713-1719.

Sarkisian, C. A., Brusuelas, R. J., Steers, W. N., Davidson, M. B., Brown, A. F., Norris, K. C., Anderson, R. M., Mangione, C. M. (2005). Using focus groups of older African Americans and Latinos with diabetes to modify a self-care empowerment intervention. *Ethn Dis, 15*(2), 283-291.

Schim, S. M., Doorenbos, A., Benkert, R., & Miller, J. (2007). Culturally Congruent Care: Putting the Puzzle Together. *J Transcult Nurs, 18*(2), 103-110.

Schneider, E. C., Zaslavsky, A. M., & Epstein, A. M. (2002). Racial Disparities in the Quality of Care for Enrollees in Medicare Managed Care. *JAMA, 287*(10), 1288-1294.

Schulman, K. A., Berlin, J. A., Harless, W., Kerner, J. F., Sistrunk, S., Gersh, B. J., Dubé, R., Taleghani, C. K., Burke, J. E., Williams, S., Eisenberg, J. M., Escarce, J. J.& Ayers, W. (1999). The Effect of Race and Sex on Physicians' Recommendations for Cardiac Catheterization. N Engl J Med, 340(8), 618-626.

Segal, S. P., Bola, J. R., & Watson, M. A. (1996). Race, quality of care, and antipsychotic prescribing practices in psychiatric emergency services. *Psychiatr Serv, 47*(3), 282-286.

Sequist, T. D., Adams, A., Zhang, F., Ross-Degnan, D., & Ayanian, J. Z. (2006). Effect of Quality Improvement on Racial Disparities in Diabetes Care. *Arch Intern Med, 166*(6), 675-681.

Shavers, V. L., & Brown, M. L. (2002). Racial and Ethnic Disparities in the Receipt of Cancer Treatment. *J. Natl. Cancer Inst., 94*(5), 334-357.

Smedley, B. D., Stith, A. Y., & Nelson, A. R. (2002). *Unequal Treatment: Confronting Racial and Ethnic Disparities in Health Care. Institute of Medicine.* Washington DC: National Academy Press.

Snowden, L. R. (2001). Barriers to effective mental health services for African Americans. *Mental Health Services Research, 3,* 181-187.

Strakowski, S. M., Flaum, M., Amador, X., Bracha, H. S., Pandurangi, A. K., Robinson, D., & Tohen, M. (1996). Racial differences in the diagnosis of psychosis. *Schizophrenia Research, 21*(2), 117-124.

Street, R. L. (1991). Information-giving in medical consultations: the influence of patients' communicative styles and personal characteristics. *Soc Sci Med, 32*(5), 541-548.

Street, R. L. (1992). Communicative styles and adaptations in physician-parent consultations. *Soc Sci Med, 34*(10), 1155-1163.

Street, R. L. (2001). *Active patients as powerful communicators: the linguistic foundation of participation in health care* (2nd ed.). Chichester: John Wiley.

Sue, D. W. (2001). Multidimensional Facets of Cultural Competence. *The Counseling Psychologist, 29*(6), 790-821.

Sue, D. W., Ivey A.E., & Pederson, P. B. (1996). *A theory of multicultural counseling and therapy*. San Francisco, CA: Brooks/Cole Publishing.

Sue, S. (2006). Cultural competency: From philosophy to research and practice. *Journal of Community Psychology, 34*(2), 237-245.

Takeuchi, D. T., Sue, S., & Yeh, M. (1995). Return rates and outcomes from ethnicity-specific mental health programs in Los Angeles. *American Journal of Public Health, 855,* 638-643.

Thom, T., Haase, N., Rosamond, W., Howard, V. J., Rumsfeld, J., Manolio, T., et al. (2006). Heart Disease and Stroke Statistics--2006 Update: A Report From the American Heart Association Statistics Committee and Stroke Statistics Subcommittee. *Circulation, 113*(6), e85-151.

Trivedi, A. N., Sequist, T. D., & Ayanian, J. Z. (2006). Impact of hospital volume on racial disparities in cardiovascular procedure mortality. *Journal of the American College of Cardiology 47(2), pp. 417-424., 47*(2), 417-424.

Ulmer, C., McFadden, B., & Nerenz, D. R. (2009). *Race, Ethnicity, and Language Data: Standardization for Health Care Quality Improvement*. Washington, DC: National Academies Press.

U.S. Census Bureau. (2008). *An Older and More Diverse Nation by Midcentury*. Retrieved from http://www.census.gov/PressRelease/www/releases/archives/population/012496.html.

U.S. Department of Health and Human Services [DHHS]. (2001a). *Mental Health: A Report of the Surgeon General*. Rockville, MD: U.S. Department of Health and Human Services, Substance Abuse and Mental Health Services Administration, Center for Mental Health Services, National Institutes of Health, National Institute of Mental Health. Retrieved from http://www.surgeongeneral.gov/library/mentalhealth/home.html.

U.S. Department of Health and Human Services [DHHS]. (2001b). *Mental Health: Culture, Race, and Ethnicity: A supplement to Mental Health: A Report of the Surgeon General*. Rockville, MD: U.S. Department of Health and Human Services, Substance Abuse and Mental Health Services Administration, Center for Mental Health Services, National Institute of Mental Health. Retrieved from http://www.surgeongeneral.gov/library/mentalhealth/cre/.

U.S. Department of Health and Human Services [DHHS]. (2003). *Developing Cultural Competence in Disaster Mental Health Programs: Guiding Principles and Recommendations*. Rockville, MD: U.S. Department of Health and Human Services, Substance Abuse and Mental Health Services Administration, Center for Mental Health Services, National Institute of Mental Health. Retrieved from http://mentalhealth.samhsa.gov/publications/allpubs/sma03-3828/default.asp.

U.S. Department of Health and Human Services [DHHS]. (2006). Cultural competence resources for health care providers (DHHS Pub. No. SMA 3828). Rockville, MD: U.S. Department of Health and Human Services, Substance Abuse and Mental Health Services Administration, Center for Mental Health Services, National Institute of Mental Health Retrieved from http://www.hrsa.gov/culturalcompetence

Valdez, A., Banerjee, K., Ackerson, L., & Fernandez, M. (2002). A Multimedia Breast Cancer Education Intervention for Low-Income Latinas *Journal of Community Health* *27*(1), 33-51.

van Ryn, M., & Burke, J. (2000). The effect of patient race and socio-economic status on physicians' perceptions of patients. *Social Science & Medicine, 50*(6), 813-828.

van Ryn, M., & Fu, S. S. (2003). Paved With Good Intentions: Do Public Health and Human Service Providers Contribute to Racial/Ethnic Disparities in Health? *American Journal of Public Health, 93*(2), 248-255.

Vega, W. A., & Rumbaut, R. G. (1991). Ethnic Minorities and Mental Health. *Annual Review of Sociology, 17*(1), 351-383.

Vernon, S. W., Tilley, B. C., Neale, A. V., & Steinfeldt, L. (1985). Ethnicity, Survival, and Delay in Seeking Treatment for the Symptoms of Breast Cancer *Cancer, 55*(7), 1563-1571.

Virnig, B. A., Lurie, N., Huang, Z., Musgrave, D., McBean, A. M., & Dowd, B. (2002). Racial Variation In Quality Of Care Among Medicare+Choice Enrollees. *Health Aff, 21*(6), 224-230.

Waidmann, T. (2009). Estimating the Cost of Racial and Ethnic Health Disparities. *The Urban Institute*.

Wang, P. S., Lane, M., Olfson, M., Pincus, H. A., Wells, K. B., & Kessler, R. C. (2005). Twelve-Month Use of Mental Health Services in the United States: Results From the National Comorbidity Survey Replication. *Arch Gen Psychiatry, 62*(6), 629-640.

Watkins, L. O. (2004). Epidemiology and burden of cardiovascular disease. *Clinical Cardiology, 27*(S3), 2-6.

Weiss, B. D. (2007). *Health literacy: can your patients understand you?* Chicago: American Medical Association and AMA Foundation. Document Number)

Weisse, C., Sorum, P., Sanders, K., & Syat, B. (2001). Do gender and race affect decisions about pain management? *Journal of General Internal Medicine, 16*(4), 211-217.

Weissman, J. S., Betancourt, J., Campbell, E. G., Park, E. R., Kim, M., Clarridge, B., Blumenthal, D., Lee, K. C., Maina, A. W. (2005). Resident Physicians' Preparedness to Provide Cross-Cultural Care. *JAMA, 294*(9), 1058-1067.

World Health Organization. (1979). *Health For All.* Paper presented at the International Conference on Primary Health Care. Retrieved from www.who.int/about/definition/en/print.html.

In: Health Psychology
Editor: Ryan E. Murphy, pp. 59-78

ISBN 978-1-61728-981-1
© 2010 Nova Science Publishers, Inc.

Chapter 3

THE DYNAMICS OF PAIN AND AFFECT: TOWARD A SALIENT PHENOTYPE FOR CHRONIC PAIN

Patrick H. Finan[1] and Howard Tennen[2]
[1]Department of Psychology, Arizona State University
[2]Department of Community Medicine, University of Connecticut

ABSTRACT

For decades, clinical evidence has suggested that the subjective experiences of pain and emotion are intertwined. More recently, neuroimaging data have supported this notion, implicating both cortical and subcortical brain regions in overlapping regulatory roles for pain and emotion. There is a need presently to focus research efforts on the identification of salient phenotypes that more fully explicate the relation of pain and emotion, specifically in the context of chronic pain. This can be accomplished through the identification of endogenous brain mechanisms that can be translated into clinically relevant markers of vulnerability and resilience, and through the description of naturalistic processes that promote or inhibit adaptation to chronic pain. The present chapter focuses on how variability in the dynamics of the affect system and its covariation with pain processes influence both brain function and daily experience with chronic pain. Specifically, the chapter addresses the roles of both positive and negative affects during states of heightened pain and provides a rationale for why characterization of affective reactivity to pain at the levels of brain function and daily process is essential to the evolution of more highly targeted treatment strategies.

INTRODUCTION

A genetic basis for individual differences in the perception of pain has been proposed (Diatchenko, Nackley, Tchivileva, Shabalina, & Maixner, 2007; Nielsen et al., 2008), and genetic variability has been identified in a variety of chronic pain conditions, including chronic low back pain (Battié, Videman, Levalahti, Gill, & Kaprio, 2007), fibromyalgia (Markkula et al., 2009), rheumatoid arthritis (Barton et al., 2008), and osteoarthritis (Valdes & Spector, 2010). The primary thrust of genetic research on chronic pain has been to better understand both the basic function of the organic precursors to chronic pain, as well as the manner in which they interact with environmental, pharmacological, and other genetic factors to predict adaptation, symptom trajectory, and treatment response. However, as with other areas of genetic inquiry, many of the reported   associations with common chronic pain conditions have never been replicated, or have been non-replicated (e.g., Gursoy, 2002; Tander et al., 2008), fueling uncertainty about the validity of the initial results.

A major threat to the validity of genetic associations is phenotypic misspecification or underspecification. A phenotype is the observable expression of the functions of a gene or set of genes. Phenotypic misspecification occurs when the phenotype chosen for study does not adequately reflect (at least partially) the true phenotype generated by the chosen genotype. To combat this problem, it is necessary to operationalize salient phenotypes that reflect both the functional workings of the target genetic variation and some process, either brain-based or subjective, that is intermediate to the disease. The purpose of the present chapter is to identify salient phenotypes that are relevant to many common chronic pain disorders. In that effort, we have chosen to describe a set of processes that show promise in both capturing genetic variation and reflecting the daily experience with chronic pain: The dynamic relations between pain and affect.

Clinical research has, for years, identified a link between the subjective experience of pain and affect in chronic pain patients (Turk & Okifuji, 2002), and epidemiological evidence suggests there is a high comorbidity between mood and anxiety disorders and chronic pain (McWilliams, Cox, & Enns, 2003; Ohayon & Schatzberg, in press). Pain is an adaptive phenomenon that alerts an organism of a sensory threat and motivates immediate behavioral change (Eccleston & Crombez, 1999). Often coupled with pain is the perception of a specific negative emotion, such as fear, anger, or despair, or a more general state of negative affect (Bruehl, Burns, Chung, Ward, & Johnson, 2002; Gaskin, Greene, Robinson, & Geisser, 1992; Turk, Robinson, & Burwinkle, 2004). Chronic pain has also been associated with a disruption in the ability to experience positive affect, independent of its association with negative affect (Zautra, Fasman et al., 2005), suggesting that the linkages between pain and affect are dynamic and involve the whole affect system, rather than a single valenced response (Cacioppo, Gardner, & Berntson, 1999). Affect can be defined as an umbrella term that encompasses specific emotions (i.e., short term, high intensity), moods (i.e., longer term, low intensity), or coping processes that result from the appraisal of personally relevant stimuli (Gross, 1998; Gross & Thompson, 2007). The coupling of pain and affect is particularly apparent among people who suffer from chronic pain, as these individuals are in a state of constant adaptation to both tonic and phasic physiological challenges. These constant challenges, in turn, lead to a persistent engagement of the affective system to aid in interpretation of the physiological state of the body and motivate behavioral change (Craig, 2003a). Despite these reported associations, the mechanisms through which pain directly influences and is influenced by the upregulation of negative affect and downregulation of positive affect are not fully understood, and subject to individual differences. Still, a growing body of evidence suggests that chronic pain processes are best characterized by their dynamic relations with both negative and positive affective states.

Medicine has already begun to respond to the empirically founded connection between pain and affect, as evidenced by the common treatment of some chronic pain conditions with anti-depressant medications (Kroenke et al., 2009), as well as the referral of many chronic pain patients to mental health care for cognitive-behavioral therapy, among other psychotherapeutic practices (Hoffman, Papas, Chatkoff, & Kerns, 2007). But treatment outcomes are still modest at best, with variability between chronic pain groups, as well as between classes of drugs and/or psychological treatment (Goldenberg, 2007; Morley & Williams, 2006). Some promise for improvement in the treatment of pain and mood symptoms in chronic pain patients lies in the description of the genetic contribution to chronic pain (Diatchenko et al., 2007).

Because the development and maintenance of many chronic pain conditions are characterized by the dynamic relations of pain and affect, and not pain alone, there is a need to establish salient candidate phenotypes for chronic pain that incorporate aspects of both phenomena. This view is supported by recent evidence that the proportion of genetic variability in pain sensitivity differs widely between responses to thermal pain stimulation and the cold pressor test (Nielsen et al., 2008). Thus, genetic variability in a particular phenotype, pain sensitivity, does not generalize across stimulus and measurement paradigms. It follows from these observations that genetic variability in chronic pain will be insufficiently explained by the examination of phenotypes that do not include the affective component of pain.

ESTABLISHING A VALID PHENOTYPE

Emerging in the broad field of behavioral genetics is the notion that advances in the statistical, computational, and molecular measurement of genetic effects on common diseases are outpacing advances in the identification and measurement of complex phenotypes (Freimer & Sabatti, 2003). Attempts to capture genetic variability at the genome-wide level have begun to bear fruit; novel variants for such chronic pain conditions as osteoarthritis (Kerkhof et al., 2010) and rheumatoid arthritis (Eyre et al., 2009) have been identified and replicated. But these gene-discovery investigations have limited explanatory reach for multifactorial disorders subject to influence from a variety of intermediate phenotypes with complex psychological loadings. Therefore, genome-wide association at the phenotypic level of disease or syndrome falls short of describing the potentially rich products of genetic variation intermediate to that association. A patient's experience with chronic pain is subject to individual differences in a variety of factors, including pain perception and tolerance (Nielsen, Price, Vassend, Stubhaug, & Harris, 2005), past trauma history (Defrin et al., 2008), depression history (Tennen, Affleck, & Zautra, 2006), and capacity for affective regulation (Finan, Zautra, & Davis, 2009; Zautra, Affleck, Tennen, Reich, & Davis, 2005). Therefore, a single association or even series of associations at the syndromal level (i.e., diagnostic status) is unlikely to translate into treatment strategies that, in fulfillment of the mandate of the biopsychosocial model of chronic pain management (Gatchel, Peng, Peters, Fuchs, & Turk, 2007), improve physiological, functional, affective, and quality of life outcomes.

A growing chorus of scholars is calling for greater focus on operationalizing phenotypes that can be systematically studied in genetic association designs (Bilder et al., 2009; Gerlai, 2002; Houle, 2010). Bilder et al. (2009) highlight several considerations for establishing a salient, valid phenotype, including: 1) identifying genetic variability in the phenotype; 2)

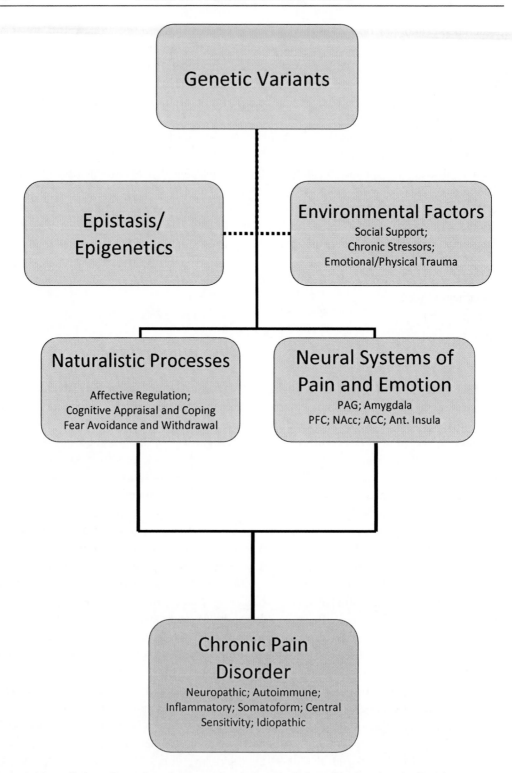

Figure 1. Naturalistic and neural mechanisms of genetic association with chronic pain disorders.

determining that the phenotype is reliable and psychometrically valid; 3) ensuring the phenotype is relevant to process-based and clinical constructs in humans; 4) ensuring the phenotype is implicated in known strategies for treatment of the disease or syndrome of interest; and 5) gathering available evidence for environmental influences on the phenotype. Building off of those suggestions, we have conceptualized a hierarchical model for establishing salient phenotypes in chronic pain research, depicted in Figure 1. In the model, genetic variants are expressed at two intermediate phenotypic levels: The neural or endophenotypic level, and the naturalistic phenotypic level. The pathways from genotype to phenotype can be modulated *in vitro* by epigenetic factors, such as plasticity in cellular signaling pathways, or epistasis characterized by gene-by-gene interactions. Additionally, environmental factors, such as stress or trauma, are likely to influence genetic effects on disease (Caspi & Moffitt, 2006). Ultimately, some combination of phenotypic expression at the endophenotypic and naturalistic phenotypic levels yields clinical symptomatology and disease. Therefore, salient phenotypes for chronic pain should be present at both the neural and naturalistic levels, and meaningfully contribute to the development, maintenance, and day-to-day experience of a particular disorder of interest. To identify salient phenotypes for chronic pain, we first provide neural evidence for the dynamic relations between pain and affect.

NEURAL EVIDENCE

Nociceptive pain transmission begins in the periphery when damaging or potentially damaging stimuli activate the primary afferent nociceptive neurons: small-diameter C- and Aδ-fibers. Small-diameter neurons are grouped into several classes according to their selective transmission of specific sensory stimuli, including mechanical and heat nociception, as well as various other forms of information regarding the state of the skin and viscera, such as innocuous changes in temperature or immune activity (Craig, 2003b). Primary nociceptors transmit pain and other interoceptive signals to the second-order nociceptive neurons, terminating in Laminae I, II, and V in the dorsal horn of the spinal cord (Craig, 2002). Second-order neurons subsequently transmit the sensory information through a variety of ascending nociceptive pathways, including the spinothalamic tract, spinoreticular pathway, spinohypothalamic pathway, and the spinoamygdalar pathway, with final projections to a variety of cortical regions (Westlund, 2005).

Descending modulatory control over sensory stimuli begins in the cortex, where it is influenced by interactive processes subserving emotion regulation. Gross and Thompson (2007) define emotions as, "...multifaceted, whole-body phenomena that involve loosely-coupled changes in the domains of subjective experience, behavior, and central and peripheral physiology," (p. 4), and emotion regulation as, "...the heterogeneous set of processes by which emotions are themselves regulated" (p. 7). Top-down regulation of emotions and, more broadly, affect involves attentional control and cognitive appraisal/reappraisal, and requires input from separate areas of the anterior cingulate cortex (ACC) and prefrontal cortex (Bush, Luu, & Posner, 2000; Ochsner, Bunge, Gross, & Gabrieli, 2002; Ochsner & Gross, 2007). Several lines of evidence support a dual process conceptualization of pain and affective regulation.

Perception of pain results in the deployment of attentional resources from the frontal and prefrontal cortexes (Legrain et al., 2009; Villemure & Bushnell, 2009), and motivates a negative affective response that involves the synchronized recruitment of the ACC and insular cortex, with downstream subcortical projections to the amygdala, thalamus, periaqueductal gray area, and brainstem (Craig, Chen, Bandy, & Reiman, 2000; Price, 2000; Rainville, 2002; Tracey & Mantyh, 2007; Tracey et al., 2002). Early imaging evidence showed that ratings of pain unpleasantness could be specifically modulated under hypnotic suggestion without additionally modulating the perception of pain intensity (Rainville, Duncan, Price, Carrier, & Bushnell, 1997), providing a neural basis for 'pain affect.' This finding was coupled with the observation that ACC activation, and not activation in the sensory cortexes, correlated with reductions in pain unpleasantness (Rainville et al., 1997). More recent studies have revealed distinct activation in the ACC for the affective component of pain processing, separate from cognitive attention to pain (Villemure & Bushnell, 2009).

Imaging studies have clarified that the entire affect system, not just negative affective circuitry, is engaged in the pain response. Pain inhibits the reward response to morphine in rodent models by activating the mesolimbic k-opioid and dopaminergic systems in the ventral tegmental area of the nucleus accumbens (Narita et al., 2004). It has been suggested that chronic activation of these descending pathways may explain the diminished ability of chronic pain patients to maintain positive affect through pain flares (Leknes & Tracey, 2008). Vogt (2005) highlights the fact that valenced affective activation in response to pain is differentiated in the cingulate gyrus, such that different subregions seem to be consistently involved in specifically-valenced responses to pain. For instance, the anterior midcingulate cortex (aMCC) is selectively activated in the dual processing of fear and pain, and the pregenual ACC (pACC) is selectively activated as ratings of pain unpleasantness to noxious stimuli increase. Additionally, the posterior midcingulate cortex (pMCC) has been associated with nociceptive recognition, but not affective response, while the subgenual anterior cingulate cortex (sACC) is associated with the storage of negatively valenced emotional memories, but is not activated in response to nociceptive stimuli (Vogt, 2005).

A point of interest is the distinction between neural activation of pain unpleasantness and positive affect. Do these constructs measure processes that anchor opposite ends of a 'pleasantness' continuum, or does neural circuitry differentiate between the two? The literature does not currently provide a resolution to this query, but one hypothesis could be that pain unpleasantness is regulated through the same circuitry that regulates positive emotions and moods, and thus exists on a bipolar continuum with positive affect, distinct from negative affect. Indeed, several studies have shown that the pACC, and not the sACC, is activated amidst pain unpleasantness (Kulkarni et al., 2005; Ploner, Gross, Timmermann, & Schnitzler, 2002). Coupled with Vogt, Berger, & Derbyshire's (2003) observations of selective pACC activation during the experience of positive emotion in response to pleasant activities, these findings provide a basis for differential neural activation for the positive versus negative affective response to pain.

Ample evidence suggests that the pain-affect relation is bidirectional, with recent work showing that the intensity of pain can be modulated by negative affective states. This directional path is encoded in cingulate, insular, amygdalar, and periaqueductal gray circuitry, providing a neural basis for a chronic pain feedback loop in which pain leads to negative affect, which further modulates the perception of pain (Wiech & Tracey, 2009). Positive affective stimuli may disrupt the feedback loop and inhibit pain through parallel descending modulatory pathways (Wiech & Tracey, 2009).

The neural basis for affective modulation of pain can be appreciated through studies that manipulate the affective state during pain challenge via presentation of pictures known to differentially activate positive and negative affective pathways in the periaqueductal gray and amygdala (Rhudy & Meagher, 2001). Meagher, Arnau, & Rhudy (2001) demonstrated that presentation of negatively valenced affective slides correlated with a reduction in threshold for pain intensity and unpleasantness during a cold pressor task, whereas presentation of positively valenced slides correlated with increased thresholds. These findings were replicated by a separate group using similar methodology (de Wied & Verbaten, 2001).

Aspects of this line of research have been evaluated in clinical chronic pain samples. Central sensitization of pain in fibromyalgia, for example, is thought to be heavily influenced by the heightened emotionality of these patients (Yunus, 2007). Imaging work has shown that brain activity in the cingulate cortex uniquely corresponds to elevations in pain intensity following heightened pain anticipation in fibromyalgia patients compared to both rheumatoid arthritis patients and healthy controls (Burgmer et al., 2010). Modulation of limbic-mediated pain intensity and unpleasantness may also be achieved through deep breathing, which produces changes in parasympathetic activity via increased activity of the insular cortex (Rosenkranz et al., 2005), as well as changes in heart rate variability in concert with changes in activity in the ACC (Matthews, Paulus, Simmons, Nelesen, & Dimsdale, 2004). In an experimental heat pain paradigm, Zautra, Fasman, Davis, and Craig (2010) demonstrated that slow deep breathing resulted in a significantly smaller reduction in pain intensity and unpleasantness for fibromyalgia patients compared to healthy controls. This finding further supports the relevance of specific pain-affect neural pathways to clinical conditions of chronic pain.

Pharmacological evidence suggests that neurotransmitter systems typically targeted for improvement of affective processing among depressed patients may also modulate pain through the selective cingulate subregion channels identified by Vogt (2005). Amitriptyline was found to reduce rectal pain-related activation in the pACC during a mental stress task, thereby implicating the serotoninergic and noradrenergic systems in the pACC-mediated regulation of pain transmission (Morgan, Pickens, Gautam, Kessler, & Mertz, 2005). This finding is important because it suggests that cingulate involvement during pain may not only be reactive. Indeed, a reduction in pACC activation following pharmacological modulation of affective processing may also reflect bidirectionality in the cingulate subregion model of the dual processing of pain and affect (Vogt, 2005).

A genetic basis for the aforementioned neural circuitry of pain and affect may be effectively explored through neuroimaging. Pezawas et al. (2005) demonstrated that the functional connections between the sACC and the amygdala may be mediated by genetic variation in the serotonin transporter polymorphism (*5HTTLPR*). Specifically, short allele carriers had less gray matter in the limbic regions compared to long-allele carriers, as well as reduced functional connectivity between the rostral sACC and the amygdala (Pezawas et al., 2005). This genetic association explained significant variation in harm avoidance, suggesting that the well-chronicled link between limbic circuitry and negative emotion may have a genetic basis in the serotonergic system. Pain avoidance is conceptually similar to harm avoidance, and has been associated with activation in the ACC (Koyama, Kato, Tanaka, &

Mikami, 2001). Thus, there is reason to hypothesize that the Pezawas et al. (2005) methodologies may be extended to address the dual processing of pain and affect.

In addition to the serotonergic system, genetic variation in the opioidergic systems may contribute to the descending modulatory pathways of pain and affect. Zubieta et al. (2001) demonstrated that sustained pain applied to the masseter muscles resulted in increases in μ-opioid activation in the dorsal ACC, lateral prefrontal cortex, insula, hypothalamus, and thalamus. Thus, prolonged pain specifically recruits an endogenous opioidergic response. However, μ-opioid receptor availability negatively correlated with affective ratings of pain as measured with the McGill Pain Questionnaire (Melzack & Katz, 1999), such that increasingly negative affective ratings of pain were found at diminishing levels of μ-opioid receptor binding potential. These findings have been extended in an effort to explain central nervous system maintenance of chronic pain in fibromyalgia. Compared to healthy controls, fibromyalgia patients have reduced μ-opioid receptor availability in the amygdala, ACC, and nucleus accumbens, suggesting opioid-mediated dysfunction in the processing of pain stimuli (Harris, Scott, Gracely, Clauw, & Zubieta, 2007). The negative correlation between affective ratings of pain and μ-opioid receptor availability was also enhanced in fibromyalgia patients compared with healthy controls (Harris et al., 2007). Indeed, a variant in the the μ-opioid receptor (A118G in *OPRM1*), which results in a 10-fold reduction in μ-opioid receptor protein (Beyer, Koch, Schröder, Schulz, & Höllt, 2004; Zhang, Wang, Johnson, Papp, & Sadée, 2005) has been found to contribute to individual differences in both experimental pain ratings (e.g., Fillingim et al., 2005; Lotsch, Stuck, & Hummel, 2006; Uhl, Sora, & Wang, 1999) and pain-related anger (Bruehl, Chung, & Burns, 2008; Bruehl, Chung, Donahue, & Burns, 2006).

The effects of the opioidergic system on the dual processing of pain and affect may be further explained through its interaction with the dopaminergic system. A common functional single nucleotide polymorphism (SNP) in the gene that codes for the catabolysis of dopamine, catechol-O-methyltransferase (*COMT*), explained variability in μ-opioid receptor activation and binding potential in limbic regions during a prolonged pain challenge (Zubieta et al., 2003). Specifically, individuals homozygous for the met^{158} allele, who are predisposed to over-expression of tonic dopamine, evidenced reduced activation of the μ-opioid receptor system in response to a prolonged pain stimulus, coupled with compensatory increases in μ-opioid receptor binding potential. Subsequent to the pain stimulus, met^{158} homozygotes reported higher pain affect scores on the McGill Pain Questionnaire as well as higher negative affect scores on the Positive and Negative Affect Schedule (Watson, Clark, & Tellegen, 1988). This set of findings establishes a genetic basis for the involvement of multiple neurotransmitter systems operating within relevant brain regions on the phenotypic expression of negative affective reactivity to pain. The choice of a prolonged pain paradigm allows for closer specification of the phenotype to chronic pain conditions in that it mirrors the "wind-up" pain phenomenon proposed to underlie the perpetuation of central sensitization in some chronic pain disorders (Meeus & Nijs, 2007).

In summary, there is sufficient neural evidence to establish four salient endophenotypes for the development of chronic pain: 1) negative affective reactivity to pain; 2) positive affective reactivity to pain; 3) negative affective modulation of pain; and 4) positive affective modulation of pain. These phenotypes appear to be most relevant to idiopathic disorders or disorders of central sensitization, but may extend to other chronic pain disorders that evince substantial inter-individual variability in both the trajectory of pain symptoms over time and the extent to which they present comorbid with affective disturbance. Relatively few genetic studies have tested for association with rigorously evaluated endophenotypes, so much work must be done to build upon and systematically replicate the existing evidence. The work by Zubieta and colleagues stands as an exemplar for how to use neuroimaging as a foundation for the identification of phenotypes that represent the dynamic relations of pain and affect, and test for genetic association across multiple theoretically-derived neural systems.

NATURALISTIC EVIDENCE

Although characterization of endophenotypes of the pain-affect system is essential to understanding the brain-based pathways through which pain and affect are evoked, there is a comparable need to establish salient phenotypes that capture the everyday patient experience with chronic pain. The application of daily or weekly process models and studies that employ intensive micro-longitudinal study designs (Affleck, Zautra, Tennen, & Armeli, 1999) to genetic association designs may be referred to as a naturalistic phenotype approach. The measurement of naturalistic phenotypes for chronic pain, then, can be defined as the repeated assessment of reliable process-oriented indicators of pain and affect in the context of one's natural environment. Whereas the selection of an endophenotype circumscribes the measurement to a more proximal indicator of the neurobiological process engendered by variation in the gene, naturalistic phenotypic measurement more closely approximates everyday processes that contribute to variation in a chronic pain disorder of interest. Even more, as a measure gets closer to real-time, the threat of recall error and bias is minimized. In studies of pain and affect, retrospective accounts have tended to be biased by and focused on peak intensity and more recent experiences rather than the ebbs and flows of an experience in daily life (Redelmeier & Kahneman, 1996; Wirtz, Kruger, Scollon, & Diener, 2003). Of course, these distal intermediate phenotypes should also be plausibly related to, and perhaps caused by, the neural processes associated with the target genetic variation. We proceed, then, by reviewing evidence from intensive micro-longitudinal studies for affective reactivity to and modulation of pain in an effort to establish salient phenotypes of the dynamic relations of pain and affect at the naturalistic level.

Zautra, Davis, and colleagues introduced the Dynamic Model of Affect (DMA) as an integrative approach to understanding the interactive relations of pain, positive affect, and negative affect in the daily lives of chronic pain patients (Davis, Zautra, & Smith, 2004; Zatura, Smith, Affleck, & Tennen, 2001). The DMA holds that positive and negative affect operate independently under normal circumstances, but become strongly negatively correlated during conditions of elevated pain. Further, the DMA predicts that psychological stress will both amplify the bipolarity of positive and negative affect, and induce a negative coupling between pain and positive affect, two constructs that are expected to be independent in the absence of uncertainty (Davis et al., 2004). In a 12-week weekly repeated measurement study of rheumatoid arthritis patients, Potter, Zautra, & Reich (2000), discovered that pain and negative affect were correlated across all weeks, while pain and positive affect were only correlated on weeks during which stress was elevated relative to a patient's own mean. Zautra et al. (2001) extended this finding to show that weeks in which pain was average or diminished produced no correlation between positive and negative affect, whereas a strong bipolar affect relation emerged on elevated pain weeks. This finding was replicated in a sample of fibromyalgia patients (Zautra et al., 2001), suggesting that the dynamic naturalistic relations between pain and affect are generalizable to chronic pain populations with distinctly different sets of organic pathology. Further, these dynamic relations among pain, positive affect, and negative affect have been captured through daily diary methods. Rheumatoid arthritis patients who completed a daily diary of pain and mood measures once per day for 30 days reported lower positive mood and higher negative mood on days in which pain was elevated (Conner et al., 2006). Thus, the dual processing of pain and affect can be consistently captured through a variety of micro-longitudinal designs.

The relation between positive and negative affect in the face of pain in tests of the DMA have followed Gross and Thompson's (2007) conceptualization of emotion regulation. Through this view, emotions or affective states of opposite valence interact in a system akin to a thermostat. As pain increases, negative affect increases and becomes more negatively correlated with positive affect. Eventually, an adaptive positive affective response must be mounted to restore homeostatic balance. Individuals differ in their ability to adaptively regulate their affective states, and this disposition has been psychometrically validated in the Trait Meta-Mood Scale (Salovey, Mayer, Goldman, Turvey, & Palfai, 1995) as a measure of mood repair. This measure has been shown to predict variation in negative affective responses following distressing stimuli (Salovey et al., 1995). For rheumatoid arthritis patients, mood repair moderated the prospective relation of pain to negative affect in a weekly assessment paradigm (Hamilton, Zautra, & Reich, 2005). Rheumatoid arthritis patients who scored higher on dispositional mood repair reported less negative affect during weeks subsequent to elevated pain weeks, relative to patients who reported less dispositional mood repair.

Hamilton, Zautra, & Reich (2007) extended those findings to show that the prospective pain-negative affect relation was dependent on the intensity of patients' initial negative affective response; as negative affective intensity increased, dispositional mood repair no longer attenuated the prospective pain-negative affect relation. Positive affective reactivity to pain (i.e., loss of positive affect in response to pain) was highest among patients who were poor affective regulators and responded to pain with low intensity negative affect.

Differences in affect and affective regulation have also been reported between chronic pain groups in weekly and daily process designs. Fibromyalgia patients reported less overall positive affect than osteoarthritis patients across 12 weeks of measurement (Zautra, Fasman et al., 2005), and this finding was replicated in a 30-day daily diary study with a different sample of the same chronic pain groups (Finan et al., 2009). Further, fibromyalgia patients evidence greater difficulty, relative to osteoarthritis patients, in sustaining positive affect on days in which pain is elevated. Finan et al. (2009) showed that fibromyalgia patients experienced greater increases in negative affect and greater decreases in positive affect on high pain days than did osteoarthritis patients. Lagged analyses did not clarify the temporal ordering of these effects, so the prospective pain-affect relation has only been reported at the weekly level.

It is important to note that the fibromyalgia-specific positive affective deficit may, too, be subject to individual differences within that diagnostic group. Higher weekly and trait positive affect has been shown to decrease the correlation between pain and negative affect in a sample of women with fibromyalgia (Zautra, Johnson, & Davis, 2005). Finding differences between chronic pain disorders in weekly and daily processes of pain and affect is an essential component in the establishment of naturalistic phenotypes for chronic pain. By showing that processes that are common across chronic pain disorders nonetheless differ in magnitude and/or quality between specific diagnostic groups with specific symptom profiles, one can have greater confidence that the phenotype selected adequately reflects naturalistic processes associated with a particular disorder. For example, although positive affective reactivity to pain may be a valid naturalistic phenotype to explore in most chronic pain disorders, it appears to be particularly applicable to fibromyalgia.

Further individual differences in the daily dynamic relations between pain and affect have been observed among people with and without a history of major depression (Conner et al., 2006; Tennen et al., 2006). Rheumatoid arthritis patients who had a history of major depression (but not current major depression) evidenced stronger daily relations of pain to both positive and negative mood than patients without a history of depression. Patients with a history of depression were also more likely than their never depressed counterparts to utilize emotional venting as a strategy to cope with distress associated with elevations in pain. That it is possible to capture individual differences in affective reactivity to pain based upon a prior depressive episode suggests that environmental influences may disrupt the neurobiological pathways from gene to neural process that affect downstream naturalistic phenomena.

A valid naturalistic phenotype must have part of its variance plausibly explained by genetic factors. Because naturalistic phenotypes are several steps removed from the functional product of genetic variation, naturalistic phenotypic specification must rely on the available literature and theory. Thus, genetic variants that are used in an association study that employs a daily process design should have some evidence base established at other levels of analysis, such as the neurobiological level, to provide a basis for concurrent validity of the naturalistic measure. The use of naturalistic phenotypes in genetic association studies across disciplines has been limited, but a few studies have employed this approach in the examination of affective states. Experience sampling (Conner, Tennen, Fleeson, & Barrett, 2009), a method used to assess psychological processes repeatedly within-day, was used to show that variation in *COMT* moderated the relation of momentary stress to negative affect in cannabis users with and without psychotic disorder (van Winkel et al., 2008). Wichers et al. (2008) found that variation in *COMT* also moderated the moment-to-moment experience of positive affect in response to positive events. Gunthert et al. (2007) utilized a daily process design to investigate the association of variation in the serotonin transporter gene (*5HTTLPR*) with the experience of anxious mood in response to daily stressors. On days when college students experienced more intense stressors, short allele carriers reported elevated feelings of anxiety, compared to long allele students. This gene X stress interaction was not replicated when measures of trait anxiety and neuroticism were substituted for the marker of daily anxiety reactivity. Thus, naturalistic phenotypic measurement may provide an advantage over single-occasion designs in detecting genetic contribution to time-variant constructs such as affect and pain.

We know of only one study that has specifically incorporated the naturalistic phenotype approach into a study of the genetic influences on chronic pain. Finan et al. (2010) utilized a 30-day electronic diary design to test for association of two common 'pain' genes with positive affective reactivity to daily pain in a sample of fibromyalgia patients. This naturalistic phenotype was selected based on the consistent finding that fibromyalgia patients exhibit an overall deficit in positive affect as well as an inability to sustain positive affect through periods of elevated pain relative to other chronic pain patients (Finan et al., 2009; Zautra, Fasman et al., 2005). A gene implicated in the opioid-mediated reward pathways of the ACC and nucleus accumbens (*OPRM1*) and a gene associated with maladaptive pain and affective outcomes in pain patients (*COMT*) were selected for study. Consistent with the authors' hypotheses, variability in the *A118G* variant in *OPRM1* was associated with greater overall positive affect across diary days. Additionally, variability in the $val^{158}met$ variant in *COMT* was associated with a reduction in positive affect on high pain days relative to low pain days. Although these findings have not yet been replicated, the likelihood that they are true (not false-positive) is increased by the reliability of the repeated measures design (Epstein, 1980). Further, the threat of phenotypic misspecification was minimized given that the phenotype was narrowly defined according to an established naturalistic relation between pain and positive affect that had already been associated with variation both within fibromyalgia and between chronic pain disorders.

SUMMARY AND CONCLUSION

This chapter has presented evidence at the neural and naturalistic levels for a broad, but salient phenotype for chronic pain characterized by the dynamic relations between pain and affect. Within this broad classification, a variety of more focused phenotypes may be tested according to affective valence, discreet emotion, type of pain pathology, and response to experimental pain stimuli. Revisiting Bilder at al.'s (2009) criteria for establishing a salient phenotype, this chapter has shown that a dual processing model of pain and affect is highly relevant for a variety of known chronic pain disorders, and that pharmacological and psychological treatment of many chronic pain disorders often center on the covariation of pain and affect. Further, we have presented evidence suggesting that genetic variation explains variation in both neural and naturalistic phenotypes of the dual processing of pain and affect.

Environmental influences on the dynamics of pain and affect can be best assessed through naturalistic phenotypic measurement, as this approach enables the participant to record in close-to-real-time the daily minor stressors and social exchanges known to engage the affect system and modulate pain perception (Bolger, DeLongis, Kessler, & Schilling, 1989; Gunthert, Cohen, Butler, & Beck, 2007). It is less clear how best to measure environmental influences on the neural circuitry of pain and affect, as 'environmental' could be defined in its traditional sense, as factors operating outside the individual, or alternatively it could be defined as extracelluar factors within the individual but outside the pathways specified by the endophenotype that may alter the genetic association with that endophenotype. One way to conceptualize environmental influences on neural circuitry is through a line of research on the insular cortex's role in interoception (Craig, 2002). Specifically, recent evidence indicates that the anterior insula is active during cue-mediated anticipation prior to experimental human touch (Lovero, Simmons, Aron, & Paulus, 2009). Thus, neural circuitry typically implicated in the perception of pain and the affective response is reactive to anticipatory cues for common environmental stimuli.

Finally, we have not addressed issues of reliability in phenotypic measurement, as this topic is vast, understudied, and deserving of a separate article. With that said, we firmly believe that careful attention must be paid to the reliability of phenotypes chosen for the study of genetic influences on the dynamics of pain and affect. At the neural level, there is some evidence to indicate the solid estimates of reliability can be obtained through fMRI, among other imaging paradigms (Aron, Gluck, & Poldrack, 2006; Caceres, Hall, Zelaya, Williams, & Mehta, 2009; Johnstone et al., 2005). Particularly, the distribution of intraclass correlation coefficients (ICCs), a common measure of reliability, in brain regions of interest in an initial fMRI scan can be calculated and used to predict between-subject differences in region-specific activation, distinct from other non-activated areas, in a second scan during a separate testing session (Caceres et al., 2009). Test-retest reliability of fMRI has specifically been demonstrated in the amygdala in the context of a fear-induction paradigm (Johnstone et al., 2005). In fact, amygdala activation in response to the presentation of fearful faces evidenced higher test-retest reliability over an eight week time period than activation following neutral stimuli (Johnstone et al., 2005).

High test-retest reliability in naturalistic phenotypic measurement derives from the repeated assessment of process variables over time. In a demonstration exceptionally relevant to our interest in naturalistic pain-affect phenotypes derived from intensive repeated observations, Epstein (1979; Epstein, 1983) showed that the reliability coefficients of indicators of positive emotions, negative emotions and (headache) pain, based on a single day of observation tended to be low. Yet when the data were aggregated over 12 days, reliability coefficients for these three constructs increased to between .75 and .90. Predictably, since measurement reliability sets the theoretical upper limit on a measure's validity, the aggregated daily indicators of pain and emotions also revealed a conceptually meaningful increase in their inter-relationships, as well as their associations with personality indicators. Also, by aggregating pain and affect on multiple occasions, pain-affect phenotypes allow investigators to demonstrate the temporal stability and cross situational consistency that define a trait (see: Epstein & O'Brien, 1985).

The development of salient, reliable phenotypes of chronic pain will be a wasted venture if a parallel effort in replicating reported genetic associations is not a major focus of research going forward. Process-oriented phenotypes at the neural and naturalistic levels may differ from one measurement paradigm or instrument to another. As mentioned earlier, reactivity to thermal pain appears to be a different phenotype than reactivity to cold pressor pain (Nielsen et al., 2008), and activation in the pACC appears to be associated with the affective component of pain, whereas activation in the sACC does not (Vogt, 2005). Even more, there is necessarily variation between scales developed to assess different dimensions of pain and affect, the endorsement of which further varies between chronic pain diagnoses. So, imagine a report of genetic association with diminished positive affect covarying with pACC activation in response to cold pressor pain among fibromyalgia patients. An ideal replication of such a finding must: a) use the identical instrument used to assess positive affect (e.g., PANAS; Watson, Clark, & Tellegen, 1988); b) use the identical imaging method used to assess pACC activation (e.g., fMRI BOLD); c) use the identical pain stimulus method; d) report identical region-specific findings (e.g., pACC activation versus sACC activation); and e) sample from the identical chronic pain population (e.g., fibromyalgia syndrome). A replication study that deviates from any of those criteria risks misspecifying the phenotype and, thus, diluting the variance captured by the genetic association. Put another way, improper replication methods increase the chance of Type II errors. That said, efforts should be made in parallel with direct replication studies to establish cross-method consistency of genetic association effects.

The dynamics of pain and affect are essential to understanding day-to-day life with chronic pain. By establishing phenotypes at the neural and naturalistic levels that capture the vicissitudes of the pain-affect relation, we hope to characterize the experience of the whole organism and, ultimately, improve therapeutic intervention at the pharmacological and psychological levels. For chronic pain patients, the experience of pain is often indelibly linked to a disturbance in the affective system, a disruption in the ability to effectively regulate emotions in the face of persistent threat. There is considerable room for improvement in how we, as scientists, define and analyze the chronic pain experience. The development and refinement of phenotypes that capture the dynamics of pain and affect offers promise in bridging that gap.

REFERENCES

Affleck, G., Zautra, A., Tennen, H., & Armeli, S. (1999). Multilevel daily process designs for consulting and clinical psychology: A preface for the perplexed. *Journal of Consulting and Clinical Psychology, 67*, 746-754.

Aron, A. R., Gluck, M. A., & Poldrack, R. A. (2006). Long-term test-retest reliability of functional MRI in a classification learning task. *Neuroimage, 29*, 1000-1006.

Barton, A., Thomson, W., Ke, X., Eyre, S., Hinks, A., Bowes, J., et al. (2008). Rheumatoid arthritis susceptibility loci at chromosomes 10p15, 12q13 and 22q13. *Nature Genetics, 40*, 1156-1159.

Battié, M. C., Videman, T., Levalahti, E., Gill, K., & Kaprio, J. (2007). Heritability of low back pain and the role of disc degeneration. *Pain, 131*, 272-280.

Beyer, A., Koch, T., Schröder, H., Schulz, S., & Höllt, V. (2004). Effect of the A118G polymorphism on binding affinity, potency and agonist-mediated endocytosis, desensitization, and resensitization of the human mu-opioid receptor. *Journal of Neurochemistry, 89*, 553-560.

Bilder, R. M., Sabb, F. W., Cannon, T. D., London, E. D., Jentsch, J. D., Parker, D. S., et al. (2009). Phenomics: The systematic study of phenotypes on a genome-wide scale. *Neuroscience, 164*, 30-42.

Bolger, N., DeLongis, A., Kessler, R. C., & Schilling, E. A. (1989). Effects of daily stress on negative mood. *Journal of Personality and Social Psychology, 57*, 808-818.

Bruehl, S., Burns, J. W., Chung, O. Y., Ward, P., & Johnson, B. (2002). Anger and pain sensitivity in chronic low back pain patients and pain-free controls: The role of endogenous opioids. *Pain, 99*, 223-233.

Bruehl, S., Chung, O. Y., & Burns, J. W. (2008). The mu opioid receptor A118G gene polymorphism moderates effects of trait anger-out on acute pain sensitivity. *Pain, 139*, 406-415.

Bruehl, S., Chung, O. Y., Donahue, B. S., & Burns, J. W. (2006). Anger regulation style, postoperative pain, and relationship to the A118G mu opioid receptor gene polymorphism: A preliminary study. *Journal of Behavioral Medicine, 29*, 161-169.

Burgmer, M., Pogatzki-Zahn, E., Gaubitz, M., Stüber, C., Wessoleck, E., Heuft, G., et al. (2010). Fibromyalgia unique temporal brain activation during experimental pain: a controlled fMRI Study. *Journal of Neural Transmission, 117*, 123-131.

Bush, G., Luu, P., & Posner, M. I. (2000). Cognitive and emotional influences in anterior cingulate cortex. *Trends in Cognitive Sciences, 4*, 215-222.

Caceres, A., Hall, D. L., Zelaya, F. O., Williams, S. C. R., & Mehta, M. A. (2009). Measuring fMRI reliability with the intra-class correlation coefficient. *Neuroimage, 45,* 758-768.

Cacioppo, J. T., Gardner, W. L., & Berntson, G. G. (1999). The affect system has parallel and integrative processing components: Form follows function. *Journal of Personality and Social Psychology, 76,* 839-855.

Caspi, A., & Moffitt, T. E. (2006). Gene–environment interactions in psychiatry: Joining forces with neuroscience. *Nature Reviews Neuroscience, 7,* 583-590.

Conner, T. S., Tennen, H., Fleeson, W., & Barrett, L. F. (2009). Experience Sampling Methods: A Modern Idiographic Approach to Personality Research. *Social and Personality Psychology Compass, 3,* 292-313.

Conner, T. S., Tennen, H., Zautra, A. J., Affleck, G., Armeli, S., & Fifield, J. (2006). Coping with rheumatoid arthritis pain in daily life: Within-person analyses reveal hidden vulnerability for the formerly depressed. *Pain, 126,* 198-209.

Craig, A. D. (2002). How do you feel? Interoception: the sense of the physiological condition of the body. *Nature Reviews Neuroscience, 3,* 655-666.

Craig, A. D. (2003a). A new view of pain as a homeostatic emotion. *Trends in Neuroscience, 26,* 303-307.

Craig, A. D. (2003b). Pain mechanisms: Labeled lines versus convergence in central processing. *Annual Reviews in Neuroscience, 26,* 1-30.

Craig, A. D., Chen, K., Bandy, D., & Reiman, E. M. (2000). Thermosensory activation of insular cortex. *Nature Neuroscience, 3,* 184-190.

Davis, M. C., Zautra, A. J., & Smith, B. (2004). Chronic pain, stress, and the dynamics of affective differentiation. *Journal of Personality, 72,* 1133-1159.

de Wied, M., & Verbaten, M. N. (2001). Affective pictures processing, attention, and pain tolerance. *Pain, 90,* 163-172.

Defrin, R., Ginzburg, K., Solomon, Z., Polad, E., Bloch, M., Govezensky, M., et al. (2008). Quantitative testing of pain perception in subjects with PTSD–Implications for the mechanism of the coexistence between PTSD and chronic pain. *Journal of Pain, 138,* 450-459.

Diatchenko, L., Nackley, A. G., Tchivileva, I. E., Shabalina, S. A., & Maixner, W. (2007). Genetic architecture of human pain perception. *Trends in Genetics, 23,* 605-613.

Eccleston, C., & Crombez, G. (1999). Pain demands attention: A cognitive-affective model of the interruptive function of pain. *Psychological Bulletin, 125,* 356-366.

Epstein, S. (1979). The stability of behavior: I. On predicting most of the people much of the time. *Journal of Personality and Social Psychology, 37,* 1097-1126.

Epstein, S. (1980). The stability of behavior. *American Psychologist, 35,* 790-806.

Epstein, S. (1983). Aggregation and beyond: Some basic issues on the prediction of behavior. *Journal of Personality, 51,* 360-392.

Epstein, S., & O'Brien, E. J. (1985). The person-situation debate in historical and current perspective. *Psychological Bulletin, 98,* 513-537.

Eyre, S., Hinks, A., Flynn, E., Martin, P., Wilson, A. G., Maxwell, J. R., et al. (2009). Confirmation of association of the REL locus with rheumatoid arthritis susceptibility in the UK population. *Annals of the Rheumatic Diseases, Retrieved April 1, 2010,* http://ard.bmj.com/content/early/2009/2011/2027/ard.2009.122887.

Fillingim, R. B., Kaplan, L., Staud, R., Ness, T. J., Glover, T. L., Campbell, C. M., et al. (2005). The A118G single nucleotide polymorphism of the [mu]-opioid receptor gene

(OPRM1) is associated with pressure pain sensitivity in humans. *Journal of Pain, 6*, 159-167.

Finan, P. H., Zautra, A., Davis, M. C., Lemery-Chalfant, K., Covault, J., & Tennen, H. (2010). Genetic influences on the dynamics of pain and affect in fibromyalgia. *Health Psychology, 29*, 134-142.

Finan, P. H., Zautra, A. J., & Davis, M. C. (2009). Daily Affect Relations in Fibromyalgia Patients Reveal Positive Affective Disturbance. *Psychosomatic Medicine, 71*, 474-482.

Freimer, N., & Sabatti, C. (2003). The human phenome project. *Nature Genetics, 34*, 15-21.

Gaskin, M. E., Greene, A. F., Robinson, M. E., & Geisser, M. E. (1992). Negative affect and the experience of chronic pain. *Journal of Psychosomatic Research, 36*, 707-713.

Gatchel, R. J., Peng, Y. B., Peters, M. L., Fuchs, P. N., & Turk, D. C. (2007). The biopsychosocial approach to chronic pain: Scientific advances and future directions. *Psychological Bulletin, 133*, 581-624.

Gerlai, R. (2002). Phenomics: fiction or the future? *Trends in Neuroscience, 25*, 506-509.

Goldenberg, D. L. (2007). Pharmacological treatment of fibromyalgia and other chronic musculoskeletal pain. *Best Practice in Research and Clinical Rheumatology, 21*, 499-511.

Gross, J. J. (1998). The emerging field of emotion regulation: An integrative review. *Review of General Psychology, 2*, 271-299.

Gross, J. J., & Thompson, R. A. (2007). Emotion regulation: Conceptual foundations. In J. J. Gross (Ed.), *Handbook of Emotion Regulation* (pp. 3-24). New York: Guilford.

Gunthert, K. C., Cohen, L. H., Butler, A. C., & Beck, J. S. (2007). Depression and next-day spillover of negative mood and depressive cognitions following interpersonal stress. *Cognitive Therapy and Research, 31*, 521-532.

Gunthert, K. C., Conner, T. S., Armeli, S., Tennen, H., Covault, J., & Kranzler, H. R. (2007). Serotonin transporter gene polymorphism (5-HTTLPR) and anxiety reactivity in daily life: A daily process approach to gene-environment interaction. *Psychosomatic Medicine, 69*, 762-768.

Gursoy, S. (2002). Absence of association of the serotonin transporter gene polymorphism with the mentally healthy subset of fibromyalgia patients. *Clinical Rheumatology, 21*, 194-197.

Hamilton, N. A., Zautra, A. J., & Reich, J. (2007). Individual differences in emotional processing and reactivity to pain among older women with rheumatoid arthritis. *The Clinical Journal of Pain, 23*, 165-172.

Hamilton, N. A., Zautra, A. J., & Reich, J. W. (2005). Affect and pain in rheumatoid arthritis: Do individual differences in affective regulation and affective intensity predict emotional recovery from pain? *Annals of Behavioral Medicine, 29*, 216-224.

Harris, R., Scott, D., Gracely, R., Clauw, D., & Zubieta, J. (2007). Differential changes in mu-opioid receptor (MOR) availability following acupuncture and sham acupuncture therapy in fibromyalgia (FM) patients. *Journal of Pain, 8*, S24.

Hoffman, B. M., Papas, R. K., Chatkoff, D. K., & Kerns, R. D. (2007). Meta-analysis of psychological interventions for chronic low back pain. *Health Psychology, 26*, 1-9.

Houle, D. (2010). Numbering the hairs on our heads: The shared challenge and promise of phenomics. *Proceedings of the National Academy of Sciences, 107*, 1793-1799.

Johnstone, T., Somerville, L. H., Alexander, A. L., Oakes, T. R., Davidson, R. J., Kalin, N. H., et al. (2005). Stability of amygdala BOLD response to fearful faces over multiple scan sessions. *Neuroimage, 25*, 1112-1123.

Kerkhof, H. J., Lories, R. J., Meulenbelt, I., Jonsdottir, I., Valdes, A. M., Arp, P., et al. (2010). A genome-wide association study identifies an osteoarthritis susceptibility locus on chromosome 7q22. *Arthritis and Rheumatism, 62*, 499-510.

Koyama, T., Kato, K., Tanaka, Y. Z., & Mikami, A. (2001). Anterior cingulate activity during pain-avoidance and reward tasks in monkeys. *Neuroscience Research, 39*, 421-430.

Kroenke, K., Bair, M. J., Damush, T. M., Wu, J., Hoke, S., Sutherland, J., et al. (2009). Optimized antidepressant therapy and pain self-management in primary care patients with depression and musculoskeletal pain: A randomized controlled trial. *Journal of the American Medical Association, 301*, 2099-2110.

Kulkarni, B., Bentley, D. E., Elliott, R., Youell, P., Watson, A., Derbyshire, S. W. G., et al. (2005). Attention to pain localization and unpleasantness discriminates the functions of the medial and lateral pain systems. *European Journal of Neuroscience, 21*, 3133-3142.

Legrain, V., Van Damme, S., Eccleston, C., Davis, K. D., Seminowicz, D. A., & Crombez, G. (2009). A neurocognitive model of attention to pain: Behavioral and neuroimaging evidence. *Pain, 144*, 230-232.

Leknes, S., & Tracey, I. (2008). A common neurobiology for pain and pleasure. *Nature Reviews Neuroscience, 9*, 314-320.

Lotsch, J., Stuck, B., & Hummel, T. (2006). The human mu-opioid receptor gene polymorphism 118A> G decreases cortical activation in response to specific nociceptive stimulation. *Behavioral Neuroscience, 120*, 1218-1224.

Lovero, K. L., Simmons, A. N., Aron, J. L., & Paulus, M. P. (2009). Anterior insular cortex anticipates impending stimulus significance. *Neuroimage, 45*, 976-983.

Markkula, R., Järvinen, P., Leino-Arjas, P., Koskenvuo, M., Kalso, E., & Kaprio, J. (2009). Clustering of symptoms associated with fibromyalgia in a Finnish Twin Cohort. *European Journal of Pain, 13*, 744-750.

Matthews, S. C., Paulus, M. P., Simmons, A. N., Nelesen, R. A., & Dimsdale, J. E. (2004). Functional subdivisions within anterior cingulate cortex and their relationship to autonomic nervous system function. *Neuroimage, 22*, 1151-1156.

McWilliams, L. A., Cox, B. J., & Enns, M. W. (2003). Mood and anxiety disorders associated with chronic pain: an examination in a nationally representative sample. *Pain, 106*, 127-133.

Meagher, M. W., Arnau, R. C., & Rhudy, J. L. (2001). Pain and emotion: Effects of affective picture modulation. *Psychosomatic Medicine, 63*, 79-90.

Meeus, M., & Nijs, J. (2007). Central sensitization: a biopsychosocial explanation for chronic widespread pain in patients with fibromyalgia and chronic fatigue syndrome. *Clinical Rheumatology, 26*(4), 465-473.

Melzack, R., & Katz, J. (1999). The McGill Pain Questionnaire: Appraisal and current status. In D. C. Turk & R. Melzack (Eds.), *Handbook of Pain Assessment* (pp. 52-163). New York: Guilford Press.

Morgan, V., Pickens, D., Gautam, S., Kessler, R., & Mertz, H. (2005). Amitriptyline reduces rectal pain related activation of the anterior cingulate cortex in patients with irritable bowel syndrome. *Gut, 54*, 601-607.

Morley, S., & Williams, A. C. C. (2006). RCTs of psychological treatments for chronic pain: Progress and challenges. *Pain, 121,* 171-172.

Narita, M., Suzuki, M., Imai, S., Narita, M., Ozaki, S., Kishimoto, Y., et al. (2004). Molecular mechanism of changes in the morphine-induced pharmacological actions under chronic pain-like state: Suppression of dopaminergic transmission in the brain. *Life Sciences, 74,* 2655-2673.

Nielsen, C. S., Price, D. D., Vassend, O., Stubhaug, A., & Harris, J. R. (2005). Characterizing individual differences in heat-pain sensitivity. *Pain, 119,* 65-74.

Nielsen, C. S., Stubhaug, A., Price, D. D., Vassend, O., Czajkowski, N., & Harris, J. R. (2008). Individual differences in pain sensitivity: Genetic and environmental contributions. *Pain, 136,* 21-29.

Ochsner, K. N., Bunge, S. A., Gross, J. J., & Gabrieli, J. D. E. (2002). Rethinking feelings: An fMRI study of the cognitive regulation of emotion. *Journal of Cognitive Neuroscience, 14,* 1215-1229.

Ochsner, K. N., & Gross, J. J. (2007). The neural architecture of emotion regulation. In J. J. Gross (Ed.), *The Handbook of Emotion Regulation* (pp. 87–109). New York: Guilford Press.

Ohayon, M. M., & Schatzberg, A. F. (in press). Chronic pain and major depressive disorder in the general population. *Journal of Psychiatric Research.*

Pezawas, L., Meyer-Lindenberg, A., Drabant, E. M., Verchinski, B. A., Munoz, K. E., Kolachana, B. S., et al. (2005). 5-HTTLPR polymorphism impacts human cingulate-amygdala interactions: A genetic susceptibility mechanism for depression. *Nature, 8,* 828-834.

Ploner, M., Gross, J., Timmermann, L., & Schnitzler, A. (2002). Cortical representation of first and second pain sensation in humans. *Proceedings of the National Academy of Sciences, 99,* 12444-12448.

Potter, P. T., Zautra, A. J., & Reich, J. W. (2000). Stressful events and information processing dispositions moderate the relationship between positive and negative affect: Implications for pain patients. *Annals of Behavioral Medicine, 22,* 191-198.

Price, D. D. (2000). Psychological and neural mechanisms of the affective dimension of pain. *Science, 288,* 1769-1772.

Rainville, P. (2002). Brain mechanisms of pain affect and pain modulation. *Current Opinion in Neurobiology, 12,* 195-204.

Rainville, P., Duncan, G. H., Price, D. D., Carrier, B., & Bushnell, M. C. (1997). Pain affect encoded in human anterior cingulate but not somatosensory cortex. *Science, 277,* 968-971.

Redelmeier, D. A., & Kahneman, D. (1996). Patients' memories of painful medical treatments: Real-time and retrospective evaluations of two minimally invasive procedures. *Pain, 66,* 3–8.

Rhudy, J. L., & Meagher, M. W. (2001). The role of emotion in pain modulation. *Current Opinion in Psychiatry, 14,* 241-245.

Rosenkranz, M. A., Busse, W. W., Johnstone, T., Swenson, C. A., Crisafi, G. M., Jackson, M. M., et al. (2005). Neural circuitry underlying the interaction between emotion and asthma symptom exacerbation. *Proceedings of the National Academy of Sciences, 102,* 13319-13324.

Salovey, P., Mayer, J. D., Goldman, S. L., Turvey, C., & Palfai, T. P. (1995). Emotional attention, clarity, and repair: Exploring emotional intelligence using the Trait Meta-Mood Scale. In J. W. Pennebaker (Ed.), *Emotion, Disclosure, and Health* (pp. 125–154). Washington, D.C.: American Psychological Association.

Tander, B., Gunes, S., Boke, O., Alayli, G., Kara, N., Bagci, H., et al. (2008). Polymorphisms of the serotonin-2A receptor and catechol-O-methyltransferase genes: A study on fibromyalgia susceptibility. *Rheumatology, 28,* 685-691.

Tennen, H., Affleck, G., & Zautra, A. (2006). Depression history and coping with chronic pain: A daily process analysis. *Health Psychology, 25,* 370-379.

Tracey, I., & Mantyh, P. W. (2007). The cerebral signature for pain perception and its modulation. *Neuron, 55,* 377-391.

Tracey, I., Ploghaus, A., Gati, J. S., Clare, S., Smith, S., Menon, R. S., et al. (2002). Imaging attentional modulation of pain in the periaqueductal gray in humans. *Journal of Neuroscience, 22,* 2748-2752.

Turk, D. C., & Okifuji, A. (2002). Psychological factors in chronic pain: Evolution and revolution. *Journal of Consulting and Clinical Psychology, 70,* 678-690.

Turk, D. C., Robinson, J. P., & Burwinkle, T. (2004). Prevalence of fear of pain and activity in patients with fibromyalgia syndrome. *Journal of Pain, 5,* 483-490.

Uhl, G. R., Sora, I., & Wang, Z. (1999). The opiate receptor as a candidate gene for pain: Polymorphisms, variations in expression, nociception, and opiate responses. *Proceedings of the National Academy of Sciences, 96,* 7752-7755.

Valdes, A. M., & Spector, T. D. (2010). The genetic epidemiology of osteoarthritis. *Current Opinion in Rheumatology, 22,* 139-143.

van Winkel, R., Hengquet, C., Rosa, A., Papiol, S., Fananas, L., De Hert, M., et al. (2008). Evidence that the COMT Val158Met polymorphism moderates sensitivity to stress in psychosis: An experience-sampling study. *American Journal of Medical Genetics. Part B, Neuropsychiatric Genetics, 147B,* 10-17.

Villemure, C., & Bushnell, M. C. (2009). Mood Influences Supraspinal Pain Processing Separately from Attention. *Journal of Neuroscience, 29,* 705-715.

Vogt, B. A. (2005). Pain and emotion interactions in subregions of the cingulate gyrus. *Nature Reviews Neuroscience, 6,* 533-544.

Vogt, B. A., Berger, G. R., & Derbyshire, S. W. G. (2003). Structural and functional dichotomy of human midcingulate cortex. *European Journal of Neuroscience, 18,* 3134-3144.

Watson, D., Clark, L. A., & Tellegen, A. (1988). Development and validation of brief measures of positive and negative affect: The PANAS scales. *Journal of Personality and Social Psychology, 54,* 1063-1070.

Westlund, K. N. (2005). Neurophysiology of Nociception. In M. Papagallo (Ed.), *The Neurological Basis of Pain* (pp. 3-19). New York: McGraw-Hill

Wichers, M., Aguilera, M., Kenis, G., Krabbendam, L., Myin-Germeys, I., Jacobs, N., et al. (2008). The catechol-O-methyl transferase Val158Met polymorphism and experience of reward in the flow of daily life. *Neurospsychopharmacology, 33,* 3030-3036.

Wiech, K., & Tracey, I. (2009). The influence of negative emotions on pain: Behavioral effects and neural mechanisms. *Neuroimage, 47,* 987-994.

Wirtz, D., Kruger, J., Scollon, C. N., & Diener, E. (2003). What to do on spring break? The role of predicted, on-line, and remembered experience in future choice. *Psychological Science, 14*, 520-524.

Yunus, M. B. (2007). Role of central sensitization in symptoms beyond muscle pain, and the evaluation of a patient with widespread pain. *Best Practice and Research in Clinical Rheumatology, 21*(3), 481-497.

Zatura, A. J., Smith, B., Affleck, G., & Tennen, H. (2001). Examinations of chronic pain and affect relationships: Applications for a dynamic model of affect. *Journal of Consulting and Clinical Psychology, 69*, 786-795.

Zautra, A. J., Affleck, G. G., Tennen, H., Reich, J. W., & Davis, M. C. (2005). Dynamic approaches to emotions and stress in everyday life: Bolger and Zuckerman reloaded with positive as well as negative affects. *Journal of Personality, 73*(6), 1511-1538.

Zautra, A. J., Fasman, R., Davis, M. C., & Craig, A. D. (2010). The effects of slow breathing on affective responses to pain stimuli: An experimental study. *Pain, 149*, 12-18.

Zautra, A. J., Fasman, R., Reich, J. W., Harakas, P., Johnson, L. M., Olmsted, M. E., et al. (2005). Fibromyalgia: evidence for deficits in positive affect regulation. *Psychosomatic Medicine, 67*, 147-155.

Zautra, A. J., Johnson, L. M., & Davis, M. C. (2005). Positive affect as a source of resilience for women in chronic pain. *Journal of Consulting and Clinical Psychology, 73*(2), 212-220.

Zhang, Y., Wang, D., Johnson, A. D., Papp, A. C., & Sadée, W. (2005). Allelic expression imbalance of human mu opioid receptor (OPRM1) caused by variant A118G. *Journal of Biological Chemistry, 280*, 32618-32624.

Zubieta, J. K., Heitzeg, M. M., Smith, Y. R., Bueller, J. A., Xu, K., Xu, Y., et al. (2003). COMT val158met Genotype affects {mu}-Opioid neurotransmitter responses to a pain stressor. *Science, 299*, 1240-1243.

Zubieta, J. K., Smith, Y. R., Bueller, J. A., Xu, Y., Kilbourn, M. R., Jewett, D. M., et al. (2001). Regional mu opioid receptor regulation of sensory and affective dimensions of pain. *Science, 293*, 311-315.

In: Health Psychology
Editor: Ryan E. Murphy, pp. 79-98

ISBN 978-1-61728-981-1
© 2010 Nova Science Publishers, Inc.

Chapter 4

HYPNOSIS AS AN ADJUNCT TO COGNITIVE-BEHAVIOURAL THERAPY INTERVENTION FOR THE TREATMENT OF FIBROMYALGIA

Antoni Castel[1,2] Rosalía Cascón[1,3] and Maria Rull[1,2,3]

[1] Pain Clinic. Hospital Universitari de Tarragona Joan XXIII. Spain
[2] Multidimentional Pain Research Group. IISPV. Universitat Rovira i Virgili. Spain.
[3] Universitat Rovira i Virgili. Spain

ABSTRACT

The purpose of this study is to explore the contributing effects of hypnosis on a cognitive-behavioural therapy intervention for the treatment of chronic pain in patients with fibromyalgia.

The study is structured in four sections. Firstly, it introduces what fibromyalgia is, why it has become a current concern for health psychology and what are the more effective treatments for this syndrome. Specifically, individual and group cognitive-behavioural therapy as part of a multidisciplinary treatment are described as commonly recognised as an effective psychological treatment in fibromyalgia patients. Also, a brief review on the use of clinical hypnosis to reduce both acute and chronic pain is offered, noting that there are only few studies that focus on fibromyalgia-related pain.

Secondly, the methods and procedures of this study are specified. A sample of patients with fibromyalgia were randomly assigned to one of the two treatment conditions: 1) Cognitive-behavioural group therapy treatment; or 2) Cognitive-behavioural group therapy treatment with hypnosis. The contents of each psychological treatment program are carefully described. To assess the efficacy of the designed treatment programs, some outcome measures were taken before and after the treatment. These variables were: pain intensity, pain quality, anxiety, depression, functionality, and some sleep dimensions such as quantity, disturbance, adequacy, somnolence, and problems index.

Thirdly, the main results from this study are exposed. The analysis shows clinically significative improvements in both psychological treatment groups. However, patients who received cognitive-behavioural group therapy plus hypnosis showed greater improvement than those who received cognitive-behavioural group therapy without hypnosis.

And finally, a conclusion on the evidences described, some limitations to be considered in following studies and some recommendations on the treatment of patients with fibromyalgia are followed.

1. INTRODUCTION

In the last two decades fibromyalgia has received a great amount of attention by clinicians, researchers, patients and even the overall society. Although the etiology of fibromyalgia (FM) is still unclear, all this attention has been translated into an effort not only to discover its etiology but also to find an effective treatment for it. However, up to this moment the majority of treatment approaches have been based largely upon pharmacological management of symptoms (Clauwn, 2009).

This research aims to compare the differential effects of two psychological treatment programs in fibromyalgia, multicomponent cognitive-behavioural therapy (CBT) and multicomponent cognitive-behavioural therapy with hypnosis, under the initial hypothesis that a CBT with hypnosis treatment should be more effective than the same CBT treatment without hypnosis.

Fibromyalgia

Fibromyalgia is a complex chronic disease entity whose main symptom is widespread non-articular pain. It is featured by the alteration in the mechanisms for pain modulation producing hyperalgesia (increased sensitivity to painful stimuli) and allodynia (sensitivity to normally nonpainful stimuli) (Busquets, Vilaplana, and Arxer, 2005).

It is currently defined by the American College of Rheumatology (ACR) classification criteria (Wolfe, Smythe, Yunus, Bennett, Bombardier, Goldenberg, Tugwell, Campbell, Abeles, Clark, Gam, Farber, Fiechtner, Franklin, Gatter, Hamay, Lessard, Lichtbroun, Masi, McCain, Reynolds, Romano, Russell, and Sheon, 1990), in which an individual is required to have both a history of widespread pain for at least three months and the finding of 11 of 18 possible tender points on examination. Tender points are located in 9 paired regions of the body, and if an individual reports pain when one of these regions is palpated with 4 kilograms of pressure, this is considered a positive tender point. Pain is considered widespread when all the following symptoms are present: pain in both sides of the body and pain above and below the waist. In addition, axial skeletal pain (cervical spine, anterior chest, thoracic spine or low back pain) must be present (Wolfe et al., 1990).

However, these classification criteria have only 88% sensitivity and 81% specificity to discriminate FM from other musculoeskeletal chronic pain conditions (Goldenberg, Burckhardt, and Crofford, 2004; Wolfe, et al., 1990). For instance, FM shares symptoms with other regional syndromes such as temporomandibular disorder or other systemic entities such as chronic fatigue syndrome. Also, there is tremendous variability within individuals whose disease manifestations match the ACR criteria (Giesecke, Williams, Harris, Cupps, Tian, Tian, Gracely, and Clauw, 2003). Some FM patients experience only pain, while other experience a wide array of additional symptoms such as numbness and tingling, headaches, irritable bowel syndrome, sleep disturbance, fatigue, cold sensitivity, complaints of cognitive dysfunction, anxiety, depression, mood disturbance, etc. (Giesecke et al., 2003; Busquets et al., 2005). Nevertheless, for all of them pain is severe and is often accompanied by stiffness, especially in the morning or after periods of rest.

Studies from the United States and Western Europe countries, report a prevalence of FM of 2% in general population (3,4% in women and 0,5% in man; see Neumann and Buskila, 2003). This prevalence increases up to 5.7% in general practice and up to 20% in rheumatology outpatients (Marder, Meenan, Felson, Reichlin, Bimbaum, Croft, Dore, Kaplan, Kaufman, and Stobo, 1991). Social and demographic characteristics associated with the presence of FM are: being female, being divorced, failure to complete high school and low income.

Despite increased knowledge about FM, there is currently no cure. The absence of any definitive treatment has resulted in a variety of pharmacological and non-pharmacological treatments (Bennet, Jones, Turk, Russell, and Matallana, 2007). The conflicting data on different treatment effectiveness has led to the development of evidence-based guidelines designed to provide patients and physicians guidance in selecting among the alternatives. Despite this attempt, there is no consensus among the main evidence-based guidelines (Häuser, Thieme and Turk, 2010). While both, the American Pain Society (APS) (2005) guideline and the Association of the Scientific Medical Societies in Germany (AWMF) (2008) assigned the highest level of recommendation to aerobic exercise, CBT, amitriptyline and multicomponent treatment. In marked contrast the European League against Rheumatism (EULAR) (2007) assigned the highest level of recommendation to a set of pharmacological treatment. According to Häuser et al. (2010) the inconsistencies across these guidelines are likely attributable to the criteria used for study inclusion, weighting systems and composition of the panels.

Regardless of the lack of consensus among the specific components, all three evidence-based guidelines agree on a multidisciplinary approach as the best approach for the management of fibromyalgia, in line with the findings of previous studies (Burckhardt, 2006; Fishbain, Rosomoff, Goldberg, Cutler, Abdel-Moty, Khalil, and Rosomoff, 1993; Goldenberger et al., 2004; Lemstra and Olszyynski, 2005; among others). These treatments include medication management, education, physical exercise and cognitive-behavioural therapy (CBT).

Cognitive-Behavioural Therapy for Chronic Pain and Fibromyalgia

Among the components of the multidisciplinary approach, the efficacy of CBT in treating various chronic pain disorders has been demonstrated in numerous studies and has been stated in numerous reviews and meta-analyses (Butler, Chapman, Forman, and Beck, 2006; Eccleston, Williams, and Morley, 2009; Gatchel and Rollings, 2008; Hoffman, Papas, Chatkoff, and Kerns, 2007; Kröner-Herwig, 2009; McCracken and Turk, 2002; Morley, Eccleston, and Williams,1999; Morley, Williams and Hussain, 2008; Ostelo, Tulder, Vlaeyen, Linton, Morley, and Assesndelf, 2005; Thorn, Cross and Walker, 2007; Tulder, Ostelo, Vlaeyen, Linton, Morley, and Assesndelf, 2000; Turk, Swanson and Tunks, 2008). For instance, the last comprehensive systematic review by Eccleston et al. (2009) in which fifty-two randomized controlled trials (RCTs) of psychological therapy studies were examined, shows that CBT has positive effects on the three outcomes assessed: pain, disability and mood. In this review, the effects of CBT has been proved markedly superior to those of behavioural therapy (BT) and treatment as usual (pharmacological management of symptoms). Although CBT effect is reported weak in improving pain and disability, the effect in mood outcomes has been shown to be higher and to be maintained at six months follow-up.

In particular with fibromyalgia, CBT has been also proved effective in producing modest outcomes across multiple domains, including pain, fatigue, physical functioning and mood (Bennett and Nelson, 2006; Burckhardt, 2006; Goldenberg et al., 2004; Rossy, Buckelew, Dorr, Hagglund, Thayer, McIntosh, Hewett, and Johnson, 1999; Williams, Cary, Groner, Chaplin, Glazer, Rodriguez and Clauw, 2002). This therapy has also received strong empirical support in FM when applied in group format (Keel, Bodoky, Urs, and Müller, 1998; Williams et al., 2002).

The conceptual bases for treating FM outpatients are: 1) patients need skills to manage their symptoms, 2) patients can learn to self-manage FM symptoms and 3) healthy practices may change symptoms and the general health conditions. The efficacy of multidisciplinary treatments depends on several factors. However, the feeling of control that the patient acquires to manage the symptoms is of great importance (Burckhardt, 2006).

Although some studies have reported evidence supporting the use of CBT in isolation for the treatment of fibromyalgia (Kaplan, Goldenberg, and Galvin-Nadeau, 1993), more recent studies plead for the benefits of combining CBT with other components such as physical therapy, occupational therapy and medication management in a multi-disciplinary program (Singh, Berman, Hadhazy, and Creamer, 1998; Turk, Okifuji, Sinclair, and Starz, 1998; White and Nielson, 1995). In particular, synergistic and greatest benefits appear to occur when combining CBT adjunctively with movement therapy (Creamer, Singh, Hochberg, and Berman, 2000; Singh et al., 1998), physical exercise (Bennett, Burckhardt, Clark, O'Reilly, Wiens, and Campbell, 1996; Gowans, Hueck, Voss, and Richardson, 1999; Lemstra and Olszynski, 2005; Mannerkorpi, Nyberg, Ahlmen, and Ekdahl, 2000).

Nevertheless, when comparing studies using this therapy for the treatment of chronic pain and fibromyalgia, a great heterogeneity regarding what are exactly its components, how they are applied, how the therapy sessions are organized, etc. emerges. Therefore, as Williams (2003) already noted and Eccleston et al. (2009) confirmed, it is difficult to evaluate the collective results of these studies because each study used a different set of skills, different labels for treatment, different formats of treatment and differing domains of outcomes to evaluate. Also, there is a considerable lack of detail in defining what exactly has been done under "CBT" label to facilitate comparison. In this regards, Eccleston et al. (2009) conclude with the recommendation of improving detailed data on quality and content of treatment.

Some attempts have been made in order to clarify the core tenets and components of CBT for the treatment of chronic pain and to homogenize them. According to Bradley (1996) and Williams (2003) and basing on the previous work of Turk and Rudy (1989), all CBT interventions share and are supported by the scientific principles of learning and cognitive change. These core tenets regarding interactions among environmental events, cognitions and behaviours that determine patients' subjective pain perceptions are compatible with Melzack and Wall's gate control theory (1965).

Thus, CBT-supported interventions for chronic pain typically include four phases or components (Bradley, 1996; Turk et al., 2008; Williams 2003). These have been described as:

education, skills acquisition for pain management, skills consolidation and generalization and maintenance of the skills learned.

The education component focuses on helping patients challenge their negative perceptions regarding their abilities, and to manage pain by making them aware of the role that thoughts and emotions play in potentiating and maintaining stress and physical symptoms. Cognitive restructuring as it is termed, includes identifying maladaptive thoughts during problematic situations, introduction and practice of coping thoughts and behaviours, shifting from self-defeating to coping thoughts, practice of positive thoughts, home-practice and follow-up (Turk et al., 2008: 217). The skills acquisition and consolidation components present more heterogeneity among studies depending on the specific skills trained. The whole repertoire include: relaxation (we include in this category all the methods of teaching the relaxation response such as progressive muscle relaxation, Schultz autogenic training, visual imagery, hypnosis and biofeedback), problem solving, activity pacing, assertiveness, pleasant activity scheduling, sleep hygiene and behavioural goal-setting. All they are aimed to provide alternative ways of thinking and behaving (Keefe, 1996; Williams, 2003). The generalization and maintenance component is aimed to solidify skills and prevent relapse by anticipating future problems so that they can think about and practice the behavioural responses that may be necessary for adaptive coping (Turk et al., 2008).

All these components are addressed to enhance patients' sense of self-efficacy by increasing a sense of control to combat the feelings of helplessness and demoralization often felt by people with chronic pain. Given the empirical results of CBT, this psychological intervention is becoming standard in chronic pain treatment (Turk et al, 2008). However, as it has been reported above, there is a great heterogeneity when implementing these four components regarding the duration, the psychological techniques used, the different formats, etc. Therefore, the attempt of this study is to be very detailed in the description of the design and development of the CBT program for our patients.

Clinical Hypnosis for Chronic Pain and Fibromyalgia

Hypnosis can be understood as ''a social interaction in which one person, designated the subject responds to suggestions offered by another person, designated the hypnotist, for experiences involving alterations in perception, memory and voluntary action'' (Kihlstrom, 1985). Recently, the interest of hypnosis in the treatment of different pain conditions has increased. This rise has been supported by extensive evidence on the efficacy of hypnotic treatment to reduce acute and chronic pain (see Barber, 1996, 2001; Elkins, Jensen and Patterson, 2007; Gay, Philippport and Luminet, 2002; Hammond, 2007; Hilgard and Hilgard, 1975; Jensen and Patterson, 2006; Lynn, Kirsch, Barabasz, Cardeña, and Patterson, 2000; Mendoza and Capafons, 2009; Montgomery, DuHamel and Redd, 2000; Patterson and Jensen, 2003; Stoelb, Molton, Jensen, and Patterson, 2009 Syrjala and Abrams, 1996).

Notwithstanding the proven benefits of hypnosis in the overall treatment for pain, the number of studies on the efficacy of hypnosis for fibromyalgic pain in particular has been scarce. Hannen, Hoenderdos, van Romunde, Hop, Mallee, Terweil, and Hekster (1991) showed than patients treated with hypnosis improved in a greater extent than those patients treated with physical therapy in the following variables: pain, fatigue and sleep disturbances. According to these authors the benefits were maintained after 24-week follow-up. In an experimental study to measure brain flow through PET functional neuroimaging, Wik, Fischer, Bragée, Finer, and Fredrikson (1999), demonstrated than patients with fibromyalgia reported less pain during hypnosis than when they were at rest. In a more recent study, Castel, Pérez, Sala, Padrol, and Rull (2007) found different effects depending on the type of suggestion used in hypnosis. In particular, suggestions for hypnotic analgesia had a greater effect over pain intensity and the sensitive dimension of pain than hypnosis followed by relaxation suggestions. In another study by Alvarez-Nemegyei, Negreros-Castillo, Nuño-Gutiérrez, Álvarez-Berzunza, and Alcocer-Martínez (2007), the effects of Ericksonian hypnosis were assessed in a sample of 43 patients. The reported effect of this treatment was a decrease in the number of tender points. However, these patients did not show any improvement in functional capacity, as measured by the Fibromyalgia Impact Questionnaire (FIQ).

Hypnosis has also proven its efficacy when combined with CBT. In particular, a meta-analytic review by Kirsch, Montgomery and Sapirsten (1995) shows that hypnosis enhances the efficacy of CBT. However, there is some controversy about its joint efficacy in experimental pain (Milling, Kirsch, Meunier, and Levine, 2002; Milling, Meunier and Levine, 2003). In the context of clinical pain, there are several studies that supported the benefits of combining hypnosis with CBT. For instance, Edelson and Fitzpatrick (1989) reported greater decrease in pain in those patients treated with hypnosis and CBT, when comparing them to those treated just with CBT. Also, Martínez-Valero, Castel, Capafons, Sala, Espejo, and Cardeña (2008) conclude from a pilot study that hypnosis could be a useful tool in the treatment of fibromyalgia when combined with CBT. Finally, in the recent work by Castel, Salvat, Sala, and Rull (2009) with a sample of 47 patients, these authors concluded that patients treated with CBT, either if combined with hypnosis or not, improved significantly more than those who just received only conventional pharmacological treatment. Their analysis also indicated that patients who received CBT with hypnosis showed greater improvement in pain intensity, affective dimension of pain and functionality than those who received CBT alone.

The main objective of our study is to compare the differential effects of two programs of psychological treatment of fibromyalgia: cognitive-behavioural multicomponent therapy (CBT) and cognitive-behavioural multicomponent therapy with hypnosis. Our hypothesis is that one cognitive-behavioural treatment of the fibromyalgia added with hypnosis would be more effective than the same cognitive-behavioural treatment alone.

2. METHODS

Treatment Programs Developed

The treatment program for the management of fibromyalgia described in this article has been developed throughout more than three years of research. The current program is the result of the development and improvement of two previous treatment programs. The reason of describing in detail the two previous treatment programs in this section is twofold: firstly, to respond to the chronic pain literature claim for more detailed data on the content of treatments in order to compare studies (Eccleston et al., 2009) and secondly, to validate and justify the components, duration and sequence of the current program as an improvement of the previous ones.

First Treatment Program

Initially, a multicomponent CBT program for the treatment of fibromyalgia was developed in a group format to optimize the available resources in the context of outpatient hospital services. This program consisted of ten 90-minute group session once weekly. After being assessed, patients were randomly assigned to one of the two treatment conditions: CBT program or CBT with hypnosis program. The only difference between both treatment programs was the inclusion of hypnosis as an adjunt to CBT in the latter.

The CBT program consisted of the following components: education, relaxation training based in slow diaphragmatic breathing, cognitive restructuring skills training, activity pacing skills training, self-instructions skills, problem solving skills, life values and relapse prevention. The diaphragmatic breathing relaxation technique was trained individually in a separate individual session the second week of treatment and was practiced at the end of the group sessions every week.

The CBT with hypnosis program consisted of the following components: education, analgesic hypnosis, cognitive restructuring skills training, activity pacing skills training, self-instructions skills, problem solving skills, life values and relapse prevention. The analgesic hypnosis was introduced in a separate individual session the second week of treatment and afterwards patients were given analgesic self-hypnosis at the end of the group sessions every week.

As it can be observed, the only difference between both treatment programs was that in the CBT with hypnosis program the diaphragmatic relaxation technique was replaced with analgesic self-hypnosis training, maintaining the same sequence, format and duration.

After completing each program, patients were individually interviewed to identify the components perceived as more useful to them. Also, the effects of the treatment were assessed by comparing pre and post treatment outcome measures. The information of this pilot treatment program was analysed to improve the design of the program but the conclusions of this first stage were not published.

Second Treatment Program

The number of sessions was increased up to twelve sessions, though maintaining the duration of each session and periodical. Also a third treatment condition was included in this phase. Therefore, patients were randomly assigned to one of the three following treatment conditions: standard care control group consisting of medication management, CBT program or CBT with hypnosis program.

The second CBT program consisted of the following components: education about fibromyalgia and theory of pain perception, relaxation training based on the body's sensations awareness, cognitive restructuring skills training, assertiveness training, activity pacing and pleasant activity scheduling training, goal-setting, problem solving skills, life values and relapse prevention.

The second CBT with hypnosis program consisted of the following components: education about fibromyalgia and theory of pain perception, analgesic hypnosis, cognitive restructuring skills training, assertiveness training, activity pacing and pleasant activity scheduling training, goal-setting, problem solving skills, life values and relapse prevention.

As in the previous program, the analgesic self-hypnosis and relaxation techniques were introduced in a separate individual format the second week of treatment and were practised in the last 20 minutes of the group sessions in the following weeks.

In this second stage of the treatment program design, patients were given an audio CD recorded by the therapist to facilitate the practice at home of self-hypnosis or relaxation (depending on which treatment condition they pertained to).

As it can be observed, the only difference between both treatment programs was that in the CBT with hypnosis program the relaxation technique training was replaced with analgesic self-hypnosis training.

As it happened with the first treatment program developed, patients were interviewed individually after completing the program to identify the components perceived as more useful to them. Also, the effects of the treatment were assessed by comparing pre and post treatment results. But in this case, the analysis of these results was published (see Castel et al., 2009). The main conclusions of the analysis were that patients who attended either CBT or CBT with hypnosis programs showed greater improvement than those patients who received only conventional pharmacological treatment. Moreover, the analysis indicated that those patients who attended the CBT with hypnosis program improved more than those who attended the CBT program without hypnosis. Whereas patients from the CBT program just improved in functionality assessed through the FIQ (Fibromyalgia Impact Questionnaire), patients who attended CBT with hypnosis program also improved significantly in pain intensity and in the affective dimension of pain measured by the MPQ (McGill Pain Questionnaire). Nonetheless, the ANOVA did not state any significant difference in the improvement among the different programs.

Third Treatment Program

This is the definitive program based on the improvements of the previous programs described above. This new treatment program was increased up to fourteen 120-minute group sessions, maintaining the weekly periodical. This third version of the CBT program was composed of the following parts: education about fibromyalgia and theory of pain perception, Schultz Autogenic Training, cognitive restructuring skills training, cognitive-behavioural therapy for primary insomnia, assertiveness training, activity pacing and pleasant activity scheduling training, goal-setting, life values and relapse prevention.

Regarding the third version of the CBT with hypnosis treatment program, this was composed of the following parts: education about fibromyalgia and theory of pain perception, hypnosis with analgesic suggestion, cognitive restructuring skills training, cognitive-behavioural therapy for primary insomnia, assertiveness training, activity pacing and pleasant activity scheduling training, goal-setting, life values and relapse prevention.

As it can be observed, this third version varied significantly from the previous versions. The differences regarding the previous programs were the introduction of a new module of cognitive-behavioural therapy for primary insomnia, the increase of the number of sessions and the duration of each session and the suppression of the problem solving training module. These changes were based on the information collected from the individual interviews with patients from the previous versions, and from the analysis of the therapist about the usefulness of each module, the sequence, the duration, etc.

This third version also introduced changes that affected specifically and separately to each of both programs. In particular, the CBT treatment program replaced the general relaxation technique with the Schultz Autogenic Training. As it happened in the previous version, the technique was introduced through an individual session by the second week and practised in the last 20 minutes of every weekly group session. Also, an audio CD recorded by the therapist was delivered to each patient to facilitate the practice at home.

In the CBT with hypnosis program, although hypnosis was maintained as an analgesic technique at the second component of the program, its use was extended as an adjunt of cognitive behavioural therapy to other components of the program. Specifically, cognitive therapy was complemented with hypnosis through visualization of the most complex situations chosen by the patient. Within hypnosis, the patient proceeded modifying the belief or emotion provoked by the concrete situation and ending with a covert self-reinforcement. The cognitive behavioural therapy for primary insomnia was complemented with an anchor consisting of visualising a blind lowering and a relaxing suggestion. The assertiveness training was complemented with the visualization of a situation previously chosen by the patient in which he/she used an adaptive assertive style and also with the suggestion of positive emotions and covert self-reinforcement. Finally, the component of activity pacing, pleasant activity scheduling training and goal-setting was complemented with the visualization of the short-place goals' achievement. To do so, a technique of future projection and visualization of the necessary steps to attain the goal was employed. Hypnosis exercises were performed at the end of each session replacing the Schultz autogenic training of the CBT program. All patients from this group were given an audio CD to practice at home. This CD only contained the analgesic hypnosis exercises. Despite of the complexity of the CBT with hypnosis program, it didn't require more time during the sessions or in the overall duration than the CBT program.

Participants

Inclusion criteria for study participation were: having a fibromyalgia diagnosis using the ACR diagnostic criteria (Wolfe et al., 1990), being between 18 years old and less than 60 years old; and having at least 6 years of education. The latter criterion was included because participation in the CBT intervention used requires minimal reading and writing abilities. Exclusion criteria were: one or more additional severe chronic medical pain conditions; significant suicidal ideation; severe psychopathology (e.g. psychosis); moderate to severe cognitive impairment; or the presence of pending litigation due to fibromyalgia.

The study sample was made up of 46 patients from the Pain Unit who accomplished the inclusion criteria. All of them were receiving standard pharmacological treatment for pain when initiated the program. Their average age was of 50.1 years old (S.D. 7.3) and the length of their history of pain was in average of 13.8 years (S.D. 9.0). From this sample, 98% were women and the remaining 2% were men. More clinical and demographic data are detailed in table 1.

Table 1. Demographic and clinical data

Group	Age (years)	Sex Male	Sex Female	Pain Duration (years)	Formal education Low	Formal education Mid	Formal education High	Marital status Single	Marital status Married	Marital status Separated	Marital status Divorce
All participants (n = 46)	50.1 SD 7.3	1 (2%)	45 (98%)	13.8 SD 9.0	19 (41%)	22 (48%)	5 (11%)	2 (4%)	32 (70%)	9 (20%)	3 (6%)
CBT (n = 27)	49.3 SD 7.8	1 (4%)	26 (96%)	11.5 SD 8.6	13 (48%)	9 (33%)	4 (14%)	1 (4%)	20 (73%)	5 (19%)	1 (4%)
CBT with Hypnosis (n = 19)	51 SD 6.9	0 (0%)	19 (100%)	15.5 SD 9.2	5 (26%)	13 (69%)	1 (5%)	1 (5%)	12 (63%)	4 (21%)	2 (11%)

Note: CBT = cognitive-behavioural treatment; CBT with Hypnosis = cognitive-behavioural treatment added with hypnosis; low education = completed their primary education; mid education = completed their secondary education; high education = completed higher education

Procedure

Patients who accomplished the inclusion criteria were invited to participate in the study. If they accepted, they were asked to sign the study consent form. In the previous week to the beginning of the treatment, demographic data were collected and several instruments of measure were administered to obtain the pre-treatment outcome measures. In the week immediately after the completion of the treatment, the same instruments of measure were again administered to obtain the post-treatment outcome measures. Pre-treatment and post-treatment outcome measures were carried out by a blinded psychologist. Patients were randomly assigned to one of the two treatment conditions: CBT program or CBT with hypnosis program.

Instruments of Measure

Numeric Rating Scale (NRS)

The patient has to indicate the maximum, minimum and usual intensities of pain suffered in the last week using a numerical scale with values ranging from 0 to 10. Value 0 indicates "no pain", while value 10 indicates "the maximum pain possible". From these three independent scores, a combined retrospective measure was obtained. This procedure has demonstrated a high degree of reliability as a measure of pain suffered during a specific period of time (Dwkin and Siegfried, 1994; Jensen, Turner, Romano, and Fisher, 1999).

Hospital Anxiety and Depression Scale (HADS, Zigmond and Snaith, 1983)

This scale evaluates the presence of anxiety and depression. It consists of 14 items, seven for each dimension. In this study, we have used the Spanish adaptation by Tejero, Guimerá, Farré, and Peri (1986).

McGill Pain Questionnaire (MPQ, Melzack, 1975)

The MPQ assesses twenty domains of pain quality that are categorized, and scored, in three global dimensions: sensory, affective and evaluative. This questionnaire was designed to provide quantitative measures of the pain experience. Although, the complete questionnaire was administered, for the purposes of this study only the sensory and affective dimensions were considered. The sensory dimension describes the pain properties in terms of duration, location, pressure, temperature, tactile sensitivity and consistency. The affective dimension describes the pain in terms of nervous tension, neurovegetative reactions and fear. In this study, we have used the Spanish adaptation by Lázaro, Bosch, Torrubia, and Baños (1994).

Fibromyalgia Impact Questionnaire (FIQ, Burckhardt, Clark and Bennett, 1991)

The FIQ is an instrument that assesses the impact of fibromyalgia on physical functioning, work status, depression, anxiety, sleep, pain, stiffness, fatigue and well-being. The test allows one total score. Higher the FIQ score is, higher is the impact of fibromyalgia on patient's life. In this study, we have used the Spanish adaptation by Rivera and González (2004).

Medical Outcomes Study (MOS) Sleep Scale (MOS, Hays and Steward, 1992)

This instrument assesses the sleep's quality and duration and produces six dimensions. Although, the complete scale was administered, for the purposes of this study only the following dimensions were considered: quantity of sleep, sleep disturbance, sleep adequacy, and sleep problems index. In this study, we have used the Spanish adaptation by Rejas, Ribera, Ruiz, and Masrramón (2007).

Statistical Analysis

First, we compared the participants in the two treatment conditions on demographic and pre-treatment outcome variables using t-tests for continuous variables and chi-square analyses for categorical variables. Next, to determinate the differences between pre-treatment and post-treatment measures, paired t-tests were performed. Finally, between treatments comparisons were performed by univariate analyses, when appropriate.

3. RESULTS

No statistically significant differences were found between the two groups of treatment on age, gender distribution, pain duration, marital status or educational level (see table 1). No significant differences were found either on the pre-treatment measures of the scales HADS, FIQ and MOS Sleep.

Table 2. Pre and post-treatment outcome measures of participants in each treatment condition

OUTCOMES	CBT ALONE (Pre-post)	CBT with HYPNOSIS (Pre-post)
PAIN INTENSITY	5.9 – 5.6	6.8 - 5.4 **
	(S.D. 1.8 – 1.4)	(S.D. 1.2 – S.D. 1.5)
PRIS	24.9 – 24.3	27.0 – 23.8 *
	(S.D. 5.7- S.D. 6.1)	(S.D. 6.1 – S.D. 4.5)
PRIA	5.3 – 3.8 *	5.0 – 2.6 **
	(S.D. 2.1 – S.D. 2.5)	(S.D. 2.4 – S.D. 1.8)
ANXIETY	13.9 – 9.2 ***	11.4 – 6.3 ***
	(S.D. 4.2 – S.D. 4.8)	(S.D. 4.5 – S.D. 3.6)
DEPRESSION	10.8 – 7.1 ***	9.6 – 5.2 ***
	(S.D. 4.5 – S.D. 5.2)	(S.D. 5.0 – S.D. 4.8)
FIQ	63.3 – 53.5 *	70.3 – 47.0 ***
	(S.D. 15.6 – 16.4)	(S.D. 15.1 – S.D. 19.1)
QUANTITY OF SLEEP	5.7 – 6.7 **	5.2 – 6.9 ***
	(S.D. 1.6 – S.D. 1.7)	(S.D. 1.7 – S.D. 1.7)
SLEEP DISTURBANCE	12.6 – 19.4 ***	12.5 – 20.7 ***
	(S.D. 5.4 – S.D. 3.1)	(S.D. 4.7 – S.D. 2.3)
SLEEP ADEQUACY	4.0 – 5.7 **	3.5 – 6.2 *

	(S.D. 2.9 – S.D. 3.6)	(S.D. 2.1 – S.D. 3.8)
SOMNOLENCE	12.3 – 13.8 **	10.5 – 14.1 ***
	(S.D. 2.7 – S.D. 3.0)	(S.D. 4.0 – S.D. 2.3)
SLEEP PROBLEMS	27.8 – 39.6 ***	25.7 – 40.9 ***
INDEX	(S.D. 9.1 – 7.6)	(S.D. 8.5 – S.D. 7.8)

* p < .05; ** p < .01; *** p < .001

Note: CBT = cognitive-behavioural treatment; PRIS = McGill Pain Questionnaire, Sensory Score; PRIA = McGill Pain Questionnaire, Affective Score; ANXIETY = HADS Anxiety Score; DEPRESSION = HADS Depression Score; FIQ = Fibromyalgia Impact Questionnaire Total Score; Quantity of Sleep, Sleep Disturbance, Sleep Adequacy, Somnolence, and Sleep Problems Index are subtests of the Medical Outcomes Study (MOS) Sleep Scale.

As it can be observed in table 2, in the CBT treatment group there were significant changes between pre and post-treatment measures on anxiety [t = 5.63; p < .0001], depression [t = 4.88; p < .01], affective dimension of pain,   [t = 3.74; p < .0001], functionality [t = 3.81; p < .01], quantity of sleep [t = -3.04; p < .01], sleep disturbance [t = -8.03; p < .0001], sleep adequacy   [t = -2.77; p < .05], somnolence [t = -3.15; p < .01], and sleep problems index [t = -7.33; p < .0001].

With regards to the CBT with hypnosis treatment group, significant changes were found between pre and post-treatment measures on pain intensity [t = 4.05; p < .01], anxiety [t = 7.23; p < .0001], depression [t = 5.61; p < .0001], sensory dimension of pain [t = 2.54; p < .05], affective dimension of pain [t = 3.64; p < .01], functionality [t = 3.81; p < .01], quantity of sleep [t = -5.73; p < .0001], sleep disturbance [t = -8.69; p < .0001], sleep adequacy [t = -2.66; p < .05], somnolence [t = -5.28; p < .0001], and sleep problems index [t = -7.94; p < .0001].

Univariate analysis (ANOVA) exhibited that the CBT with Hypnosis program was more effective than the CBT program in modifying pain intensity [F(1,45) = 5.16; p < .05], functionality (FIQ) [F(1,45) = 8.12; p < .01], and somnolence [F(1,45) = 6.52; p < .05].

4. CONCLUSION

The obtained results support the hypothesis of this study, that is, to say a cognitive-behavioural treatment for fibromyalgia complemented with hypnosis is more effective than the same cognitive-behavioural treatment without hypnosis. These results are clinically relevant given that they provide information about the benefits of CBT when applied alone or with another procedure such as hypnosis.

The cognitive-behavioural group treatment program for fibromyalgia without hypnosis has proven to be effective in the modification of certain clinical variables. In particular, patients attaining this treatment program improved significantly in anxiety, depression, affective domain of pain, functionality, and variables of sleep such as quantity, disturbance, adequacy, somnolence and index of problems. On the contrary, there were not significant differences between pre and post-treatment outcomes either on pain intensity or on the sensorial domain of pain. This is in line with what other controlled studies found when analysing the efficacy of CBT alone with fibromyalgia patients (see for instance Castel et al.,

2009; Nicassio, Radojevic, Weisman, Schuman, Kim, Schoenfeld-Smith, and Krall, 1997; Redondo, Justo, Moraleda, Velayos, Puche, Zubero, Hernández, Ortells, and Pareja, 2004; Vlaeyen, Teeken-Gruben, Goossens, Rutten-van Mölken, Pelt, Van Eek, and Heuts, 1996; William et al., 2002). However, not all the studies in which CBT has been applied as only treatment have had the same results. Specifically, CBT treatments for juvenile fibromyalgia show contradictory results, since some authors have reported comparable results to those shown above (Kashikar-Zuck, Swain, Jones, and Graham, 2005), while others have described significant improvements on pain intensity, functionality and other symptoms (Degotardi, Klass, Rosemberg, Fox, Gallelli, and Gottlieb, 2006).

In our study patients who attended CBT with hypnosis program improved significantly in all the assessed variables. Concretely, the pacients group of the CBT with hypnosis had improved in more variables and in more extend than the pacients group of the CBT without hypnosis. When both treatments are statistically compared using ANOVA, adding hypnosis demonstrated to improve the effects of CBT program for fibromyalgia in pain intensity, functionality and day-somnolence. Nonetheless, we should not underestimate the efficacy of the CBT without hypnosis program, although it didn't improve the intensity or the sensory dimension of pain.

Finally, it's also important to notice that the CBT program and the CBT program with hypnosis described in this study are the outcome of the improvement and development of previous programs, in particular of two previous versions. The progressive development of this program has assumed a model of research-action, wherein the analysis of previous results has allowed improving and developing the treatment program. This process has increased the validity and effectiveness of the last version of this program.

As it has already been stated in the opening sections of this article, the CBT programmes for the management of pain usually includes education, behavioural goal-setting, relaxation training (normally progressive muscle relaxation or controlled diaphragmatic breathing), pleasant activity scheduling, cognitive restructuring, assertiveness and relapse prevention (Bennet and Nelson, 2006). Regarding this trend, our program includes the usual components of this type of programmes, but also incorporates CBT for primary insomnia, a less frequent component in the up to now developed programmes for patients with chronic pain (Espie, 2006; Tang, 2009). Another innovation of our program regarding the more usual programs for the treatment of chronic pain, has been the choice of Schultz Autogenic Training as the method for relaxation. Nevertheless, changes not affected only the CBT component of the new program. Changes were also introduced in the hypnotic component of the program. As it was explained before, in order to perform CBT program, hypnosis was used not only as an analgesic technique, but also as a technique that would increase the effects of the cognitive and behavioral contents of the CBT program,

Nonetheless, some limitations of this study should be considered when interpreting the results. The first limitation regards to the relatively small sample size which limits the generalization of the results. The second limitation has to do with the lack of previous assessment of the patients' expectations about the treatment. It is possible that the differences found were due to differences in patients' expectations about each treatment condition. Measuring those expectations would allow controlling these possible effects (Jensen and Patterson, 2005, 2006; Kirsch 1999). The third limitation concerns the lack of previous assessment of the hypnotic susceptibility of those patients who participated in the CBT with hypnosis program. However, in clinical samples the hypnotic susceptibility has not the same predictive value than in samples made up with healthy individuals (Jensen, Hanley, Engel, Romano, Barber, Cardenas, Kraft, Hoffman, and Patterson, 2005). The fourth and last limitation derives from not performing any long-term or medium-term follow-up assessment of the patients allowing the estimation of therapeutical benefits maintenance. However, there is some evidence that supports the maintenance of therapeutical benefits in patients treated with hypnosis over 6 to 12-month follow-up (Hannen et al., 1991; Jensen, Barber, Hanley, Engel, Romano, Cardenas, Kraft, Hoffman, and Patterson, 2008).

Notwithstanding the above limitations, the results obtained are encouraging and in line with previous studies that demonstrate the efficacy of CBT for patients with fibromyalgia. Also, and more importantly, this study contributes evidence about the additive effects of hypnosis when complemented with CBT. These effects are mainly a decrease in pain intensity and an improvement in sleep and functionality. Therefore, it can be concluded that hypnosis is an adequate complement of CBT for the treatment of patients with fibromyalgia.

REFERENCES

Alvarez-Nemegyei J, Negreros-Castillo A, Nuño-Gutiérrez J, Álvarez-Berzunza J, Alcocer-Martínez LM. (2007). Eficacia de la hipnosis ericksoniana en el síndrome de fibromialgia en mujeres. *Revista Médica del Instituto Mexicano de Seguro Social, 45* (4): 395-401.

Barber J. (1996). *Hypnosis and suggestion in the treatment of pain. A clinical guide.* New York: Norton Company Inc.

Barber J. (2001). Hypnosis. En: Loeser JD, editor. *Bonica's management of pain.* Philadelphia: Lippincott Williams and Wilkins, p: 1768-1778.

Bennett R, Nelson D. (2006). Cognitive behavioral therapy for fibromyalgia. *Nature Clinical Practice Rheumatology, 2* (8): 416-424.

Bennett RM, Burkhardt CS, Clark SR, O'Reilly CA, Wiens AN, Campbell SM (1996). Group treatment of fibromyalgia: a 6 month outpatients program. *Journal of Rheumatology, 23*: 521-528.

Bradley LA. (1996). Cognitive-behavioral therapy for chronic pain. En: R.J. Gatchel, D.C. Turk (Eds.). *Psychological approaches to pain management: a practitioner's handbook.* New York, EEUU: The Guilford Press; p. 131-147.

Burckhardt CS. (2006). Multidisciplinary approaches for management of fibromyalgia. *Current Pharmaceutical Design, 12*: 59-66.

Burckhardt CS, Clark SR, Bennett RM. (1991). The Fibromyalgia Impact Questionnaire: Development and validation. *Journal of Rheumatology, 18*:728-33.

Busquets C, Vilaplana J, Arxer A. (2005). Dolor musculoesquelético de origen mecánico e inflamatorio. En: Rull M, editor. *Dolor musculoesquelético.* La Coruña, Spain: SED, p. 63-103.

Butler AC, Chapman JE, Forman EM, Beck AT. (2006). The empirical status of cognitive-behavioral therapy: a review of meta-analyses. *Clinical Psychology Review, 26:* 17-31.

Bennett RM, Jones J, Turk DC, Russell IJ, Matallana L. (2007) An internet survey of 2596 people with fibromyalgia. *BMC Musculoeskeletal Disorder, 8*: 27.

Bradley L.A. (1996) Cognitive-behavioral therapy for chronic pain. In: RJ Gatchel and DC Turk (Eds.) *Psychological Approaches to Pain Management: A Practitioner's Handbook.* New York: The Guildford Press: 131-147.

Castel A, Pérez M, Sala J, Padrol A, Rull M. (2007). Effect of hypnotic suggestion on fibromyalgic pain: Comparison between hypnosis and relaxation. *European Journal of Pain, 11*: 463-468.

Castel A, Salvat M, Sala J, Rull M. (2009). Cognitive-behavioural group treatment with hypnosis: a randomized pilot trial in fibromyalgia. *Contemporary Hypnosis, 26*: 48-59.

Chambless, D.L. y Hollon, S.D. (1998). Defining empirically supported therapies. *Journal of Consulting and Clinical Psychology, 66,* 7-18

Clauw DJ. (2009). Fibromialgia: An overview. *The American Journal of Medicine, 122*: S3-S13.

Creamer P, Singh BB, Hochberg MC, Berman BM. (2000). Sustained improvement produced by nonpharmacologic intervention in fibromyalgia: results of a pilot study. *Arthritis Care and Research, 13*: 198-204.

Degotardi PJ, Klass ES, Rosenberg BS, Fox DG, Gallelli KA, Gottlieb BS. (2006). Development and evaluation of a cognitive-behavioral intervention for juvenile fibromyalgia. *Journal of Pediatric Psychology, 31*: 714-723.

Dworkin RH, Siegfried RN. (1994). Are all those pain ratings necessary? [letter to the editor]. *Pain, 58*: 279.

Eccleston C, Williams ACDC and Morley S (2009) Psychological therapies for the management of chronic pain (excluding headache) in adults (Review), *Cochrane Database of Systematic Reviews, Issue 2*: 2-101.

Edelson J, Fitzpatrick JL. (1989). A comparison of cognitive-behavioral and hypnotic treatments of chronic pain. *Journal of Clinical Psychology, 45*: 316-323.

Elkins G, Jensen MP, Patterson DR. (2007). Hypnotherapy for the management of chronic pain. *International Journal of Clinical and Experimental Hypnosis, 54*: 303-315.

Espie CA. (2006). *Overcoming insomnia and sleep problems: A self-help guide using cognitive-behavioral techniques.* London: Robinson.

Fishbain DA, Rosomoff HL, Goldberg M, Cutler R, Abdel-Moty E, Khalil TM, Rosomoff RS. (1993). The prediction of return to the workplace after multidisciplinary pain center treatment. *The Clinical Journal of Pain, 9* (1): 3-15.

Gay M, Philipport P, Luminet O. (2002). Differential effectiveness of psychological interventions for reducing osteoarthritis pain: A comparison of Erickson hypnosis and Jacobson relaxation. *European Journal of Pain, 6*: 1-16.

Gatchel RJ and Rollings KH (2008) Evidence-informed management of chronic low back pain with cognitive behavioral therapy, *Spine Journal, 8*: 40-44.

Giesecke T, Williams DA, Harris RE, Cupps TR, Tian X, Tian TX, Gracely RH, Clauw DJ. (2003). Subgrouping of fibromyalgia patients on the basis of pressure-pain thresholds and psychological factors. *Arthritis and Rheumatism, 48*: 2916-2922.

Goldenberg DL, Burckhardt C, Crofford L. (2004). Management of fibromyalgia syndrome. *JAMA, 17*: 2388-2395.

Gowans SE, de Hueck A, Voss S and Richardson MA (1999) A randomized controlled trial of exercise and education for individuals with fibromyalgia. *Arthritis Care Research, 12*:120-128.

Green JP, Barabasz AF, Barrett D and Montgomery GH (2005). Forging ahead: The 2003 APA Division 30 definition of hypnosis. *International Journal of Clinical and Experimental Hypnosis*, 53:259-264.

Haanen HCM, Hoenderdos HTW, van Romunde LKJ, Hop WCJ, Mallee C, Terweil JP, Hekster GB. (1991). Controlled trial of hypnotherapy in the treatment of refractory fibromyalgia. *Journal of Rheumatology, 18*: 72-75.

Hammond DC. (2007). Review of the efficacy of clinical hypnosis with headaches and migraines. *International Journal of Clinical and Experimental Hypnosis, 55:* 207-219.

Häuser W, Thieme K, Turk DC. (2010) Guidelines on the management of fibromyalgia syndrome- A systematic review. *European Journal of Pain, 14*: 5-10.

Hays RD, Steward AL. (1992). Sleep measures. En A.L. Steward y J.E. Ware (Eds.). *Measuring functioning and well-being: the Medical Out-comes Study approach*. Durham (NC): Duke University Press; p. 235-259.

Hildgard ER, Hilgard JR. (1975). *Hypnosis in the relief of pain*. Los Altos, CA: Williams Kaufmann, Inc.

Hoffman BM, Papas RK, Chatkoff DK, Kerns RD (2007) Meta-analysis of psychological interventions for chronic low back pain. *Health Psychology, 26*:1-9.

Jensen MP, Barber J, Hanley MA, Engel JM, Romano JM, Cardenas DD, Kraft GH, Hoffman AJ, Patterson DR. (2008). Long-term outcome of hypnotic-analgesia treatment for chronic pain in persons with disabilities. *International Journal of Clinical and Experimental Hypnosis, 56*: 156-169.

Jensen MP, Hanley MA, Engel JM, Romano JM, Barber J, Cardenas DD, Kraft GH, Hoffman AJ, Patterson DR. (2005). Hypnotic analgesia for chronic pain in persons with disabilities: A case series. *International Journal of Clinical and Experimental Hypnosis, 53*: 198-228.

Jensen MP, Patterson DR. (2005). Control conditions in hypnotic-analgesia clinical trials: challenges and recommendations. *International Journal of Clinical and Experimental Hypnosis, 53*: 170-197.

Jensen MP, Patterson DR. (2006). Hypnotic treatment of chronic pain. *Journal of Behavioral Medicine, 29*: 95-123.

Jensen MP, Turner JA, Romano JM, Fisher LD. (1999). Comparative reliability and validity of chronic pain intensity measures. *Pain, 83*: 157-162.

Kaplan KH, Goldenberg DL and Galvin-Nadeau M (1993) The impact of a meditation-based stress reduction program on fibromyalgia. *General Hospital Psychiatry, 15*:284-289.

Kashikar-Zuck S, Swain NF, Jones BA, Graham TB. (2005). Efficacy of cognitive-behavioral intervention for juvenile fibromyalgia syndrome. *Journal of Rheumatology, 32*: 1594-1602.

Keefe FJ (1996) Cognitive behavioral therapy for managing pain. *Clinical Psychologist, 49*:4-5.

Keel PJ, Bodoky C, Urs G, Müller W. (1998). Comparison of integrated group therapy and group relaxation training for fibromyalgia. *The Clinical Journal of Pain, 14*: 232-238.

Kihlstrom JK. (1985). Hypnosis. *Annual Review of Psychology, 36*: 385-418.

Kirsch I. (1999). Hypnosis and Placebos: Response Expectancy as a Mediator of Suggestion Effects. *Anales de Psicología, 15* (1): 99-110.

Kirsch I, Montgomery G, Sapirsten G. (1995). Hypnosis as an adjunct to cognitive-behavioral psychotherapy: a meta-analysis. *Journal of Consultant Clinical Psychology, 63*: 214-220.

Kröner-Herwig B (2009) Chronic pain syndromes and their treatment by psychological interventions. *Current Opinion in Psychiatry,* *22*:200-204.

Lázaro C, Bosch F, Torrubia R, Baños JE. (1994). The development of a Spanish Questionnaire for assessing pain: preliminary data concerning reliability and validity. *European Journal of Psychological Assessment, 10*: 145-151.

Lemstra M, Olszynski WP. (2005). The effectiveness of multidisciplinary rehabilitation in the treatment of fibromyalgia. *Clinical Journal of Pain, 21*: 166-174.

Lynn SJ, Kirsch I, Barabasz A, Cardeña E, Patterson DR. (2000). Hypnosis as an empirically supported clinical intervention: The state of the evidence and a look to the future. *International Journal of Clinical and Experimental Hypnosis, 48:* 239-259.

Mannerkorpi K, Nyberg B, Ahlmen M and Ekdahl C (2000) Pool exercise combined with an education program for patients with fibromyalgia syndrome. *Journal of Rheumatology,* *27*:2473-2481.

Marder WD, Meenan RF, Felson DT, Reichlin M, Bimbaum NS, Croft JD, Dore RK, Kaplan H, Kaufman RL , Stobo JD. (1991). The present and future adequacy of rheumathology manpower. A study of health care needs and physician supply. *Arthritis and Rheumatism, 34*: 1209-1217.

Martínez-Valero C, Castel A, Capafons A, Sala J, Cardeña E. (2008). Hypnotic treatment synergizes the psychological treatment of fibromyalgia: a single pilot study. *American Journal of Clinical and Hypnosis, 50*: 311-321.

McCracken LM and Turk DC (2002) Behavioral and cognitive-behavioral treatment for chronic pain: outcome, predictors of outcome and treatment process, *Spine, 27*: 2564-2573.

Melzack R. (1975). The McGill pain questionnaire: major properties and scoring methods. *Pain, 1*: 277-299.

Melzack R. & Wall, P.D. (1965) Pain mechanisms: a new theory. *Science, 50*: 971-979.

Mendoza ME, Capafons A. (2009). Eficacia de la hipnosis clínica: resumen de su evidencia empírica. *Papeles del psicólogo, 30*: 98-116.

Milling LS, Kirsch I, Meunier SA, Levine MR. (2002). Hypnotic analgesia and stress inoculation training: Individual and combined effects in analog treatment of experimental pain. *Cognitive Therapy and Research, 26*: 355-371.

Milling LS, Meunier SA, Levine MR. (2003). Hypnotic enhancement of cognitive-behavioral interventions for pain: an analogue treatment study. *Health Psychology, 22*: 406-413.

Morley S, Eccleston C, Williams A. (1999). Systematic review and meta-analysis of randomized controlled trials of cognitive behavior therapy and behavior therapy for chronic pain in adults, excluding headche. *Pain, 80*: 1-13.

Morley S, Williams A, Hussain S (2008) Estimating the clinical effectiveness of cognitive-behavioral therapy in the clinic: evaluation of a CBT informed pain management program. *Pain, 137*: 670-680.

Montgomery GH, DuHamel KN, Redd WH.(2000). A meta-analysis of hypnotically induced analgesia: how effective is hypnosis? *International Journal of Clinical and Experimental Hypnosis, 48*: 138-153.

Neumann L, Buskila D. (2003). Epidemiology of fibromyalgia. *Current Pain and Headache Reports, 7*: 362-368.

Nicassio PM, Radojevic V, Weisman MH, Schuman C, Kim J, Schoenfeld-Smith K, Krall T. (1997). A comparison of behavioral and educational interventions for fibromyalgia. *Journal of Rheumatology, 24*: 2000-2007.

Ostelo RWJG, Tulder MW van, Vlaeyen JWS, Linton SJ, Morley SJ, Assesndelf WJJ.(2005). Behavioral treatment for chronic low-back pain. *Cochrane Database Systematic Review.* 2005 Jan *25*;(1):CD002014.

Patterson DR, Jensen MP. (2003). Hypnosis and clinical pain. *Psychological Bulletin, 129*: 138-153.

Redondo JR, Justo CM, Moraleda FV, Velayos YG, Puche JJ, Zubero JR, Hernández TG, Ortells LC, Pareja MA. (2004). Long-term efficacy of therapy in patients with fibromyalgia: a physical exercise-based program and a cognitive-behavioral approach. *Arthritis and Rheumatism, 51*: 184-192.

Rejas J, Ribera MV, Ruiz M, Masrramón X. (2007). Psychometric properties of the MOS (Medial Outcomes Study) Sleep Scale in patients with neuropathic pain. *European Journal of Pain, 11*: 329-340.

Rivera J, González T. (2004). The Fibromyalgia Impact Questionnaire: a validated Spanish version to assess the health status in women with fibromyalgia. *Clinical and Experimental Rheumatology, 22:* 554-60.

Rosenstiel AK, Keefe FJ. (1983). The use of coping strategies in chronic low back pain patients: relationships to patient characteristics and current adjustment. *Pain, 17*: 33-44.

Rossy LA, Buckelew SP, Dorr N, Hagglund KJ, Thayer JF, McIntosh MJ, Hewett JE, Johnson JE. (1999). A meta-analysis of fibromyalgia treatment interventions. *Annals of Behavioral Medicine, 21*: 180-191.

Singh BB, Berman BM, Hadhazy VA, Creamer P. (1998). A pilot study of cognitive behavioral therapy in fibromyalgia. *Alternative Therapies in Health and Medicine, 4*: 67-70.

Soriano J, Monsalve V. (1999). Valoración, afrontamiento y emoción en pacientes con dolor crónico. *Boletín de Psicología, 62:* 43-64.

Stoelb BL, Molton IR, Jensen MP, Patterson DR. (2009). The efficacy of hypnotic analgesia in adults: a review of the literature. *Contemporary Hypnosis, 26*: 24-39.

Syrjala KL, Abrams JR. (1996). Hypnosis and imagery in the treatment of pain. In: RJ Gatchel, DC Turk DC, editors. *Psychological approaches to pain management: a practitioner's handbook.* New York, EEUU: The Guilford Press; p.231-258.

Tang NKY. (2009). Cognitive behavioral therapy for abnormalities of chronic pain patients. *Current Rheumatology Reports, 11*: 451-460.

Tejero A, Guimerá EM, Farré JM, Peri JM. (1986). Uso clínico del HAD (Hospital Anxiety and Depression Scale) en población psiquiátrica: Un estudio de su sensibilidad, fiabilidad y validez. *Revista del Departamento de Psiquiatría de la Facultad de Medicina de la Universidad de Barcelona, 13*: 233-238.

Thorn BE, Cross TH, Walker BB. (2007). Meta-analyses and systematic reviews of psychological treatments for chronic pain: relevance to an evidence-based practice. *Health Psychology, 1*: 10-12.

Tulder MW van, Ostelo RWJG, Vlaeyen JWS, Linton SJ, Morley SJ, Assesndelf WJJ. (2000). Behavioural treatment for chronic low-back pain. A systematic review within the framework of the Cochrane back review group. *Spine, 26*: 270-281.

Turk, D.C. & Rudy, T.E. (1989) A cognitive-behavioral perspective on chronic pain: Beyond the scalpel and syringe. In C.D. Tollison (Ed.) *Handbook of Chronic Pain Management* (pp.222-236). Baltimore: Williams & Wilkins.

Turk DC, Okifuji A, Sinclair JD and Starz TW (1998) Interdisciplinary treatment for fibromyalgia syndrome: clinical and statistical significance. *Arthritis Care Research, 11*:186-195.

Turk DC, Swanson KS, Tunks ER (2008) Psychological approaches in the treatment of chronic pain patients- When pills, scalpels and needles are not enough. *The Canadian Journal of Psychiatry, 53*: 213-223.

Turner JA, Mancl L, Aaron LA. (2006) Short- and long-term efficacy of brief cognitive-behavoral therapy for patients with chronic temporomandibular disorder pain: a randomized, controlled trial. *Pain 121*:181-194.

Vlaeyen JW, Teeken-Gruben NJ, Goossens ME, Rutten-van Mölken MP, Pelt RA, van Eek H, Heuts PH. (1996). Cognitive-educational treatment of fibromyalgia: a randomized clinical trial. I. Clinical effects. *Journal of Rheumatology, 23*: 1237-1245.

White KP and Nielson WR (1995) Cognitive behavioural treatment of fibromyalgia syndrome: a follow-up assessment. *Journal of Rheumatology*, 22: 717-721.

Wik G, Fischer H, Bragée B, Finer B, Fredrikson M. (1999). Functional anatomy of hypnotic analgesia: a PET study of patients with fibromyalgia. *European Journal of Pain, 3*: 7-12.

Williams, D.A. (2003) Psychological and behavioural therapies in fibromyalgia and related syndromes. *Best Practice and Research Clinical Rheumatology. 17*: 649-665.

Williams DA, Cary MA, Groner KH, Chaplin W, Glazer LJ, Rodriguez AM, Clauw DJ. (2002). Improving physical functional status in patients with fibromyalgia: a brief cognitive behavioral intervention. *The Journal of Rheumatology, 29*: 1280-1286.

Wolfe F, Smythe HA, Yunus MB, Bennett RM, Bombardier C, Goldenberg DL, Tugwell P, Campbell SM, Abeles SM, Clark P y col. (1990). The American College of Rheumatology 1990 criteria for the classification of fibromyalgia: report of the multicenter criteria committee. *Arthritis and Rheumatism, 33*: 160-172.

Zigmond AS, Snaith RP. (1983). The Hospital Anxiety and Depression Scale. *Acta Psychiatrica Scandinava, 67*: 361-370.

In: Health Psychology
Editor: Ryan E. Murphy, pp. 99-111

ISBN 978-1-61728-981-1
© 2010 Nova Science Publishers, Inc.

Chapter 5

CAN TECHNOLOGY IMPROVE THE TREATMENT OF CHRONIC INSOMNIA? A REVIEW OF BEST PRACTICES

*Norah Vincent**

Department of Clinical Health Psychology, Faculty of Medicine, University of Manitoba
PZ-251, 771 Bannatyne Avenue, Winnipeg, Manitoba, R3E 3N4

ABSTRACT

The use of technology to treat common health problems, such as chronic insomnia, is a growing trend in the health psychology field. The experience of persistent insomnia, as defined by a difficulty with falling asleep, staying asleep, and/or early morning awakening, coupled with sleep-related daytime impairment affects a large number (10%) of adults (Morin, LeBlanc, Daley, Gregoire, & Merette, 2006). Those with chronic insomnia are at an increased risk for a number of health problems (Elwood, Hack, Pickering, Hughes, & Gallacher, 2006; Crum, Storr, Chan, & Ford, 2004) and laboratory based studies show that restricting the sleep of healthy individuals to 50 to 75% of that normally obtained often produces unrecognizable impairments in vigilance and working memory (Van Dongen, Maislin, Mullington, & Dinges, 2003). The two main treatments for chronic insomnia consist of cognitive behavioral therapy and pharmacotherapy, however, consumers often express a preference for cognitive behavioral therapies (Morin, Gaulier, Barry, & Kowatch, 1992; Vincent & Lionberg, 2001). In response to this need, a variety of intervention websites and handheld microcomputer devices have been developed to provide cognitive behavioral intervention to those with this problem. Additionally, the potential use of telehealth to treat individuals with this problem will be discussed. This paper will review these new technologies and highlight the evidence base for these approaches. Additionally, considerations regarding who might most benefit from using these supports will be examined, as will receptivity to these innovations. Implications of the use of technology for the delivery of cognitive behavioral therapy services will be discussed.

---

* Phone (204) 787-3272; Fax: (204) 787-3755;
Email: NVincent@exchange.hsc.mb.ca

INTRODUCTION

With a healthcare system capitalizing on powerful new information technologies and applying them to the problem of improving health, this is a ripe time to be involved in the dissemination of evidence-based treatments. Many individuals have a high level of comfort with technology and routinely consult with the world wide web before visiting with their healthcare specialist. Insomnia is one common health problem where a variety of treatment-related information is easily obtainable on the world wide web. Insomnia is a chronic condition for 10% of the adult population (Morin et al., 2006) and has been described as an international public health problem (Espie, 2009). Far from being just a nuisance, individuals with insomnia disorder are at increased risk for stroke (Elwood et al., 2006), diabetes (Cappuccio, Strazzullo, D'Ella, & Miller, 2010) , obesity (Gangwisch, Malaspina, Boden-Albala, & Heymsfield, 2005), alcohol abuse (Crum et al., 2004), depressive episodes (Breslau, Roth, Rosenthal, & Andreski, 1996; Ford & Kamerow, 1989), automobile accidents (Balter & Uhlenhuth, 1992), and workplace absenteeism (Daley et al., 2009; Godet-Cayre et al., 2006). Unsettling are findings from experimental studies which illustrate that reducing the sleep of healthy individuals to 50 to 75% of that normally obtained produces cumulative, often unrecognizable, deficits in vigilance and working memory (Van Dongen et al., 2003).

The two main treatments for insomnia include pharmacotherapy and cognitive behavioral therapy (CBT). There have been a number of research trials comparing the two approaches (McClusky, Milby, Switzer, Williams & Wooten, 1991; Jacobs, Pace-Schott, Stickgold, & Otto, 2004; Morin, et al., 2009; Sivertsen et al., 2006; Vallieres, Morin, & Guay, 2005). Riemann and Perlis (2009) recently reviewed efficacy studies in this area and concluded that there are comparable short-term outcomes between CBT and benzodiazepine receptor agonists, but that CBT has better durability in the long-run. Perhaps fortunately, research has shown that individuals with insomnia often express a preference for cognitive behavioral therapy (Morin et al., 1992; Vincent & Lionberg, 2001).

Despite the widespread occurrence of chronic insomnia, research suggests that a significant proportion of individuals with sleep problems do not seek any treatment (Leblanc, Belanger, Merette, Savard & Morin, 2009), often due to lack of awareness and accessibility of treatment options (Stinson, Tang, & Harvey, 2006). Such factors have spurred research interest in the production of accessible self-administered treatments for insomnia (Vincent & Holmqvist, 2010). A recent review of this literature suggests that self-administered forms of CBT for insomnia (e.g., manuals, audiotapes, television, video, Internet, or telephone consultation) can be effective in reducing symptoms of insomnia (Currie, 2008). Some of the newer self-administered forms of CBT for insomnia are delivered with the aid of technology. For example, Riley and colleagues (2010) developed a sophisticated sleep device which is worn on the wrist and delivers behavioral treatment for insomnia. A number of other investigators have created online CBT programs for insomnia (Ritterband et al., 2009; Strom et al., 2004; Suzuki et al., 2008; Vincent & Lewycky, 2009) which can be accessed from the user's home. More recent developments pertain to the use of telemedicine or telehealth to deliver cognitive behavioral treatment for insomnia to those at a distance (Holmqvist, Vincent, & Walsh, 2010). These approaches will now be reviewed.

New Technologies in the Treatment of Insomnia

Riley and colleagues (2010) developed a sleep key device which delivers stimulus control and sleep restriction therapy using a small handheld computer worn on the wrist or attached to the bed. The device emits a low volume tone every 10 minutes which allows for live sampling of sleep. If awake when the tone sounds, users press a button on the sleep device to store their data. Additionally, users input information regarding their bedtimes and wake-up times, as well as time out of bed. In so doing, the sleep device allows for the assessment of sleep efficiency and total sleep time. Using this information, the users of the sleep key receive information regarding an appropriate bedtime based on the prior night of sleep consistent with the sleep restriction strategy (Spielman, Saskin, & Thorpy, 1987). After 4 days with the same bedtime, the program signals that bedtime should occur 15 minutes earlier than the prior night, provided that sleep efficiency exceeds 90%. If sleep efficiency does not exceed this amount, the device shifts the bedtime to 15 minutes later. When users are awake for more than 30 minutes during the night, which is indicated by a response to 3 consecutive sleep prompts, the device signals the user to remove themselves from bed. This allows for the strengthening of the association between sleepiness and the bedroom environment consistent with a stimulus control strategy (Bootzin, 1977).

Online Treatments

Another technological advance in the area of insomnia is online treatment. There have been 4 online programs for insomnia which have been developed and evaluated in the past few years (Ritterband et al., 2009; Strom et al., 2004; Suzuki et al., 2008; Vincent & Lewycky, 2009). All of the programs involve users logging on to a website, often daily, to enter information about their sleep and to complete modules or cores. At the time of publication of these interventions, common to each program were materials related to sleep restriction therapy, education and instruction pertaining to stimulus control, cognitive therapy, sleep hygiene, and relaxation therapy. Some of the programs have also included relapse prevention (Ritterband et al., 2009) and help with hypnotic medication tapering (Strom et al., 2004; Vincent & Lewycky, 2009). Several of the programs include calculators which provide appropriate bedtimes given sleep diary information based on the sleep restriction strategy (Ritterband et al., 2009; Strom et al., 2004; Vincent & Lewycky, 2009). These programs vary in length from 2 to 9 weeks and each of these programs has unique features.

Unique Features of Online Programs

In the context of a very brief 2-week treatment, Suzuki et al.'s (2008) Japanese program clearly emphasizes adherence. This program requires users to select a reward for themselves for practicing with selected interventions for a sufficient duration. Users are awarded "virtual tokens" depending on their performance. Participants who achieve a set goal for the virtual tokens are sent a message of congratulations and positive encouragement, and given advice about which behaviors would be most effective to adopt for better sleep. A weekly summary provided to each user describes the user's adherence for that week and their sleep quality and analyzes the relationship between the two variables.

The most unique aspect of Ritterband et al's (2009) *SHUTi* program is the clever animation used to help individuals identify problematic sleep hygiene habits. Users view a bedroom scene and can click on various objects in the scene to receive sleep hygiene tips and information. These authors also employ quizzes and brief games to enhance learning in this text-based program. This program is more similar to a video game than any of the other currently available programs. The second noteworthy aspect of Ritterband and colleagues work was their use of email reminders. These automated reminders are sent to users at a time when they are to begin a new core or module, and mid-week to encourage the entry of sleep diaries and the implementation of learned strategies. The use of reminders would seem to be important as Ritterband and colleagues have the most lengthy program (9 weeks) of those studied, and it is well known that adherence to online interventions diminishes as program length increases (Wangberg, Bergmo, & Johnsen, 2008). Lastly, unlike the other online programs, users of this program are required to complete a core before a new one will be available and in this way forces compliance.

Strom et al.'s (2004) Swedish online program is a primarily text-based program which is unique in soliciting participant email feedback on a regular basis. To encourage engagement, users are asked to send questions or comments to the authors about the program. In turn, they receive an individual email response. Frequent queries are posted on a FAQ (frequently asked questions) area on the site.

Vincent and Lewycky's (2009) *RETURN2SLEEP* program is unique in relying primarily on audiovisual clips as the main method to deliver information. Users fill out "sneak peek" questionnaires to assess which aspect of the upcoming module may be most relevant to them. Also, like Suzuki et al. (2008), graphs provide daily feedback about progress in areas of sleep efficiency and sleep quality. Submission of weekly adherence logs are reinforced through text messages, and users are given an opportunity to view the adherence data of others who have previously used the program. Unique to this program, and based on user feedback, are links to a blog, facebook, and twitter which allows for social support/networking opportunities regarding the treatment of insomnia.

Telemedicine/Telehealth

Teleconferencing technology (i.e., telehealth) is increasingly being used to augment access to services for individuals in rural and remote regions. A satellite or ground link connects the healthcare provider to a patient. Patients are then able to see, hear, and talk to healthcare providers on a television screen. Telehealth can be employed to link patients into cognitive behavioral treatment groups for insomnia or to link to an individual psychologist who provides sleep services. For group treatments, the individual linking becomes a group member, and the rest of the group and the healthcare provider can see and communicate with the remote individual. This allows for an easy demonstration of therapeutic techniques as well as individualized feedback and support. To our knowledge, there has been no formal study of the effectiveness of using telehealth in the treatment of insomnia. We are currently beginning a randomized controlled trial with 96 individuals with chronic and comorbid insomnia who live in rural and remote regions, to determine whether CBT is more effective using telehealth delivery than online delivery.

EVIDENCE-BASE FOR NEW TECHNOLOGIES

There has been a high degree of rigor in the evaluation of new technologies in the area of insomnia perhaps because the very technology under study makes the collection of data very straightforward. For example, each of the technologies described above (with the exception of telehealth) has been evaluated in a randomized controlled trial although most of these trials did not compare the new technology to an alternative treatment, and there was an absence of both an attention placebo control condition and of blinding. Additionally, most of the participants under study have been those with chronic primary insomnia which is not overly reflective of the population of those with chronic insomnia, many of whom have comorbid conditions. Of these RCTs, 3 have employed community-recruited individuals and excluded those with comorbid medical and psychiatric conditions (Riley et al., 2010; Ritterband et al., 2009; Strom et al., 2004), one included referred and community-recruited individuals with comorbid and primary insomnia (Vincent & Lewycky, 2009), and one included individuals who were "interested in improving their sleep quality" but not necessarily having disturbed sleep (Suzuki et al., 2008).

Sleep Key

In the context of an RCT, the sleep key device (Riley et al., 2010) was delivered with a self-help manual and compared to a control condition consisting of self-help manual alone. Relative to the control condition, results showed that there were no significant improvements in any of the sleep parameters or in a more global rating of insomnia severity. It is worth noting that this was a more stringent test of the efficacy of the technology relative to the internet studies, all of which employed a waiting list control group. Despite the absence of statistically significant differences, one-third of the participants in the active condition had sleep efficiencies > 90% at the post-treatment period relative to 9% of those in the control condition. Of note, this gap narrowed at the 12-week follow-up period. Similarly, at the post-treatment period, 19% of those in the active treatment group compared to 0 in the control group, did not have clinically significant insomnia using the Insomnia Severity Index (Bastien, Vallieres, & Morin, 2001). Again, this difference became non-significant at the 12-week follow-up period.

Online Treatments

Results from the online program evaluations have demonstrated that online intervention produces significant improvements in sleep, with the exception of one investigation (Suzuki et al., 2008). This is perhaps not surprising as Suzuki and colleagues employed a very brief 2-week intervention with a group of people that may have had relatively good sleep quality at the start. In the remaining online studies, insomnia severity significantly improved in the two studies that measured this variable (Ritterband et al., 2009; Vincent & Lewycky, 2009) and the degree of maladaptive attitudes about sleep was significantly reduced in the two studies that assessed this variable (Strom et al., 2004; Vincent & Lewycky, 2009). Results from sleep diary data differed between the studies; Strom et al. (2004) reported significant improvements in wake time at night, total sleep time, and sleep efficiency (time asleep/total time spent in bed). Ritterband et al. (2009) indicated significant improvements in the number of nocturnal awakenings, wake time at night, and sleep efficiency. Vincent & Lewycky (2009) noted significant improvements in sleep quality and daytime fatigue. These programs appear to have slightly different effects despite very similar treatment components although the effects are more similar than different.

Telemedicine/Telehealth

There is no evidence that telehealth delivery of cognitive behavioral therapy for insomnia is effective at this point in time, however, research in other settings has demonstrated that psychological interventions can be effectively delivered via telehealth with benefits similar to in-person delivery of services. For example, research with chronic pain patients showed that a 10-week mindfulness-based intervention, relative to waiting list control, improved quality of life, pain ratings, and catastrophizing, however those in an in-person treatment group condition had significantly lower usual pain ratings (Gardner-Nix, Backman, Barbati & Grummit, 2008).

METHODOLOGICAL ISSUES IN USING TECHNOLOGY IN RANDOMIZED TRIALS

One methodological issue flagged by a number of investigators in the studies reviewed is that many sleep diary parameters tend to spontaneously improve over time in waiting list control groups. This makes the determination of change more difficult to show in intervention conditions, and also suggests that there may be a placebo effect in operation. Future investigations might want to consider an attention placebo group. A second issue highlighted by Riley et al. (2009) but noted by other investigators, is that a large percentage of individuals receiving CBT using technology, relative to controls, end up in the normative range on the study variables at the post-treatment period. Riley noted that 38% of those in the intervention condition reported that their sleep was much or very much improved, compared to none in the control condition suggesting that there may be a bimodal response. Therefore, identification of moderators of treatment should be an important next step for these investigations. Hebert, Vincent, Lewycky, and Walsh (2010) reported that adults with insomnia who had higher levels of self-efficacy regarding completion of an online program for insomnia, and more social support were more likely to adhere to some components of the intervention. Further, those with a less severe presentation of insomnia and those with psychiatric comorbidity were more likely to drop-out. More investigation into who most benefits from online treatment of insomnia is a worthwhile area of study.

RECEPTIVITY

Receptivity to technological advances can be assessed by multiple sources; patients, providers, and healthcare administration. Most of the investigations utilizing technology in the treatment of insomnia have assessed patient receptivity.

Patient-Rated

Using the sleep key device, Riley et al., (2010) reported that participants rated this intervention as moderately easy to use [mean rating of 6.3 using a scale ranging from 1 (extremely difficult) to 10 (extremely easy)] and moderately satisfying [6.2 on a scale ranging from 1 (extremely dissatisfied) to 10 (extremely satisfied)]. Participant receptivity to intervention websites have been discussed in many of the online investigations for insomnia. Strom et al. (2004) reported that online treatment for insomnia was described by patients as convenient, private, and allowing for the freedom to control the amount and duration of contact. Vincent and Lewycky (2009) assessed satisfaction with online treatment for insomnia using the Client Satisfaction Questionnaire (Attkisson & Zwick, 1982) and found that it was relatively high (M = 25.1 out of possible 32.0, SD = 4.66) but somewhat less than that reported by a comparison in-person group at the same site with an identical protocol (M = 26.72, SD = 3.82) (Vincent, Holmqvist, Walsh, & Lewycky, 2009). A secondary analysis of a larger RCT showed that there was a significant association between locus of control and satisfaction with online treatment for insomnia. Those with a more internal sleep locus of control at pre-treatment tend to be more satisfied with online treatment at the conclusion of the program (Vincent, Lewycky, Walsh, & Holmqvist, 2009). Thorndike et al. (2008) assessed the ease and convenience of the web program studied by Ritterband et al. (2009). Using the Internet Intervention Utility Questionnaire for SHUTi, users found the program mostly easy or very easy to use, understandable, and mostly or very enjoyable.

Outside of the area of insomnia, recent research shows that individuals with chronic conditions view the information content (i.e., level of detail, specificity, practicality) of intervention websites as the single most important feature (Kerr, Murray, Stevenson, Gore, & Nazareth, 2006). Using focus group methodology, these authors noted that patients are favorably predisposed to being informed about what to expect of a chronic condition, treatments available, possible complications, relevant medications, local services and resources, new research and areas of scientific uncertainty, and other people's experiences or personal stories. Importantly, focus group participants noted that they particularly liked being able to control how much information they accessed at any one time and to easily find the correct level of detail for them. Online interventions for insomnia have not been as rigorously assessed from the patients' point of view.

In the context of a randomized clinical trial (in-progress) comparing telehealth to online treatment for chronic insomnia, we have found that 80% of participants would prefer to receive online treatment when presented with a balanced description of the two options (Holmqvist, Vincent, & Walsh, 2010). One of the central objections to telehealth has been lack of accessibility and reduced flexibility. Users of telehealth continue to require that appointments be scheduled by the healthcare system and that they travel to the nearest telehealth facility to link up with the host site. Thus it would seem that the various technologies are being viewed favorably by users although individuals may have more clear preferences.

Provider-Rated

The biggest challenge to dissemination of insomnia treatment may be the uptake of technology among providers. From a physician perspective, concerns regarding giving up a professional-centered relationship and having to answer more questions from patients about healthcare puts a larger premium on the physician having good communication skills (McMullan, 2006). A focus group with family physicians conducted in a mid-sized Canadian city in 2008 showed that physicians were favorably predisposed to referring patients for online treatments provided that the material on the site was evidence-based, that patients reported being satisfied with use of the site, and that physicians did not have to answer many questions about the site content (Vincent, Walker, & Katz, 2008).

Concerns regarding giving away expertise, misuse of materials by patients, and lost revenue are issues for psychologists working in the area of sleep medicine. We surveyed a small number of users (n = 15) of online treatment for insomnia as to whether they would see a psychologist in the future for a sleep problem (Vincent, Holmqvist, Lewycky, & Hart-Swain, 2009). Of those surveyed, 73% (11/15) indicated that they would do so. Further, these individuals consistently rated it as very important that this psychologist be a sleep specialist. The image was that online treatment experience produced a highly educated consumer who was also more knowledgable about the type of help that they wished to receive. Moreover, users of online treatment anticipated that their knowledge about cognitive behavioral therapy would assist them if they saw a psychologist by increasing their awareness of areas of treatment to target which could guide the interaction. Far from letting the practitioner determine what was the most appropriate treatment, individuals' penchant for becoming more self-reliant emerged as a strong factor in guiding the exchange with the healthcare provider.

Administration-rated

Healthcare administrators may be favorably predisposed to the use of technology in delivering healthcare due to the potential for cost offset. The direct costs associated with outpatient visits for insomnia are sizeable and were estimated at $11.96 billion per year in the USA in 1995 (Walsh & Engelhardt, 1999) and $191.2 million in the province of Quebec, Canada in 2002 (Daley et al., 2009). Medications, insomnia-related absenteeism and lost productivity, and costs associated with hospitalization are other large expenses (Daley et al., 2009; Walsh & Engelhardt, 1999). There is little available data on the cost-offset of using Riley and colleagues (2010) sleep key. Of users of online treatment for insomnia, Thorndike et al. (2008) reported that at least 50% reported that doctor visits and telephone calls to physicians about their insomnia were reduced. Amongst a sub-sample of referred outpatients, Vincent et al., (2009b) reported that significantly fewer completers of online treatment, relative to waiting list controls, elected to join a 6-week group treatment for insomnia when offered such an opportunity (20% vs 71%). There have been no formal investigations of the cost effectiveness of online treatment for insomnia, however, recent opinion papers have described the stepped care approach to the treatment of insomnia. These papers have highlighted that health technology be the first line insomnia treatment in such an approach (Edinger, 2009; Espie, 2009). At our site, our outpatient program is set up as a stepped care model which allows individuals to select the level of intervention appropriate for their needs. Initially, a low intensity intervention (online treatment) is offered, followed by an opportunity for a single-session consultation, followed by an opportunity for group treatment, followed by an opportunity for in-person treatment. Stepped care is not only prudent fiscally, but providing patients with treatments of their choice has been associated with better adherence and outcomes (Raue, Schulberg, Heo, Klimstra, & Bruce, 2009). There have been no investigations of the cost-effectiveness of treating insomnia using telemedicine/telehealth.

IMPLICATIONS

The potential use of technology in the treatment of insomnia seems undeniable. With a growing and aging population, the need for more sleep services has been compellingly argued (Botteman, 2009). In stark juxtaposition to this situation, is the lack of growth in the number of providers dedicated to supplying sleep services. There will be pressure on the healthcare system to provide more access to evidence-based treatment for insomnia in the ensuing years. Educational programs in sleep medicine might consider training regarding the dissemination of sleep services and methods to evaluate the adequacy of such services. It is expected that there will be a growing proliferation of websites offering "insomnia treatments". Although most of these sites are purely educational and non-interactive, interactive websites are not inexpensive to develop and update. Interactivity is important in efficacy and there is evidence that patients with chronic conditions prefer updated sites (Kerr et al., 2006). Currently, there are numerous such programs commercially available, with little to no data to support their effectiveness. To enhance the dissemination of insomnia treatment using these technologies, developers might consider developing parallel models for physician-providers using either written materials, email or mobile phone summaries, or abbreviated websites with FAQ areas highlighted. In this manner, physicians may feel more equipped and knowledgeable about the sites that their patients are visiting. Further, maximum dissemination of treatments for insomnia will require making providers, such as family physicians, aware of these technologies. Far from reducing the business of health psychologists practicing in this area, intervention websites and sleep devices may actually further increase the demand for services.

CONCLUSION

Recent technological advances in the area of insomnia such as the development of online websites and handheld computer devices have the potential to be broadly disseminated. These technologies have undergone preliminary evaluation and results are supportive of their efficacy. Research shows that these innovations have been very favorably received by individuals with chronic insomnia. Less is known about the receptivity among providers and healthcare administrators. It is anticipated that administrators will be positively predisposed to these approaches due to the cost-saving nature of these developments. Although the degree to which providers will want to use technology in their practices is unknown at this time, to achieve maximum dissemination of these evidence-based approaches may require that special provisions be made to enhance provider receptivity. Implications of these developments are that more of those with chronic insomnia will be effectively treated regardless of their locale, and that health psychologists have an opportunity to be at the leading edge of these developments. Due to the wealth of data that these technologies produce, there is a very rich climate to develop research programs around these technologies. Use of handheld devices and online websites could be employed as a first step of care in a stepped care model in traditional healthcare settings, but also could be used more broadly used to disseminate cognitive behavioral therapy to those around the world.

REFERENCES

Attkisson, C. C., & Zwick, R. (1982). The Client Satisfaction Questionnaire: Psychometric properties and correlations with service utilization and psychotherapy outcome. *Evaluation and Program Planning, 5,* 233-237.

Balter, M. B., & Uhlenhuth, E. H. (1992). New epidemiologic findings about insomnia and its treatment. *Journal of Clinical Psychiatry, 53*(Suppl.), 34-42.

Bastien, C. H., Vallieres, A., & Morin, C. M. (2001). Validation of the Insomnia Severity Index as an outcome measure for insomnia research. *Sleep Medicine, 2,* 297-307.

Bootzin, R. R. (1977). Effects of self-control procedures for insomnia. In R. B. Stuart (Ed.), *Behavioral management: Strategies, techniques, and outcomes* (pp. 176–195). New York: Brunner/Mazel.

Botteman, M. (2009). Health economics of insomnia therapy: Implications for policy. *Sleep Medicine, 10*(Suppl. 1), S22-S25.

Breslau, N., Roth, T., Rosenthal, L., & Andreski, P. (1996). Sleep disturbance and psychiatric disorders: A longitudinal epidemiological study of young adults. *Biological Psychiatry, 39,* 411-418.

Cappuccio, F. P., D'Elia, L., Strazzullo, P., & Miller, M. A. (2010). Quantity and quality of sleep and incidence of type 2 diabetes. *Diabetes Care, 33,* 414-420.

Crum, R. M., Storr, C. L., Chan, Y.-F., & Ford, D. E. (2004). Sleep disturbance and risk for alcohol-related problems. *The American Journal of Psychiatry, 161,* 1197-1203.

Currie, S. R. (2008). Self-help therapies for insomnia. In P. Watkins, & G. Clum (Eds.), *Handbook of self-help therapies* (pp. 215-241). New York, NY: Taylor and Francis.

Daley, M., Morin, C. M., Leblanc, M., Gregoire, J. P. Savard, J., & Baillargeon, L. (2009). Insomnia and its relationship to health-care utilization, work absenteeism, productivity and accidents. *Sleep Medicine, 10,* 427-438.

Edinger, J. D. (2009). Commentary: Is it time to step up to stepped care with our cognitive-behavioral insomnia therapies? *Sleep, 32,* 1539-1541.

Elwood, P., Hack, M., Pickering, J., Hughes, J., & Gallacher, J. (2006). Sleep disturbance, stroke, and heart disease events: Evidence from Caerphilly cohort. *Journal of Epidemiology and Community Health, 60,* 69-73.

Espie, C. A. (2009). "Stepped care": A health technology solution for delivering cognitive behavioral therapy as a first line insomnia treatment. *Sleep, 32,* 1549-1558.

Ford, D. E., & Kamerow, D. B. (1989). Epidemiologic study of sleep disturbances and psychiatric disorders: An opportunity for prevention? *Journal of the American Medical Association, 262,* 1479-1484.

Gangwisch, J. E., Malaspina, D., Boden-Albala, B., & Heymsfield, S. B. (2005). Inadequate sleep as a risk factor for obesity: Analyses of the NHANES I. *Sleep, 28,* 1289-1296.

Gardner-Nix., J., Backman, S., Barbati, J., & Grummitt, J. (2008). Evaluating distance education of a mindfulness-based meditation programme for chronic pain management. *Journal of Telemedicine Telecare, 14,* 88-92.

Godet-Cayré, V., Pelletier-Fleury, N., Le Vaillant, M., Dinet, J., Massuel, M.-A., & Léger, D. (2006). Insomnia and absenteeism at work. Who pays the cost? *Sleep, 29,* 179-184.

Hebert, E. A., Vincent, N., Lewycky, S., & Walsh, K. (in press). Attrition and adherence in the online treatment of chronic insomnia. *Behavioral Sleep Medicine.*

Holmqvist, M., Vincent, N., & Walsh, K. (2010). Thinking inside the box: Treating chronic insomnia using telehealth or internet. Symposium presentation at: Annual Convening of the Canadian Psychological Association, Winnipeg, MB.

Kerr, C., Murray, E., Stevenson, F., Gore, C., & Nazareth, I. (2006). Internet interventions for long-term conditions: Patient and caregiver quality criteria. *Journal of Medical Internet Research, 8*(3), e13.

Jacobs, G. D., Pace-Schott, E. F., Stickgold, R., & Otto, M. W. (2004). Cognitive behavior therapy and pharmacotherapy for insomnia: A randomized controlled trial and direct comparison. *Archives of Internal Medicine, 164,* 1888-1896.

Leblanc, M., Belanger, L., Merette, C., Savard, J., & Morin, C. M. (2009). Epidemiology of insomnia in a Canadian population-based sample. Paper presented at the 4th Conference of the Canadian Sleep Society, Toronto, Canada.

McClusky, H. Y., Milby, J. B., Switzer, P. K., Williams, V., & Wooten, V. (1991). Efficacy of behavioral versus triazolam treatment in persistent sleep-onset insomnia. *American Journal of Psychiatry, 148,* 121-126.

McMullan, M. (2006). Patients using the internet to obtain health information: How this affects the patient-health professional relationship. *Patient Education and Counseling, 63,* 24-28.

Morin, C. M., Bootzin, R. R., Buysse, D. J., Edinger, J. D., Espie, C. A., & Lichstein, K. L. (2006). Psychological and behavioral treatment of insomnia: Update of the recent evidence (1998-2004). *Sleep, 29,* 1398-1414.

Morin, C.M., Gaulier, B., Barry, T., & Kowatch, R. A. (1992). Patient's acceptance of psychological and pharmacological therapies for insomnia. *Sleep, 15,* 302-305.

Morin, C. M., LeBlanc, M., Daley, M., Gregoire, J.P., & Mérette, C. (2006). Epidemiology of insomnia: prevalence, self-help treatments, consultations, and determinants of help-seeking behaviors. *Sleep Medicine, 7*(2), 123-130.

Morin, C. M., Vallieres, A., Guay, B., Ivers, H., Savard, J., Merette, C., & Baillargeon, L. (2009). Cognitive behavioral therapy, singly and combined with medication, for persistent insomnia: A randomized controlled trial. *Journal of the American Medical Association, 301,* 2005-2015.

Riemann, D., & Perlis, M. L, (2009). The treatments of chronic insomnia: A review of benzodiazepine receptor agonists and psychological and behavioural therapies. *SleepMedicine Reviews, 13,* 205-214.

Riley, W. T., Mihm, P., Behar, A. & Morin, C. M. (2010). A computer device to deliver behavioral interventions for insomnia. *Behavioral Sleep Medicine, 8,* 2-15.

Ritterband, L. M., Thorndike, F. P., Gonder-Frederick, L. A., Magee,J. C., Bailey, E. T., Saylor, D. K., & Morin, C. M. (2009). Efficacy of an internet-based behavioral intervention for adults with insomnia. *Archives of General Psychiatry, 66,* 692-698.

Silvertsen, B., Omvik, S., Pallesen, S., Bjorvatn, B., Havik, O. E., Dvale, G., & Nordhus, I. H. (2006). Cognitive behavioral therapy vs zopiclone for treatment of chronic primary insomnia in older adults: A randomized controlled trial. Journal *of the American Medical Association, 295,* 2851-2858.

Spielman, A. J., Saskin, P., & Thorpy, M. J. (1987). Treatment of chronic insomnia by restriction of time in bed. *Sleep, 10,* 45–56.

Stinson, K., Tang, N. K., & Harvey, A. (2006). Barriers to treatment seeking in primary insomnia in the United Kingdom: A cross-sectional perspective. *Sleep, 1,* 1643-1646.

Strom, L., Pettersson, R., & Andersson, G. (2004). Internet-based treatment for insomnia: A controlled evaluation. *Journal of Consulting and Clinical Psychology, 72,* 113-120.

Suzuki, E., Tsuchiya, M., Hirokawa, K., Tniguchi, T., Mitsuhashi, T., & Kaawakami, N. (2008). Evaluation of an internet-based self-help program for better quality of sleep among Japanese workers: A randomized controlled trial. *Journal of Occupational Health, 50,* 387-399.

Thorndike, F. P., Saylor, D. K., Bailey, E. T., Gonder-Frederick, L., Morin, C. M., & Ritterband, L. M. (2008). Development and perceived utility and impact of an intervention for insomnia. *E-Journal of Applied Psychology, 4,* 32-42.

Vallieres, A., Morin, C. M., & Guay, B. (2005). Sequential combinations of drug and Cognitive behavioral therapy for chronic insomnia: An exploratory study. *Behaviour Research and Therapy, 43,* 1611-1630.

Van Dongen, H.P., Maislin, G,, Mullington, J.M., & Dinges, D. F. (2003). The cumulative cost of additional wakefulness: dose-response effects on neurobehavioral functions and sleep physiology from chronic sleep restriction and total sleep deprivation. *Sleep, 26,* 117-126.

Vincent, N., & Holmqvist, M. (2009). Low intensity interventions for chronic insomnia. In J. Bennett Levy, D. Richards, P. Farrand, H. Christensen, K. Griffiths, D. Kavanagh, B. Klein, M. Lau, J. Proudfoot, L. Ritterband, J. White, & C. Williams (Eds.) *The Oxford Guide to Low Intensity CBT Interventions.* Oxford, UK: Oxford University Press.

Vincent, N., Holmqvist, M., Lewycky, S., & Hart Swain, K. (2009). Logging on for nodding off: Empowering individuals to improve their dleep. *The Behavior Therapist, 32*(6), 123-126.

Vincent, N., & Lionberg, C. (2001). Treatment preference and patient satisfaction in chronic insomnia. *Sleep, 15,* 411-417.

Vincent, N., & Lewycky, S. (2009). Logging on for better sleep: RCT of the effectiveness of online treatment for insomnia. *Sleep, 32,* 807-815.

Vincent, N., Lewycky, S., Walsh, K., & Holmqvist, M. (2009). *Locus of control as a mediator of online treatment for insomnia.* Poster session presented at the Annual

Convening of the Association for the Advancement of Behavior and Cognitive Therapy (ABCT), New York, NY.

Vincent N, Walker J, Katz A. (2008). Self-administered therapies in Primary Care. In P. Watkins, G. Clum (Eds.), *Handbook of self-help therapies* (pp.387-418). New York, NY: Taylor and Francis.

Walsh, J. K., & Engelhardt, C. L. (1999). The direct economic costs of insomnia in the United States for 1995. *Sleep, 22*(Suppl. 2), 5386.

Wangberg, S. E., Bergmo, T. S., & Johnsen, J. (2008). Adherence in internet-based interventions. *Patient Preference and Adherence, 2*, 57-65.

In: Health Psychology
Editor: Ryan E. Murphy, pp. 113-125

ISBN 978-1-61728-981-1
© 2010 Nova Science Publishers, Inc.

Chapter 6

BENEFIT FINDING PREDICTS IMPROVED EMOTIONAL HEALTH FOLLOWING CARDIAC REHABILITATION

Bruce W. Smith, Paulette J. Christopher, Laura E. Bouldin,
Erin M. Tooley, Jennifer F. Bernard, and J. Alexis Ortiz
University of New Mexico, United States
Albuquerque, New Mexico, United States

ABSTRACT

Objective

The purpose of this study was to determine whether benefit finding was related to better emotional health in cardiac patients following cardiac rehabilitation. Benefit finding refers to the ability to find something positive or grow in response to a stressful event.

Design

Participants were cardiac patients (21% female and 22% ethnic minority) in a 12 week cardiac rehabilitation program. Benefit finding was assessed before and after the rehabilitation program. The main hypotheses were that benefit finding would predict increased positive emotion and decreased negative emotion at follow up when controlling for baseline emotion and other potential predictors of emotional health. The main outcome measures were positive and negative emotion following the rehabilitation program.

Results

Path analyses showed that benefit finding was related to more positive emotion and less negative emotion at follow-up when controlling for other predictors of emotion at follow up. In addition, positive reframing coping and income were related to more positive emotion, ethnic minority status was related to more negative emotion, and tangible social support was related to less negative emotion at follow-up.

Conclusion

Benefit finding may improve emotional health during cardiac rehabilitation. Health psychology interventions should focus on enabling cardiac patients to find more benefits in the process of coping with and recovering from heart disease.

INTRODUCTION

The experience of having a life-threatening health condition has been associated with many negative consequences including increased stress and emotional distress. Recently, researchers have begun to assess positive consequences such as increased appreciation of life, better relationships with others, and spiritual growth (Calhoun & Tedeschi, 2006). These changes have been referred to by a variety of names including "posttraumatic growth" (Tedeschi & Calhoun, 1996), "stress-related growth" (Park, Cohen, & Murch, 1996), and "benefit finding" (Mohr et al. 1999). Researchers have consistently found that at least half of those with life-threatening illnesses such as cancer, heart disease, or HIV/AIDS have reported finding at least one benefit (Affleck, Tennen Croog, & Levine, 1987; Milam, 2006; Petrie, Buick, Weinman, & Booth, 1999) as a result of having the illness.

Although the perception of having found benefits may be valuable in itself, one of the most important questions is whether benefit finding is related to health. Helgeson, Reynolds, and Tomich (2006) conducted a meta-analysis where they examined the concurrent relationship between benefit finding and various measures of health. They found a moderate, positive relationship between benefit finding and both positive well-being and intrusive-avoidant thoughts and a small, negative relationship between benefit finding and depression. There was no relationship between benefit finding and anxiety, global distress, quality of life, or subjective physical health. However, these concurrent relationships could be confounded or attenuated by the two equally plausible possibilities that (1) worse health could be the impetus for benefit finding and (2) benefit finding could lead to better health (Park & Helgeson, 2006).

Thus, prospective studies are particularly important in understanding the relationship between benefit finding and health in life-threatening illnesses. However, relatively few studies have examined the prospective relationship between benefit finding and health. On the one hand, benefit finding was related to reductions in cardiac mortality following a heart attack (Affleck et al. 1987), better well-being after cancer surgery (Schwarzer, Luszczynska, Boehmer, Taubert, & Knoll, 2006), and reduced depression in HIV/AIDS patients (Milam, 2004). On the other hand, benefit finding was related to greater negative affect in breast cancer patients (Tomich & Helgeson, 2004). In other studies, the effect of benefit finding on health has been curvilinear (Lechner, Carver, Antoni, Weaver, & Phillips, 2006) or depended on moderating factors such as personality or ethnicity (Milam, 2006).

There are several strategies that may be useful in clarifying the prospective relationship between benefit finding and health. First, researchers could focus more on the same specific aspects of health rather than using global measures. In their meta-analysis, Helgeson et al. (2006) point out that health measures have included too many broad and different constructs for consistent results to emerge. Second, health changes could be examined in briefer time intervals to better understand when the relationship between benefit finding and health may change. Most studies have used longer intervals making it difficult to know how the effects of benefit finding on health may emerge (Affleck et al. 1987; Milam, 2004; Schwarzer et al. 2006). Third, researchers could examine the same diseases in greater depth rather than taking the "shot-gun" approach of studying a greater variety of convenience samples. Several of the significant findings (e.g., Affleck et al. 1987) and the null findings (e.g., Tomich & Helgeson, 2004) are striking and call for closer examination with similar samples.

The purpose of the current study was to apply these strategies in trying to better understand the prospective effects of benefit finding on health. We decided to focus on cardiac patients since the Affleck et al. (1987) finding that benefit finding was related to reduced morbidity 8 years after a heart attack was so striking and potentially important. Although other studies have examined benefit finding in cardiac disease (Chan, Lai, & Wong, 2006; Petrie et al. 1999; Sheikh, 2004), they have not more closely examined the prospective relationship between benefit finding and health. In addition, we wanted to examine the timeframe of cardiac rehabilitation as a briefer interval where it might be possible to see significant changes in health (Sheikh & Marotta, 2008). Finally, we decided to focus on positive and negative emotion since they may represent specific and relatively independent aspects of health (Zautra, 2003), may be mediators of long-term health in cardiac patients (Kubzansky & Thurston, 2007), and are related to several risk factors for cardiac morbidity (Tully, Baker, Turnbull, & Winefield, 2008).

Our hypotheses were that benefit finding at the start of cardiac rehabilitation would be related to increased positive emotion and decreased negative emotion at the end of the program. We expected benefit finding to be related to increased positive emotion because of two-factor theory associating positive events with positive emotions (Zautra, 2003) and the cross-sectional findings associating benefit finding and well-being (Helgeson et al. 2006). We expected benefit finding to be related to decreased negative emotion because of the buffering role that positive events may play in the midst of health stressors (Davis, Zautra, & Smith, 2004). Finally, we controlled for baseline emotion and demographics, disease-related variables, and psychosocial variables that may also be related to emotion at follow-up (Rozanski & Kubzansky, 2005).

METHODS

Participants

The sample consisted of 77 men and women who completed the cardiac rehabilitation program of New Heart Center for Wellness, Exercise, and Cardiac Rehabilitation in Albuquerque, New Mexico. The mean age was 64.43 years (SD = 9.69) and 21% were female. The mean income range was between $60,000 and $70,000 and the mean years of education was 15.24 (SE = 2.88). The proportion married was 76% and the ethnic breakdown was 78% Caucasian, 21% Hispanic, and 1% Native American. The study was conducted in compliance with the Institutional Review Board of the University of New Mexico and informed consent was obtained by trained research assistants.

The requirements for participating in the New Heart cardiac rehabilitation program include having had a myocardical infarction (MI), coronary artery bypass surgery (CABG), having a stent installed, having value repair or replacement, or having had a heart transplant. Of the 77 participants in this study, 47% had an MI, 40% had CABG, 57% had a stent installed, 7% had valve repaired or replaced, and 0% had a heart transplant. The most common cardiac conditions were coronary artery disease (88%), hyperlipidemdia (74%), and hypertension (58%).

Procedures

The participants were recruited for the study during an orientation meeting for the New Heart cardiac rehabilitation program. Approximately 50% of those who were told about the study gave consent for us to use data from questionnaires completed during the course of the program. They were not paid for their participation in the study. The data for this study were taken from a questionnaire completed at the beginning of the program and upon on the completion of the program.

The New Heart program primarily focuses on increasing exercise and physical activity but also targets improving diet and coping with stress. After doing an initial walk test, an exercise physiologist meets with the patient to develop an individualized program for exercising 3 days a week for 12 weeks. During the first week of the program, the patients meet with a dietician to develop a plan for a more heart healthy diet. Finally, there is a weekly stress management group that patients are encouraged to attend on an as needed basis.

Measures

Benefit Finding
The benefit finding measure was created for this study based on a review of main domains assessed by benefit finding and posttraumatic growth measures (Tedeschi & Calhoun, 1996; Mohr et al. 1999; Park et al. 1996). The items included "better relationships with others", "greater appreciation of life," "developing new interests," "becoming a stronger person," "making new friends," "finding more meaning in life," and "spiritual growth." The instructions were "For each of the statements below, please indicate the amount of positive change you have experienced as a result of having problems with your heart." The items were responded to on a five point scale and Cronbach's alpha was .936.

Optimism
This was assessed with the Life Orientation Test Revised (LOTR; Scheier, Carver, & Bridges, 1994). The LOTR includes three positively worded items (e.g., "I'm always optimistic about my future") and three negatively worded items (e.g., "I hardly ever expect things to go my way"). The items were scored on a five point scale. Cronbach's alpha was .741.

Social Support

The social support items were selected from the *Medical Outcomes Study Social Support Survey* (MOS-SSS; Sherbourne & Stewart, 1991). The items with the strongest correlations with the emotional/informational support (referred to as "emotional support" in this study) and tangible support scales were selected including four of the eight emotional-informational support items (e.g., "someone who understands your problems") and two of the four tangible support items (e.g., "someone to help you with your daily chores if you were sick"). The items were scored on a five point scale and Cronbach alphas were .931 for emotional support and .932 for tangible support.

Spirituality

This was assessed using three items that have frequently been used to assess dispositional spirituality and religiosity (Fetzer, 1999). These items were "to what extent do you consider yourself a spirituality person?," "to what extent do you consider yourself a religious person?," and "how often do you attend spiritual/religious services?" The items were scored on a seven point scale and Cronbach's alpha was .834.

Coping

Active coping and positive reframing are consistently associated with better emotional outcomes. We assessed these variables using the Brief COPE because of their consistent association with better emotional outcomes (Carver, 1997). Active coping and positive reframing were each assessed by two items (e.g., "I've been taking action to try to make the situation better" and "I've been looking for something good in what has been happening", respectively). These items were scored on a four point scale and Cronbach's alphas were .701 for active coping and .709 for positive reframing.

Positive and Negative Emotion

Positive and negative emotion during the past two weeks was assessed using 10 items from the Mood Adjective Checklist (Larsen & Diener, 1992). The positive emotion items were "happy," "lively," "stimulated," "peppy," "active," and "cheerful" and the negative emotion items were "nervous," "blue," "anxious", and "sad." These items were scored on a seven point scale. Cronbach's alpha was .862 for positive emotion and .851 for negative emotion.

Statistical Analyses

Independent samples were used to compare the drop-outs and completers on baseline variables. Paired t-tests were used to compare the pre and post rehab emotion scores. Correlation and partial correlation analyses were used to examine the relationship between the study variables and emotion at baseline and follow up. Path analyses were used to examine the relationship between the baseline predictors and emotion at follow up. SPSS 16.0 was used for the correlation analyses and AMOS 4.0 was used for the path analyses. An alpha level of $p < .05$ was used as the statistical test for all analyses.

RESULTS

The descriptive statistics for the variables assessed at baseline are displayed in Table 1. The means or percentages are shown for 147 patients who began the cardiac rehabilitation program, the 70 patients who dropped out before completing the program, and the 77 patients who completed the 12 week program and were examined for pre-post changes in emotional health for the current study. The only significant differences between drop-outs and completers were that completers were older, had more years of education, and a higher number of exercise days at baseline.

Did Positive and Negative Emotion Change From Pre to Post Cardiac Rehabilitation?

We examined pre-post changes in emotion for the completers and for those divided into high and low benefit finding using a median split. First of all, there was a large, significant increase (d = .812, t = 7.221, p < .001) from baseline (M = 3.06, SD = 1.08) to follow up (M = 3.86, SD = .88) in positive emotion. For those high in benefit finding, there was a very large, significant increase (d = .944, t = 6.337, p < .001) from baseline (M = 3.23, SD = 1.13) to follow up (M = 4.15, SD = 0.79) in positive emotion. For those who low on benefit finding, there was a medium-large sized, significant change (d = .714, t = 4.068, p < .001) from baseline (M = 2.90, SD = 1.01) to follow up (M = 3.58, SD = .89) in positive emotion.

Table 1. Descriptive Statistics for the Baseline Variables

	All Participants (n=147)	Drop-Outs (n=70)	Completers (n=77)
Benefit Finding	1.98 (1.23)	1.86 (1.20)	2.08 (1.25)
Demographics			
Age	62.98 (10.41)	61.39 (11.00)[a]	64.43 (9.69)[a]
Years Education	14.51 (2.96)	13.71 (2.86)[b]	15.24 (2.88)[b]
Income Range	$60-70K	$60-70K	$60-70K
Female	23.81%	27.14%	20.78%
Ethnic Minority	21.43%	20.71%	22.15%
Cardiac Conditions			
Heart Attack	40.14%	32.86%	46.75%
CABG Surgery	40.14%	40.00%	40.26%
Stent Installed	53.74%	50.00%	57.14%
Program Variables			
Exercise Days	27.12 (11.94)	18.37 (11.92)[c]	34.52 (3.23)[c]
Days to Complete	-	-	113.43 (26.13)
Personal Resources			
Optimism	3.92 (0.69)	3.92 (0.68)	3.91 (0.71)
Emotional Support	4.12 (1.00)	4.08 (1.02)	4.16 (0.99)

Tangible Support	4.24 (1.08)	4.20 (1.14)	4.27 (1.03)
Spirituality	4.28 (1.63)	4.42 (1.58)	4.15 (1.67)
Coping Strategies			
Active Coping	2.44 (0.63)	2.42 (0.66)	2.45 (0.61)
Positive Reframing	2.06 (0.75)	2.11 (0.69)	2.02 (0.76)
Emotion			
Positive Emotion	3.19 (1.06)	3.30 (1.03)	3.09 (1.09)
Negative Emotion	1.64 (1.15)	1.76 (1.19)	1.53 (1.11)

Note. Means are displayed with standard deviations are in parentheses. Superscripts indicate that the means or percentages are significantly different at p < .05.

Second, there was small, non-significant decrease (d = -.175, t = -1.595, ns) from baseline (M = 1.52, SD = 1.11) to follow up (M = 1.32, SD = 1.17) in negative emotion. For those high in benefit finding, there was a small-medium sized, significant decrease (d = -.398, t = -2.441, p < .05) from baseline (M = 1.60, SD = 1.11) to follow up (M = 1.22, SD = 1.24) in negative emotion. In contrast, for those low in benefit finding there was almost no change (d = .009, t = .057, ns) from baseline (M = 1.44, SD = 1.12) to follow up (M = 1.43, SD, 1.10) in negative emotion.

Did Benefit Finding Predict Positive Emotion at Follow Up?

The results of the analyses of the potential predictors of positive emotion are presented in Table 2. At baseline, optimism, emotional support, active coping, and positive reframing were related to more positive emotion. At follow-up, benefit finding, income, optimism, active coping, and positive reframing were related to more positive emotion. The partial correlations showed that benefit finding, income, and positive reframing were all still related to more positive emotion at follow up when controlling for baseline positive emotion. Thus, our first hypothesis that benefit finding would be related to more positive emotion at follow-up was supported.

Table 2. Correlations and Partial Correlations between Baseline Variables and Positive and Negative Emotion at Baseline and Follow Up

	Positive Emotion			Negative Emotion		
	Baseline[a]	Follow[b]	Follow[c]	Baseline[a]	Follow[b]	Follow[c]
Benefit Finding	.101	.321**	.316**	.205*	-.060	-.237*
Demographics						
Age	.042	-.097	-.140	-.283**	-.183	-.030
Years Education	.126	.058	-.141	-.218+	-.170	.148+

Table 2 (Continued)

Income Range	.024	.262*	.292*	-.036	-.149	-.156+
Female	-.007	.025	.033	.070	.002	-.045
Ethnic Minority	-.013	.016	.027	.149+	.278*	.237*
Cardiac Conditions						
Heart Attack	-.060	-.082	-.060	-.113	.110	.211+
CABG Surgery	-.016	.052	.071	.010	-.095	.122
Stent Installed	.044	.020	-.003	.009	.038	.039
Personal Resources						
Optimism	.364**	.363**	.217+	-.440**	-.464**	-.292*
Spirituality	.134	.085	.018	-.102	-.047	.012
Emotional Support	.209*	.125	.019	-.115	-.230*	-.201+
Tangible Support	.084	-.127	-.170	-.137+	-.370**	-.358**
Coping Strategies						
Active Coping	.404**	.247*	.046	-.336**	-.234*	-.058
Positive Reframing	.383**	.420**	.280*	-.290**	-.201+	-.047

Note. [a]Baseline correlations include the full sample (n = 147). Follow up correlations include the participants assessed at both baseline and follow up (n = 77). [c]Partial correlations controlling for baseline benefit finding. +p < .10, *p < .05, **p < .01.

Did Benefit Finding Predict Negative Emotion at Follow Up?

The results of the analyses of the potential predictors of negative emotion are also displayed in Table 2. At baseline, age, optimism, active coping, and positive reframing were related to less negative emotion and benefit finding was related to more negative emotion. At follow-up, optimism, emotional support, tangible support, and active coping were related to less negative emotion and ethnic minority status was related to more negative emotion. The partial correlations showed that optimism and tangible support were still related to less, and ethnic minority status was still related to more negative emotion at follow up when controlling for baseline negative emotion. In addition, benefit finding was related to less negative emotion when baseline negative emotion was controlled. Thus, our second hypothesis that benefit finding would be related to less negative emotion at follow up was supported.

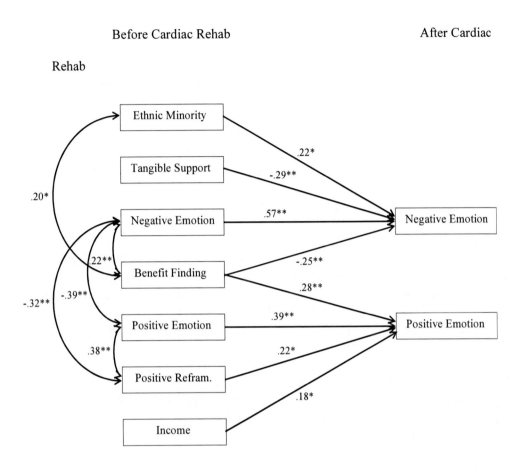

Figure 1. Path model predicting positive and negative emotion at follow up from baseline variables. *p < .05, **p < .01.

Does Benefit Finding Predict Emotion at Follow Up in a Multivariate Model?

We conducted path analyses to examine the multivariate predictors of emotion at follow up. To develop a path model, we began with all of the significant univariate predictors of either positive emotion or negative emotion at follow up and also included positive and negative emotion at baseline. We then deleted all non-significant paths and variables with no significant paths to positive or negative emotion at follow up. The final model is displayed in Figure 1 and provided a good fit for the data ($\chi2$ = 19.029, df = 16, p = 0.267, CFI = .999, TLI = .997, RMSEA = .036). The only significant predictor of both less negative emotion and more positive emotion was benefit finding. In addition, positive reframing coping and income were related to more positive emotion, ethnic minority status was related to more negative emotion, and tangible social support was related to less negative emotion at follow-up.

CONCLUSION

The purpose of this study was to determine whether benefit finding was related to better emotional health in cardiac patients who completed a 12 week cardiac rehabilitation program. We predicted and found that benefit finding was related to increased positive emotion and decreased negative emotion when controlling for baseline emotion and other important predictors. These findings are consistent with Affleck et al. (1987) regarding a prospective relationship between benefit finding and better health. In addition, they are in accord with the idea that emotion may mediate the effects of benefit finding on long-term cardiac morbidity (Kubzansky & Thurston, 2007; Tully et al. 2008). A useful next step might be to examine changes in both emotion and cardiac health at brief time intervals (e.g., three months) over a period of years to empirically test this potential link.

Why was benefit finding related to increased positive emotion and decreased negative emotion at follow-up? First, positive events have been uniquely associated with increased positive emotion (Zautra, 2003). Second, although positive events may generally be less related to negative emotion, they may be particularly important in reducing negative emotion during times of high stress (Davis et al. 2004). Third, benefit finding may have particularly strong effects in the context of cardiac rehabilitation and recovery from cardiac disease. The fact that people have already perceived positive changes as a result of having cardiac disease may have built a sense of hope and self-efficacy about achieving more positive change in a rehabilitation program. This may enhance positive emotion through increased engagement in the program and reduce negative emotions regarding losses and fears of future cardiac events.

The difference between concurrent and prospective relationships between benefit finding and emotion clearly supports the value of prospective studies. The fact that this relationship changed in a relatively short period of time suggests that cardiac rehabilitation may be an important time for examining the effects of benefit finding. Why was the concurrent relationship between benefit finding and emotion different from the prospective relationship? We suspect this may be at least partially due to the fact that benefit finding was assessed relatively close to a stressful cardiac event. Being closer to such a stressor may have reduced the chance that any perceived benefits would have had time to significantly influence positive emotional health (Schwarzer et al. 2006). In addition, the close proximity to a stressful event may have led to a simultaneous increase in negative emotions and the process of finding benefits, thus resulting in a positive correlation between them (Park & Helgeson, 2006).

The other findings regarding the predictors of emotion at follow up also deserve comment. The relationship between positive reframing and positive emotion is consistent with two-factor theory (Zautra, 2003) and the idea that positive appraisals may increase positive emotion. The relationship between tangible support and negative emotion suggests that tangible support is important for reducing distress in cardiac patients but may not necessarily involve an increase in pleasant experiences. The positive relationship between ethnic minority status and negative emotion raises questions about how well cardiac rehabilitation programs are adapted for ethnic minority patients (Sheikh & Marotta, 2008). Finally, the relation between income and positive emotion suggests that economic resources may be important for recovering cardiac patients.

The main clinical implication of this study is that interventions that increase benefit finding may be important for cardiac patients. This is supported by the relationship that we found between benefit finding and improved emotional health and the well-established relationship between emotional health and prognosis for cardiac patients (Kubzansky & Thurston, 2007; Tully et al. 2008). The kinds of interventions that may increase benefit finding have been described by Calhoun and Tedeschi (1999). These interventions may include expressive writing about perceived benefits and cognitive-behavioral stress management programs that may target benefit finding. A good time to implement such an intervention may be before or during cardiac rehab because that may be a time when the effects of benefit finding are particularly important.

This study also has important limitations. First, the sample was primarily men and future studies should include a larger proportion of women. Second, there was a large amount of attrition from the pre to post rehab assessments although this is common in cardiac rehabilitation programs (Petrie & Weinmann, 1996). Third, the benefit finding measure was created for this study although it closely mirrors the items on other benefit finding and growth scales and was highly internally consistent. Fourth, the benefits reported were perceived benefits and future studies should attempt to assess actual benefits with additional measures and observer reports.

In summary, this study found that benefit finding was related to better emotional health in cardiac patients following the completion of a cardiac rehabilitation program. Benefit finding before rehabilitation was related to more positive emotion and less negative emotion after rehabilitation. These findings are consistent with previous research showing positive effects for benefit finding in cardiac patients and suggest that short-term changes in emotional health may be a process by which benefit may affect cardiac morbidity. Future research should attempt to better understand the effects of benefit finding for cardiac patients by assessing emotion and indicators of cardiac health over longer time periods and determine whether benefit finding interventions improve emotional health and the long-term prognosis of cardiac patients.

AUTHOR NOTE

Bruce W. Smith, Paulette J. Christopher, Laura E. Bouldin, Erin M. Tooley, Jennifer F. Bernard, and J. Alexis Ortiz for the University of New Mexico.

We thank Dr. Richard D. Lueker, P. Goldyn Taylor, and the staff and patients of the New Heart Center for Wellness, Exercise, and Cardiac Rehabilitation in Albuquerque, New Mexico for their generous support of this research project.

REFERENCES

Affleck, G., Tennen, H., Croog, S., & Levine, S. (1987). Causal attribution, perceived benefits, and morbidity after a heart attack: An 8-Year study. *Journal of Consulting and Clinical Psychology*, 55, 29-35.

Calhoun, L.G., & Tedeschi, R.G. (1999). *Facilitating posttraumatic growth: A clinician's guide.* New York: Lawrence Erlbaum.

Calhoun, L. G., & Tedeschi, R. G. (Eds.). (2006). *Handbook of posttraumatic growth: Research and practice.* Mahweh, NJ: Lawrence Erlbaum.

Carver, C. S. (1997). You want to measure coping but your protocol's too long: Consider the Brief COPE. *International Journal of Behavioral Medicine, 4,* 92-100.

Chan, I. W. S., Lai, J. C. L., & Wong, K. W. N. (2006). Resilience is associated with better recovery in Chinese people diagnosed with coronary heart disease. *Psychology & Health, 21,* 335-349.

Davis, M. C., Zautra, A. J., & Smith, B. W. (2004). Chronic pain, stress, and the dynamics of affective differentiation. *Journal of Personality, 72,* 1133-1160.

Fetzer Institute. (1999). *Multidimensional Measurement of Religiousness/Spirituality for Use in Health Research: A Report of the Fetzer Institute/National Institute on Aging.* Kalamazoo, MI: John E. Fetzer Institute.

Helgeson, V. S., Reynolds. K. A., & Tomich. P. L. (2006). A meta-analytic review of benefit finding and growth. *Journal of Consulting and Clinical Psychology, 74,* 797-816.

Kubzansky, L. D., & Thurston, R. C. (2007). Emotional vitality and incident coronary heart disease. *Archives of General Psychiatry, 64,* 1393-1401.

Larsen, R., & Diener, E. (1992). Promises and problems with the circumplex model of emotion. In M. S. Clarke (Ed.), *Emotion* (pp. 25-59). Newbury Park, CA: Sage.

Lechner, S. C., Carver C. S., Antoni, M. H., Weaver, K. E., & Phillips, K. M. (2006). Curvilinear associations between benefit finding and psychosocial adjustment to breast cancer. *Journal of Consulting and Clinical Psychology, 74,* 828-840.

Milam, J. (2004). Posttraumatic growth among HIV/AIDS patients. *Journal of Applied Social Psychology, 34,* 2353-2376.

Milam, J. (2006). Posttraumatic growth and HIV disease progression. *Journal of Consulting and Clinical Psychology, 74,* 817-827.

Mohr, D. C., Dick, L. P., Russo, J. P., Boudewyn, A. C., Likosky, W., & Goodkin, D. E. (1999). The psychological impact of multiple sclerosis: Exploring the patient's perspective. *Health Psychology, 18,* 376-382.

Park, C. L., Cohen, L. H., & Murch, R. L. (1996). Assessment and prediction of stress-related growth. *Journal of Personality, 64, 71-105.*

Park, C. L., & Helgeson, V. S. (2006). Introduction to the special section: Growth following highly stressful life events – current status and future directions. *Journal of Consulting and Clinical Psychology, 74,* 791-796.

Petrie, K. J., Buick, D. L., Weinman, J., & Booth, R. J. (1999). Positive effects of illness reported by myocardial infarction and breast cancer patients. *Journal of Psychosomatic Research ,47,* 537-543.

Petrie, K.J., & Weinman, J. (1996). Role of patients' view of their illness in predicting return to work and functioning after myocardial infarction: Longitudinal study. *British Medical Journal, 312,* 1191-1194.

Rozanski, A., & Kubzansky, L. D. (2005). Psychologic functioning and physical health: A paradigm of flexibility. *Psychosomatic Medicine, 67,* S47-53.

Scheier, M. F., Carver, C. S., & Bridges, M. W. (1994). Distinguishing optimism from neuroticism (and trait anxiety, self-mastery, and self-esteem): A reevaluation of the Life Orientation Test. *Journal of Personality and Social Psychology, 67,* 1063-1078.

Schwarzer, R., Luszczynska, A., Boehmer, S., Taubert, S., & Knoll, N. (2006). Changes in finding benefit after cancer surgery and the predition of well-being one year later. *Social Science & Medicine, 63,* 1614-1624.

Sheikh, A. I. (2004). Posttraumatic growth in the context of heart disease. *Journal of Clinical Psychology in Medical Settings, 11,* 265-273.

Sheikh, A. I., & Marotta, S. A. (2008). Best practices in counseling in cardiac rehabilitation settings. *Journal of Counseling and Development, 86,* 111-119.

Sherbourne, C. D., & Stewart, A. L. (1991). The MOS social support survey. *Social Science and Medicine, 32,*705-714.

Tedeschi, R. G., & Calhoun, L. G. (1996). The Post-Traumatic Growth Inventory: Measuring the positive legacy of trauma. *Journal of Traumatic Stress, 9,* 455-471.

Tomich, P. L., & Helgeson, V. S. (2004). Is finding something good in the bad always good? Benefit finding among women with breast cancer. *Health Psychology, 23,* 16-23.

Tully, P. J., Baker, R. A., Turnbull, D., & Winefield, H. (2008). The role of depression and anxiety symptoms in hospital readmissions after cardiac surgery. *Journal of Behavioral Medicine, 31,* 281-90.

Zautra, A. J. (2003). *Emotions, stress, and health.* New York: Oxford University Press.

In: Health Psychology
Editor: Ryan E. Murphy, pp. 127-135

ISBN 978-1-61728-981-1
© 2010 Nova Science Publishers, Inc.

Chapter 7

NEGOTIATING BLAME AS A FAT CHILD'S PARENT: A CASE STUDY

Riina Kokkonen[*]

Department of Psychology, University of Eastern Finland
Joensuu, Finland

ABSTRACT

In recent years, the so-called "fatness epidemic" has been subjected to critical examination by different researchers questioning the biomedical definition of fatness as a self-induced health risk and focusing on the discrimination and blame directed at fat people. Attention has also been paid to the ways fat people themselves interpret and account for their fatness in the prevailing negative atmosphere, but the viewpoints of *the parents of fat children* have received less attention. As the primary caretakers, parents are often the ones blamed for their child's weight and are easily viewed as somehow "improper" parents. It is therefore important to look at the ways these parents interpret and manage the ambient messages implying their deviance from the norms of "good" parenthood. In this chapter, my aim is to take this subject up for discussion by presenting an analysis of the interviews of two mothers whose children have been determined to be "overweight" or "obese" by health care. These interviews are part of my current study concerning the ways the parents of Finnish fifth-graders discuss their children's health and their own role and responsibilities as parents. These two interviews stood out as clear exceptions to the other interviews, for they revolved around the issues of the child's weight and the blaming of the parents. I will present a close reading of these two interviews and analyze the multiple ways the mothers discursively and rhetorically managed the blame and tried to position themselves as worthy parents.

---

[*] Address:
Psychology, University of Eastern Finland
P.O. Box 111
FIN-80101 Joensuu, Finland
Gsm: +358-050-344 7254
E-mail: riina.kokkonen@uef.fi

INTRODUCTION

During the last twenty years, the concern over the fatness of the population has increased steadily in western societies. The discussion is largely guided by the biomedical point of view, which defines fatness as a significant health risk, even a disease in itself, and a result of a "wrong" lifestyle. Children in particular are seen to be in danger, and parental vigilance is called for to prevent and control childhood fatness and the future health problems associated with it.

Despite its hegemonic status, the biomedical point of view is currently challenged by a growing body of work on fatness from non-medical points of view, such as social, legal, and humanistic ones (e.g., Braziel & LeBesco, 2001; Gard & Wright, 2005; Harjunen, 2009; Saguy & Almeling, 2008; Solovay, 2000). What these recent studies share, though varied in their theoretical and analytical orientations, is a critical view of the biomedical point of view and the current societal panic stemming from it. On the basis of critical analyses of medical publications and popular media texts, it has been pointed out, for instance, that the results concerning the causes of fatness and the possible health risks associated with it are far from unambiguous and that the media play a central role in the construction of the fear of fatness by means of exaggerated representations. The aim of these studies has been to call attention to the strong moral aspects of the fatness "epidemic", such as the way the prevailing healthist culture discusses fatness as a self-inflicted health risk, holding that it is everyone's duty to pursue and maintain a healthy body, which easily increases the already strong burden of blame that fat people carry (e.g., Gard & Wright, 2005; Saguy & Almeling, 2008). Significantly, some of these critical studies of fatness have given a voice to fat people themselves, exposing the pervasive moral denigration and discrimination that they encounter (e.g., Harjunen, 2009).

What has not yet been addressed to the best of my knowledge, however, is the perspective of the parents of a fat child. While adults are regarded as responsible for their own weight, children are mainly viewed as victims rather than perpetrators of the "epidemic", as Throsby (2007, p. 1567) points out. It is the primary carers, the parents, that are viewed as responsible and therefore blamed if the child exceeds the limits of "normal" weight. In the media, parents, especially mothers, are accused of neglecting their children by letting them eat unhealthy food, for instance (e.g., Saguy & Almeling, 2008). These moral evaluations are also found in lay discussions on children's fatness. In my analysis of an Internet discussion on the topic, I found that the parents, mothers in particular, were mainly viewed as the primary cause of the child's fatness and were depicted as having a "lousy" character, being unable to create an "adequate" emotional bond with the child, or engaging in "faulty" child-rearing practices (Kokkonen, 2009). It seems important, then, to look at the ways these parents themselves account for their children's fatness and deal with the ambient messages implying that they deviate from the norms of "good" parenthood. The aim of this chapter is to bring this very subject up for discussion: I present a discursive analysis of the interviews of two Finnish mothers whose children were defined as "overweight" or "obese" in health care.

CHILDREN'S FATNESS AND PARENTHOOD: THE FINNISH CONTEXT

In Finland, the discussion on fatness can be described as very similar to that in other western countries, such as the UK and the US. It tends to be dominated by the biomedical point of view: through the last decade, fatness, especially that of children, has been one of the main concerns of Finnish health experts, and the topic is continually brought up in the popular media as well. Various programmes and guidelines, such as the Current Care Guideline (Finnish Paediatric Society, 2005), have been initiated and constructed in order to reduce and prevent childhood fatness. The "healthy" and "normal" development of children is regularly monitored in health check-ups by child health centres and school health care. A central part of these check-ups is measuring the child's height and weight and comparing them with the average of his or her age group by means of height/weight charts. For children under school age, if a child's weight is 10-20 % above average, s/he is considered "overweight", and if over 20 %, "obese". For school-aged children, the corresponding limits are 20-40 % and over 40% (Finnish Paediatric Society, 2005)

Finland also mirrors other western countries in the way personal responsibility for one's health is understood. Current Finnish health promotion relies on the general ideal of the autonomous, rational and responsible individual and encourages people to control their eating and to exercise regularly in order to maintain a "healthy" body (Pajari, Jallinoja, & Absetz, 2006). As to children's health, parents are viewed as responsible. In the ideal of "good" parenthood, the attributes of proper child-rearing defined by psychology, such as setting clear, consistent rules and interacting with children, are intertwined with health consciousness: for instance, parents must set clear and permanent rules concerning food and eating and show a good example of healthy living (Kokkonen, 2009).

DATA AND METHODOLOGY

The two thematic interviews that I focus on are part of my current study of the ways the parents of Finnish 5th-graders (20 mothers and 8 fathers) discuss their children's health and their own role and responsibilities as parents. I asked the parents, for instance, about their child's physical health and development in general and about the family's health-related practices, such as nutrition and physical exercise. The child's weight was a theme the two mothers in question brought up without any prompting, which clearly shows that it was a salient topic for them.

My approach to the analysis is influenced by a particular version of discursive psychology that combines aspects of ethnomethodology, conversation analysis, and post-structuralism (Edley & Wetherell, 2001). The discursive perspective has been adopted and proved useful in studies of morality in relation to health issues, including fatness, as it enables a detailed analysis of the way people construct and negotiate moral tensions in situated interaction (e.g., Jolanki, 2004; Throsby, 2007; Wiggins, 2009). My starting point is that when using language, people actively construct versions of things and of themselves and counter alternative constructions in order to defend themselves, for instance, but that they do so within the limits set by the prevailing socio-historical context and the discourses (i.e., clusters of interrelated meanings and practises) it entails. In the case of children's fatness and parenthood, the key discourses setting limits to the parents' talk can be identified as the biomedical discourse, defining the concepts of "normal" and "healthy", and the discourse of "proper" parenthood, defining how the parents should raise their children in terms of psychology and health-consciousness (see Kokkonen, 2009). In my analysis I read the interviews in relation to these discourses and focus on the ways the mothers counter possible moral accusations: I analyze how they account for their children's fatness and construct themselves as worthy parents by rhetorical and discursive means.

ANALYSIS

Case 1

The first case is that of a mother whose sons (a fifth-grader and his older brother) have been defined as "overweight" or "obese" in health care.

At the very beginning of the interview, when I ask the mother to describe the physical development of her fifth-grader son, she depicts him as having always been tall in relation to his peers and *"otherwise robust, too."* She explicitly constructs the issue of her son's weight as a moral one by describing how she has been criticised by *"the child clinic auntie"* (i.e., a nurse) in health care. Next she describes a situation in which a doctor told her that because her son happened to be robust, it was impossible to make him slim.

> He even showed with his hands that if the child is shaped like this, around the shoulders and all, there's just no way of making him slim.[i]

In this way, by vividly describing the opinion of a medical authority that is higher up in the hierarchy of health care professionals than a nurse is, she counters the blame and mitigates the possibility of her having effected her son's fatness (Edwards & Potter, 1992)

Later in the interview, the logic of the mother's argumentation changes from mitigating her responsibility as a parent to proving that she has made conscious efforts to manage her son's weight. When I ask her whether she has sought health-related information, she mentions visits to a nutrition therapist's office to talk about her son's fatness. She discussed the family's food and eating habits with the therapist and sought better courses of action. She describes the food choices she makes in the grocery store by means of several contrasts (Atkinson, 1984):

> So that was the nutrition therapist's advice. When you buy a big jar, you pay much less per kilo than you do when you buy a small jar. So I took the small jar anyway.

> So this is what we always go through, whether to buy a big bag or a little bag. Weighing things in the balance. Like non-fat milk and regular milk.

By means of these contrasts, she positions herself as a responsible parent who follows expert advice, does not try to save money at the expense of health, and also teaches her children how to make the right choices in terms of healthy, non-fattening food. She explicitly categorizes foods in moral terms on the basis of their assumed "fatteningness": *"so here we have the choices again: eat a piece of chocolate, bad, eat a piece of sugared sweets, less bad.*" She also mentions that her son likes white bread but that the nutrition therapist has advised her to minimize its consumption.

> So we have sort of taken that advice, but then again, sometimes consented to his eating white bread but every once in a while pointed out that there's rye bread too, would you like some? [And he always says] "I just don't like it."

Here she mitigates the parents' possibilities of controlling their son's eating and weight management by referring to the son's food preferences: they have tried to persuade him to eat rye bread but he does not like it. In this way, she constructs herself as being in line with contemporary expert views of "good" parenting: parents are nowadays expected to avoid forcing and to allow the child to make some decisions concerning food (Coveney, 2000, p. 130-131). When I ask what kind of eater her son is, the mother answers:

> Well, I work at a day-care centre, so I've been thinking it's funny, why didn't our boys turn out to be those poor eaters so they wouldn't be too fat.

This can also be interpreted as a way of hers to mitigate her responsibility for her son's weight management. She categorizes children contrastively into *good eaters* and *poor eaters* and places her sons in the first category; the boys have, as if by chance, become *good eaters,* and that contributes to their current weight problem. The mother continues by describing the family rules of eating: *You eat what you eat now, and if you don't care for it, I'll put it away and you can't have anything at other times.* In this way, she constructs herself as a responsible parent: she makes the main decisions concerning food and dinner times and thus does her best to control the boys' innate tendency to be *good eaters.* At the end of the interview she once more brings up her sons' fatness and the possible interpretations people may make of it:

> Surely people form an image of what our lifestyle is like, but in a way I don't agree. (…) Really, there's been discussions with the kids, like, why am I fat though we drink light pop, or why am I fat though I eat so much salad, or why am I fat though I exercise so much (…), or why am I fat though I don't eat sweets every day like little Venla, for example, who goes to the kiosk every day.

Here we see that she is well aware that people may evaluate the family's lifestyle negatively. Once more she tries to prove that she is a responsible parent by listing examples of the family's healthy choices. The reference to little *Venla* also includes a hint that some people are just more prone to gain weight than others, regardless of lifestyle.

Case 2

The other mother, too, did intensive rhetorical work when talking about the way her youngest two daughters' weight had been evaluated in health care. In contrast to the previous mother, however, her argumentation focused on denying the problem status of her daughters' weight.

This mother, too, explicitly constructs the issue as a moral one at the beginning of the interview. When I ask her about her memories of the health check-ups of her fifth-grader daughter, she says this daughter's height and weight had been defined as "normal", whereas the younger two *have got flak from the hospital about how fat they are, these normally proportioned children.* And she continues,

> Okay, so the girls' height-weight curves have swung a bit, but on the other hand Jatta, the third-grader, is approaching the stage where the weight increases first, then the height. And Jessika was categorized as a dumpling. In my view, she really is no dumpling. Then I asked the doctor, I said show me where it is, where should we start slimming this four-year-old.(...) The doctor raised the girl's smock and just couldn't say where she should slim down, only that she is like, sort of big.

Here she admits that her second daughter's weight has increased in relation to her height but constructs this as a normal part of children's physical development, which determines when the more rapid phase of height growth begins. She continues by accounting how her youngest daughter has been defined as "a dumpling" and denies this definition by vividly describing her encounter with a medical authority: even the doctor had to admit that there was nothing extra in the girl's body that needed to be reduced, that it is just the way she was built. Her argumentation continues intensely:

> You see, if they're hungry, I can't very well keep a little kid of that age hungry, and it's normal food that we eat. (...) Of course, extreme or abnormal obesity is an entirely different matter than our little bit of overweight, but I'm afraid these things may cause children huge traumas and lead to anorexia and bulimia and who knows what. (...) And when we were going to the doctor's, my middle one told me, "Look mom, I ate three hamburger patties at school", and we were going there straight after lunch. So, then she was judged to be fat.

Here the mother constructs herself as a good parent by appealing to her daughter's best interest (it is not right to let her go hungry) and by categorizing the food they eat as "normal". Next she builds a contrast between her daughter's weight and "real" obesity: the daughter's weight is not high enough to jeopardize her health. She reinforces the contrast by the extreme formulation (Pomerantz, 1986) "extreme or abnormal obesity." She also says she worries that weight-related comments might cause traumas (note again the extreme formulation "huge traumas") and lead to eating disorders. Her expression "anorexia and bulimia and who knows what" is an example of a three-part list, which is often used to reinforce one's argument (Jefferson, 1990). In this case, the list highlights the possible negative effects of commenting on the child's weight: the third part of the list suggests that anorexia and bulimia stand only as examples of a larger group of serious disorders. The mother also tells me how they went to check-up straight after school lunch, implying that the daughter's weight was high because of the large amount of food eaten and that the food also caused the daughter to appear a bit plump. When I ask her about the discussions she has had with her daughters about the issue, she says,

> We have talked a lot, and I have said that as long as you eat real food, proper food and have healthy eating habits and exercise as much as you do, we will not worry about that matter.

Here we can see a three-part list again (proper food, healthy eating habits, and exercise). By constructing the list, the mother gives ample evidence of her family's life styles and signals that because they lead a healthy life, there is no reason to make an issue of the daughters' weight. At the end of the interview, as we talk about the current societal concern over fatness, she takes up the issue once more:

> The problem is who gets to decide when one is fat. I just don't think these kids of mine are fat. If they really were fat I'd be cooperating with the doctors one hundred per cent.

Here the mother questions the limits of fatness set by the experts and also the experts' right to determine who is fat. In addition, she tries to prove that she is a responsible parent: if her daughters' weight were *really* a problem, she would do her very best to solve it. Finally, however, she admits:

> Well, I have had them spend more time outdoors, on the sly, so to speak. (…) One really can't do more. If it's in the genes, they are what they are.

Though she has persistently emphasized that she does not see her daughters having a weight problem, she still admits that she has undertaken weight management action. This can be seen to reflect the force of the biomedical discourse: a "good" parent cannot disregard the experts' comments on weight. Finally, as a closure of sorts, she mitigates her possibilities of making a difference by referring to genetic inheritance.

CONCLUSION

My purpose in this chapter was to contribute to critical studies of fatness by bringing up the perspective of the fat child's parent. All through the interviews of the two mothers, they pondered on their children's weight and the expert comments on it. The rich argumentation they engaged in can be seen to exemplify the "moral burden" carried nowadays by the parents of children defined as "overweight" or "obese."

The mother of the two boys did not try to deny that her sons' weight was too high but took this notion for granted. She mitigated her responsibility by referring to factors at least partly beyond her control, such as the innate build of her boys. The other mother's argumentation focused more on opposing the biomedical discourse. She did not deny the notion, as such, that fatness is problematic, but she did question the limits of harmful fatness set by the experts: she denied that her daughter's weight was high enough to be considered a problem. Both mothers, in addition to mitigating their responsibility or denying the problem status of the child's weight, also managed the blame by assuring that they were responsible parents. They constructed themselves as perfectly in line with the ideal of "good" parenthood, in which psychological notions intertwine with health-consciousness: they depicted themselves, for instance, as setting limits to food consumption but avoiding forcing, talking to their children about life styles, and being supportive. Thus they denied doing the very things the parents of fat children are accused of, such as being indifferent and letting the child eat fattening food (Kokkonen, 2009).

The ways these mothers managed blame seem quite similar to the ones found in studies of fat adults. Wiggins (2009) found that patients who came to weight management services accounted for their weight in two major ways when participating in group meetings with the practitioners: they either denied having done the blameworthy things (such as eating fattening food) or located the blame outside individual control (by depicting their fatness as innate, for instance). Similarly, the weight-loss surgery patients interviewed by Throsby (2007) explained their fatness and thus managed the blame by referring to factors outside individual control, such as genes, but simultaneously highlighted their conscious efforts to manage their weight. But there are also some differences. In contrast to the mothers in my study, Throsby's interviewees described different life events, such as divorce or moving house, which had led them to neglect weight management. The claim was that there are phases in life where healthy lifestyles are just not among the priorities. Presumably, this way of accounting for fatness is not as readily available for the parents of fat children as it is for fat adults. After all, parents are obliged to act for the child's best interest – always and in any circumstances. Therefore, a confession of acting otherwise might be viewed as highly condemnable. Significantly, the patients in Throsby's study also explained their fatness by describing their parents, especially mothers, as being absent and substituting food for love; thus parents are blamed not only by "outsiders" but also by fat adults. In the light of these findings, we may ask whether it is even more reprehensible in a way to be a parent of a fat child than a fat adult

As the "moral panic" surrounding fatness shows no signs of subsiding, further research is obviously needed to examine the parents' possibilities of resisting the identity of a "bad" parent they are constantly offered. One important aspect to consider is the genderedness of parenthood: as mothers are still viewed in western countries as the primary parents, they are also the ones blamed for children's fatness (Kokkonen, 2009; Saguy & Almeling, 2008). It would therefore be useful to interview both mothers *and* fathers and to examine their possible differences in accounting for the child's weight. In addition, the parents' blame management should also be studied in other contexts than the research interview, such as encounters with health professionals.

REFERENCES

Atkinson, M. (1984). *Our masters' voices: The language and body language of politics*. London: Methuen.

Braziel, J. E., & LeBesco, K. (2001). *Bodies out of bounds: Fatness and transgression*. Berkeley: University of California Press.

Coveney, J. (2000). *Food, morals and meaning: The pleasure and anxiety of eating*. London: Routledge.

Edley, N., & Wetherell, M. (2001). Jekyll and Hyde: Men's constructions of feminism and feminists. *Feminism & Psychology*, 11(4), 439-457.

Edwards, D., & Potter, J. (1992). *Discursive psychology*. London: Sage.

Finnish Paediatric Society (2005). Käypä hoito –suositus: Lasten lihavuus [Current care guideline: Childhood obesity]. *Duodecim*, 121(18), 2016-2024.

Gard, M., & Wright, J. (2005). *The obesity epidemic: Science, morality and ideology*. New York: Routledge.

Harjunen, H. (2009). *Women and fat: Approaches to the social study of fatness*. Jyväskylä: University of Jyväskylä.

Jefferson, G. (1990). List-construction as a task and resource. In G. Psathas (Ed.), *Interaction competence* (pp. 63-92). Washington DC: University Press of America.

Jolanki, O. (2004). Moral argumentation in talk about health and old age. *Health:*, 8(4), 483-503.

Kokkonen, R. (2009). The fat child – a sign of "bad" motherhood? An analysis of explanations for children's fatness on a Finnish website. *Journal of Community & Applied Social Psychology*, 19(5), 336-347.

Pajari, P. M., Jallinoja, P., & Absetz, P. (2006). Negotiation over self-control and activity: An analysis of balancing in the repertoires of Finnish healthy lifestyles. *Social Science & Medicine*, 62(10), 2601-2611.

Pomerantz, A. (1986). Extreme case formulations: A way of legitimizing claims. *Human Studies*, 9(2-3), 219-229.

Saguy, A. C., & Almeling, R. (2008). Fat in the fire? Science, the news media, and the "obesity epidemic". *Sociological Forum*, 23(1), 53-83.

Solovay, S. (2000). *Tipping the scales of justice: Fighting weight-based discrimination*. Amherst, NY: Prometheus Books.

Throsby, K. (2007). "How could you let yourself get like that?": Stories of the origins of obesity in accounts of weight loss surgery. *Social Science & Medicine*, 65(8), 1561-1571.

Wiggins, S. (2009). Managing blame in NHS weight management treatment: Psychologizing weight and "obesity". *Journal of Community and Applied Social Psychology*, 19(5), 374-387[1] The extracts are presented in close English translations provided by a professional translator. I have deleted some words that do not affect the point of the extract. The sign (…) indicates that a whole phrase has been deleted.

In: Health Psychology
Editor: Ryan E. Murphy, pp. 137-144

ISBN 978-1-61728-981-1
© 2010 Nova Science Publishers, Inc.

Chapter 8

TRUST IN HEALTH CARE: CONCEPTUAL ISSUES AND EMPIRICAL RESEARCH

Rocio Garcia-Retamero[1,2] and Yasmina Okan[1]*
[1]Universidad de Granada (Spain),
[2]Max Planck Institute for Human Development, Berlin (Germany)

ABSTRACT

Over the past few decades, there has been a shift from an emphasis on medical paternalism to the recognition of the importance of an informed patient. A balance may be achieved by encouraging patients and physicians to share decision making. Patients' trust in their physician has been suggested as a crucial factor influencing patients' willingness to participate in decision making. Investigating which variables influence trust in physicians and in heath care institutions, therefore, becomes more essential than ever. Our aim in this chapter is to examine the conceptual issues and empirical research regarding patients' trust in the different constituents of the health care system. First, we explain the meaning of trust and provide an overview of the instruments that have been developed to measure the concept. Second, we describe different types of trust and some of the variables that influence each of them. Third, we explain the impact of trust in health care systems and discuss the elements of trust that may be particularly important in this context. Finally, we describe several relevant results that emerge from a review of the literature on the topic and open avenues for future research. We conclude that empirical research clearly complements theory and suggests that developing a trustworthy health care system requires more than competent physicians. More importantly, it needs health

* Send correspondence to:
Rocio Garcia-Retamero
Facultad de Psicologia,
Universidad de Granada
Campus Universitario de Cartuja s/n,
18071 Granada (Spain)
Tel: 0034 958 246240
Fax: 0034 958 246239
Email: rretamer@ugr.es

workers that have the motivation and capacity for empathetic understanding of patients, as well as institutions that sustain ethical behaviors and so provide a basis for trust.

INTRODUCTION: THE CONCEPT OF TRUST

Trust has been a central topic in different academic disciplines, leading to the existence of a wide range of definitions of this concept. These different conceptualizations, however, share some common characteristics. In particular, factors such as competence, compassion, privacy and confidentiality, reliability and dependability, and communication are widely considered to be core components in the conceptualization of trust (Pearson & Raeke, 2000).

Trust has been defined as "the optimistic acceptance of a vulnerable situation in which the trustor believes the trustee will care for the trustor's interests" (Hall, 2006; Hall, Dugan, Zheng, & Mishra, 2001). According to Gilson (2006), this definition emphasizes several key features of trust. First, it implies that trust is a relational notion, that is, it emerges from a set of inter-personal behaviors. These behaviors are guided by sets of institutional rules, laws, and customs. At the micro level, we can distinguish several types of trust relations: between an individual patient and a physician, between two physicians, as well as between a physician and her manager. At the macro level, we can consider patient and public trust in physicians and managers in a particular health care organization and in the whole health care system (Calnan & Rowe, 2006). Second, the definition of trust involves a notion of vulnerability and risk, and it is rooted in the expectation that the other will have concern for one's own interests. That is, trust appears to be necessary to cope with situations which have an element of uncertainty regarding the motives, intentions, and future actions of other individuals and organizations that we depend on (Calnan & Rowe, 2006; Mayer, Davis, & Schoorman, 1995). Trust appears to be particularly important in the health care area because this is a setting characterized by uncertainty regarding the competence and intentions of the physician on whom the patient is reliant (Alaszweski, 2003; Calnan & Rowe, 2004). The need for interpersonal trust emerges from the vulnerability associated with being ill as well as from the information asymmetries and unequal relationships specific to the medical domain. This explains why most definitions of trust combine expectations about ability, competence, and knowledge of the physician with expectations about her ethics, integrity, and motives (Gilson, 2006; Hall et al., 2001).

INSTRUMENTS THAT MEASURE TRUST AND EMPIRICAL FINDINGS ON THE TOPIC

Trust research started to gain momentum with the 1990 publication of Anderson and Dedrick's trust in physician scale (Anderson & Dedrick, 1990). Recently, trust continues to gain increasing attention in the medical and health literatures. The dominant focus of this research is on patients' interpersonal trust in a specific physician. The number of studies concerning dimensions of trust in broader medical institutions is considerably smaller (Hall, 2006). Despite this limitation, several interesting points emerge from the existent literature on the topic (see Calnan & Rowe, 2006, and Hall, 2006 for the reviews). First, in addition to the scale noted above, several research groups have published different scales to measure medical trust (see Hall et al., 2002; Kao, Green, Davis, Koplan, & Cleary, 1998a; Leisen & Hyman, 2001; Safran et al., 1998b; Thom, Ribisl, Steward, & Luce, 1999). The majority of these scales focuses on measuring a patient's trust in his or her individual physician, although recently new scales have been developed to measure different aspects such as trust in the health care organization (e.g., LaVeist, Isaac, & Williams, 2009). Second, regarding the core of patient trust, researchers tend to agree that trust depends heavily on a patient's overall assessment of a physician's personality and professionalism, and that it is driven fundamentally by the vulnerability of patients seeking care in a compromised state of illness (Hall, 2006). Accordingly, trust in physicians consists of the following factors, ordered by importance: loyalty or caring, competency, honesty, and confidentiality (Hall et al., 2002; Kao et al., 1998a; Mechanic & Meyer, 2000; Thom et al., 1999). All reported trust scales that include these dimensions have high internal reliability and good construct validity in that they show expected associations with other measures, such as a positive correlation with the length of the relationships. Some of them have been found to have good predictive validity for outcomes expected to be sensitive to trust, such as following treatment recommendations and staying with the same physician (Thom, Hall, & Pawlson, 2004).

DIFFERENT TYPES OF TRUST AND FACTORS THAT AFFECT THEM

Research into trust relations has also explored: (1) the nature and form of trust in terms of its *different types* and (2) the *factors that build, sustain, or detract from trust* (Calnan & Rowe, 2006). Research exploring the *different types* of trust suggests that although patients' trust in a specific physician, in their medical insurer, and in the medical profession shares some commonalities, these types of trust are related to different sets of predictor variables (Balkrishnan, Dugan, Camacho, & Hall, 2003). Some studies suggest that trust in the medical profession is related to a larger extent to patients' willingness to seek care and follow recommendations than other types of trust (Balkrishnan et al., 2003; Trachtenberg, Dugan, & Hall, 2005). It has also been observed that while patients retain high levels of trust in individual physicians ("your own doctor"; Calnan & Sanford, 2004; Mainous, Baker, Love, Perreria Gray, & Gill, 2001; Tarrant, Stokes, & Baker, 2003), lower levels of trust are found for health care institutions (Calnan & Sanford, 2004). In fact, patients' trust in their personal physicians has stronger elements of faith than does trust related to other social or economic areas – perhaps comparable to the form of trust that exists in intimate or fraternal interpersonal relationships (Hall, 2006). The existence of this difference entails that the relationship between the perceived performance of the health care system at the micro-level and the perceived quality of health care provision at the macro-level is a complicated one. System trust and interpersonal trust can complement and influence each other (Mechanic & Schlesinger, 1996; Van der Schee, Braun, Calnan, Schnee, & Groenewegen, 2007), and therefore research is needed to examine the specific ways in which institutional trust influences interpersonal trust and vice-versa.

Although research on trust in healthcare has mostly focused on the patient, there have also been some attempts to analyze the role of the families' trust. Trust between the family and the healthcare provider can also affect the patient's health outcomes (Lynn-McHale &

Deatrick, 2000), but further research still needs to be conducted to examine health care providers' trust in families.

Research focusing on the *factors that build trust* suggests that these factors differ according to the type of trust being examined. Factors that can encourage patients' trust in clinicians include the clinician's technical competence, the establishment of a common understanding, and the management of patients' perception of self-confidence (Dibben & Lean, 2003). Trust is built incrementally but it can be diminished following events that lead to a perceived betrayal (Rushton, Reina, & Reina, 2007).

On the other hand, factors such as the availability of good quality care or the existence of institutional guarantees (e.g. inspections of health care quality and protection of patients' rights) have been suggested to affect the development of institutional or public trust (Van der Schee et al., 2007). However, the role of these factors in enhancing institutional trust has not been demonstrated empirically, and it is not clear whether they would constitute causes or consequences of a higher level of trust in health care systems. Thus, research is needed to establish the factors that help to develop institutional trust (Rowe & Calnan, 2006).

CONSEQUENCES OF TRUST IN THE HEALTH CARE SYSTEM

There is substantial evidence that trust mediates health care processes. In fact, it has been argued that trusting patient-physician relations have a direct therapeutic effect (Mechanic, 1998), although evidence to support such claims is still scarce mainly because of the lack of intervention studies examining the effect of trust on health outcomes (Calnan & Rowe, 2006). There is a broad agreement that trust has an indirect influence on health outcomes through its impact on patient satisfaction, adherence to treatment, and continuity with a provider. Trust also encourages patients to access health care and to disclose the information necessary to make an accurate and timely diagnosis (Calnan & Rowe, 2004; Hall et al., 2001; Mechanic, 1998). Trust, therefore, underpins patient behaviors which are important for an effective treatment. Trust is also a quality indicator, as illustrated by the large number of patients suggesting that high quality doctor-patient interactions are characterized by high levels of trust (e.g., see Safran et al., 1998a). From an organizational perspective trust is believed to be important in its own right, that is, it is intrinsically important for the provision of effective health care and has even been described as a collective good, similar to social capital (Gilson, 2006; Hall et al., 2001; Rothstein, 1998). Specific organizational benefits that might be derived from trust as a form of social capital include the reduction in transition costs due to lower surveillance and monitoring costs and the general increase in efficiency (Gilson, 2003). It has been argued that trust also has some costs and dangers. Although trust may provide legitimacy for the exercise of power, trusting too much, without caution, may also enable the abuse of power in the form of exploitation, domination or conspiracy against others (Warren, 1999). This is a particular danger for health care given the vulnerability of all patients, but particularly those from disadvantaged backgrounds, in relation to health care providers (Gilson, 2006).

FUTURE RESEARCH NEEDS

Despite the rapidly increasing body of empirical research investigating the different dimensions, determinants, and consequences of trust in healthcare, some important aspects still need to be addressed in future research. First, several empirical studies have reported correlations between trust and factors such as patient satisfaction. However, it is not always clear whether these factors constitute causes or consequences of trust. More studies exerting a rigorous experimental control are needed in order to infer the directionality of the relationships between the aforementioned variables and trust (Hall et al., 2001). In particular, experiments are needed to establish the causal link between trust and health outcomes and also to test interventions designed to improve patients' trust in their physician (Pearson & Raeke, 2000).

Second, as pointed out by Hall et al. (2001), the majority of studies exploring trust in healthcare have frequently been conducted in populations where minorities were underrepresented. However, there is evidence that trust in the physician can differ as a function of race or ethnicity. Namely, nonwhite patients have been found to have lower levels of trust in their physicians than white patients (Boulware, Cooper, Ratner, LaVeist, & Powe, 2003; Doescher, Saver, Franks & Fiscella, 2000; Kao, Green, Zaslavsky, Koplan, & Cleary, 1998b) but higher levels of trust in their health insurance plans (Boulware, Cooper, Ratner, LaVeist, & Powe, 2003). This result calls into question the generalizability of some of the reported findings to the general population. Future research should therefore be more sensitive to contextual factors such as race or ethnicity, which can directly influence trust.

Third, as noted above, the factors that play a role in the development of institutional trust, as well as the relationships between this type of trust and interpersonal trust should be explored further. Furthermore, some authors have pointed out the necessity to conduct inter-country comparisons to address this issue, since the importance of the different types of trust can vary depending on the specific health system (Rowe & Calnan, 2006). This claim is supported by empirical results showing that public trust in health care professionals and institutions varies between different countries (Van der Schee et al., 2007), a finding that suggests that cultural differences can be crucial in the level of trust placed on health care.

Last but not least, further research should also address the impact that changes in health plans can have on trust. In particular, managed care plans that have been implemented in the United States have considerably altered treatment practices, shifting the control of expenditures from the physicians to broad organizational structures. It has been argued that managed care arrangements such as financial incentives for physicians or utilization review can undermine the trust relationship between the patient and the physician (Mechanic & Schlesinger, 1996). However, other authors argue that the claim that managed care diminishes patients' trust in physicians is unjustified (Buchanan, 2000) or even that managed care can enhance patients' trust in some circumstances (Gray, 1997). More research is needed to determine the ways in which managed care has influenced trust in health care and, more crucially, the direction this influence will take in the future.

CONCLUSION

Taken together, empirical research clearly complements theory and suggests that developing a trustworthy health care system requires more than competent physicians (Gilson, 2006). More importantly, it needs health workers that have the motivation and capacity for empathetic understanding of patients, as well as institutions that sustain ethical behaviors and so provide a basis for trust.

REFERENCES

Alaszweski, A. (2003). Risk, trust and health. *Editorial Health, Risk and Society, 5*, 235–240.

Anderson, L., & Dedrick, R. F. (1990). Development of the trust in physician scale: A measure to assess interpersonal trust in patient physician relationships. *Psychological Reports, 67*, 1091–1100.

Balkrishnan, R., Dugan, E., Camacho, F. T., & Hall, M.A. (2003) Trust and satisfaction with physicians, insurers, and the medical profession. *Medical Care, 41*, 1058–1064.

Boulware, L. E., Cooper, L. A., Ratner, L. E., LaVeist, T. A., & Powe, N. R. (2003). Race and trust in the health care system. *Public Health Reports, 118*, 358–365.

Buchanan, A. (2000). Trust in managed care organizations. *Kennedy Institute of Ethics Journal, 10*, 189–212.

Calnan, M., & Rowe, R. (2004). *Trust in health care: An agenda for future research*. London: The Nuffield Trust.

Calnan, M., & Rowe, R. (2006). Researching trust relationships in health care. *Journal of Health Organization and Management, 20*, 349–358.

Calnan, M., & Sanford, E. (2004). Public trust in health care: The system or the doctor? *Quality and Safety in Health Care, 13*, 92–97.

Dibben, M. R., & Lean, M. E. J. (2003). Achieving compliance in chronic illness management: Illustrations of trust relationships between physicians and nutrition clinic patients. *Health, Risk & Society, 5*, 241–258.

Doescher, M. P., Saver, B. G., Franks, P., & Fiscella, K. (2000). Racial and ethnic disparities in perceptions of physician style and trust. *Archives of Family Medicine, 9, 1156–1163.*

Gilson, L. (2003). Trust and the development of health care as a social institution. *Social Science and Medicine, 56*, 1453–1468.

Gilson, L. (2006). Trust in health care: Theoretical perspectives and research needs. *Journal of Health Organization and Management, 20*, 359–375.

Gray, B. H. (1997). Trust and trustworthy care in the managed care era. *Health Affairs, 16*, 34–49.

Hall, M. A. (2006). Researching medical trust in the United States. *Journal of Health Organization and Management, 20*, 456–467.

Hall, M. A., Dugan, E., Zheng, B., & Mishra, A. (2001). Trust in physicians and medical institutions: What is it, can it be measured, and does it matter? *Milbank Quarterly, 79*, 613–639.

Hall, M. A., Zheng, B., Dugan, E., Camacho, F., Kidd, K., Mishra, A., & Balkrishnan, R. (2002). Measuring patients' trust in their primary care providers. *Medical Care Research and Review*, *59*, 293–318.

Kao, A., Green, D. C., Davis, N. A., Koplan, J. P., & Cleary, P. D. (1998a). Patient's trust in their physicians: Effects of choice, continuity, and payment method. *Journal of General Internal Medicine*, *13*, 681–686.

Kao, A., Green, D. C., Zaslavsky, A. M., Koplan, J. P., & Cleary, P. D. (1998b). The relationship between method of physician payment and patient trust. *Journal of the American Medical Association*, *280*, 1708–1714.

LaVeist, T. A., Isaac, L. A., Williams, K. P. (2009). Mistrust of health care organizations is associated with underutilization of health services. *Health Services Research*, *44*, 2093–2105.

Leisen, N., & Hyman, M. R. (2001). An improved scale for assessing patients' trust in their physicians. *Health Marketing Quarterly*, *19*, 23–42.

Lynn-McHale, D. J., & Deatrick, J. A. (2000). Trust between family and health care provider. *Journal of Family Nursing*, *6*, 210–230.

Mainous, A., Baker, R., Love, M., Pereira Gray, D., & Gill, J. (2001). Continuity of care and trust in one's physician: Evidence from primary care in the US and the UK. *Family Medicine*, *33*, 22–27.

Mayer, R., Davis, J., & Schoorman, F. (1995). An integrative model of organization trust. *Academic Management Review*, *23*, 438–458.

Mechanic, D. (1998). Functions and limits of trust in providing medical care. *Journal of Health Politics, Policy and Law*, *23*, 661–686.

Mechanic, D., & Meyer, S. (2000). Concepts of trust among patients with serious illness. *Social Science and Medicine*, *51*, 657–668.

Mechanic, D., & Schlesinger, M. (1996). The impact of managed care on patients' trust in medical care and their physicians. *Journal of the American Medical Association*, *275*, 1693–1697.

Pearson, S. D., & Raeke, L. H. (2000) Patients' trust in physicians: Many theories, few measures, and little data. *Journal of General Internal Medicine*, *15*, 509–513.

Rothstein, B. (1998). *Just institutions matter: The moral and political logic of the universal welfare state*. Cambridge: Cambridge University Press.

Rowe, R., & Calnan, M. (2006). Trust relations in health care: The new agenda. *European Journal of Public Health*, *16*, 4–6.

Rushton, C. H., Reina, M. L., & Reina, D.S. (2007). Building trustworthy relationships with critically ill patients and families. *AACN Advanced Critical Care*, *18*, 19–30.

Safran, D., Taira, D., Rogers, W., Kosinski, M., Ware, J., & Tarlov, A. (1998a). Linking primary care performance to outcomes of care. *Journal of Family Practice*, *47*, 213–220.

Safran, D., Kosinski, M., Tarlov, A. R., Rogers, W. H., Taira, D. A., Lieberman, N., & Ware, J. E. (1998b). The primary care assessment survey: Tests of data quality and measurement performance. *Medical Care*, *36*, 728–739.

Tarrant, C., Stokes, T., & Baker, R. (2003). Factors associated with patients' trust in their GP: A cross-sectional survey. *British Journal of General Practice*, *53*, 798–800.

Thom, D. H., Ribisl, K. M., Steward, A. L., & Luce, D. A. (1999). Further validation and reliability testing of the trust in physician scale. *Medical Care, 37,* 510–517.

Thom, D. H., Hall, M. A., & Pawlson, L. G. (2004). Measuring patients' trust in physicians when assessing quality of care. *Health Affairs, 23,* 124–132.

Trachtenberg, F., Dugan, E., & Hall, M.A. (2005). How patients' trust relates to their involvement in medical care. *The Journal of Family Practice, 54,* 344–352.

Van der Schee, E., Braun, B., Calnan, M., Schnee, M., & Groenewegen, P. P. (2007). Public trust in health care: A comparison of Germany, The Netherlands, and England and Wales. *Health Policy, 81,* 56–67.

Warren, M. E. (1999). *Democracy and trust.* Cambridge: Cambridge University Press.

In: Health Psychology
Editor: Ryan E. Murphy, pp. 145-153

ISBN 978-1-61728-981-1
© 2010 Nova Science Publishers, Inc.

Chapter 9

IMPROVING THE PUBLIC HEALTH IMPACT OF INTERNET-DELIVERED INTERVENTIONS

Rik Crutzen
Maastricht University/CAPHRI

ABSTRACT

The key problem in Internet-delivered interventions is high rates of attrition: people leave the website before actually using it. The aim of this chapter is to better understand compatibility between design and user needs. Thereby we can improve the public health impact of Internet-delivered interventions targeting health risk behaviours (e.g., a sedentary lifestyle, high fat intake, and cigarette smoking) by retaining website visitors' attention through "interactional richness" and thus creating a more positive user experience. Such a positive user experience leads to increased "e-retention" (i.e., the actual use of the intervention by the target group once they access its website). Previous studies assessed and favourably evaluated the efficacy of Internet-delivered interventions without considering use data, whereas the public health impact of an intervention largely depends on the actual use of the intervention website by the target group. Furthermore, the development and application of theories regarding e-retention is timely, since no such theories currently exist. I therefore developed an integrative theoretical framework that provides a theory-driven solution for a practice-based problem with direct applications within the mushrooming field of Internet-delivered interventions.

INTRODUCTION

Today's main causes of deaths and diseases with the highest burden of illness and health care costs in western countries (e.g., cardiovascular diseases, cancer) can be significantly reduced by preventing health risk behaviours (e.g., a sedentary lifestyle, high fat intake and cigarette smoking). Health promotion thus also implies a need for interventions to motivate people to behave in a healthy manner and to give them the skills to put this behaviour into practice. The explosive growth of the Internet has caused an increase in Internet-delivered interventions, because they fit in with the omnipresence of the Internet in people's daily lives.

Fully utilizing the potential of these interventions should decrease the burden of illness and health care costs related to today's major diseases, as these costs are largely attributable to people's behaviour (Goetzel, Anderson, Whitmer, Ozminkowski, Dunn, & Wasserman, 1998).

According to Glasgow and colleagues (Glasgow, 2007; Glasgow, Vogt, & Boles, 1999), however, evaluation of the public health impact of an intervention cannot be limited to merely assessing efficacy, but also needs to take the use of the intervention into account. Internet-delivered interventions targeting health risk behaviours related to chronic diseases (e.g., a sedentary lifestyle, high fat intake and cigarette smoking) can effectively change behaviour if people actively use these interventions (Myung, McDonnell, Kazinets, Seo, & Moskowitz, 2009; Neville, O'Hara, & Milat, 2009; Portnoy, Scott-Sheldon, Johnson, & Carey, 2008; Van den Berg, Schoones, & Vliet Vlieland, 2007; Vandelanotte, Spathonis, Eakin, & Owen, 2007). However, high rates of attrition (i.e., drop-out) are characteristic of the Internet (Eysenbach, 2005) and evidence from efficacy trials indicates that e-retention (i.e., the actual use of the interventi+on by the target group once they access the website) is very low, especially when Internet-delivered interventions are implemented in real life (*in vivo*) rather than in a research setting (*in vitro*) (Bennett & Glasgow, 2009; Evers, Cummins, Prochaska, & Prochaska, 2005). For example, server statistics of an intervention promoting heart-healthy behaviours showed that 285,146 visitors from unique IP addresses landed on the home page in a 36-month period, but 56.3% of these left the intervention website within 30 seconds (Brouwer et al., e-pub ahead of print). This touches upon the critical issue in Internet-delivered interventions: how can behaviour change ever be achieved if people are not or hardly exposed to the actual intervention?

Three different aspects of exposure can be distinguished in Internet-delivered interventions (Crutzen, De Nooijer, Brouwer, Oenema, Brug, & De Vries, 2008a; 2008b): (1) accessing the intervention website, i.e. visiting it for the first time, (2) staying on the intervention website to actually use it (e-retention) and (3) revisiting the intervention website (if necessary). The first of these, promoting a first visit, depends largely on the dissemination of the intervention and its social embedding (Crutzen, De Nooijer, Brouwer, Oenema, Brug, & De Vries, 2009b; Crutzen, De Nooijer, & De Vries, 2008). The second aspect is the main focus of this chapter, because there is no theory- or evidence-based insight into e-retention. Although previous studies did explicitly describe theory used to develop the content of the Internet-delivered intervention, these theories primarily related to behaviour determinants or behaviour change (Christensen, Griffiths, & Farrer, 2009; Crutzen, De Nooijer, Brouwer, Oenema, Brug, & De Vries, in press). The third aspect (revisiting) only applies to interventions that are intended to be used multiple times, and is partly covered by this chapter, since retaining website visitors and creating a positive user experience is a prerequisite for revisiting.

INTERACTIONAL RICHNESS

The key to increased e-retention is interactional richness (Figure 1). The concept of interactional richness is based on structuration theory (Giddens, 1984), a sociological theory that regards the interactions between structures and actors as a highly interdependent and co-evolving duality. The central idea of structuration theory, when applied to an online context, is that the characteristics of a website (i.e., its structure) shape a two-way online interaction and exchange of information with website visitors (actors) (Van Oppen, 2007).

Interactional richness consists of two components: media richness and information richness, because use and satisfaction depend on the medium as well as the information it provides (DeLone & McLean, 2003). Based on interactivity theory (Rafaeli, 1988; Song & Zinkhan, 2008), media richness is defined as the extent to which a website facilitates user control (e.g., freedom of choice (Chiou, 2008)), provides two-way communication, and is responsive to user needs. Information richness is defined as visitors' perceptions of the extent to which the website provides relevant, accurate, comprehensible and comprehensive information. Media richness and information richness can each be manipulated and validly measured (Liu, 2003; Muylle, Moenaert, & Despontin, 2004; Song & Zinkhan, 2008).

Interactional richness has a direct positive relation with utilitarian value (UV; i.e., usefulness) and hedonic value (HV; i.e., appreciation). Both are subjective measures, as indicated by the dotted line in Figure 1. Contrary to what common sense might suggest, media richness is not only related to HV (Koufaris, 2002; Mummalameni, 2005) but also to UV (Kim, Fiore, & Lee, 2007), while information richness is not only related to UV (Ballantine, 2005), but also to HV (De Wulf, Schillewaert, Muylle, & Rangarajan, 2006). Together, UV and HV constitute the two-dimensional concept of user experience (Mathwick, Malhotra, & Rigdon, 2001; Mathwick, Malhotra, & Rigdon, 2002), which refers to what a person thinks and feels during and after a visit to an intervention website (Crutzen, De Nooijer, Brouwer, Oenema, Brug, & De Vries, 2009a). The main idea, as I have described in more detail elsewhere (Crutzen et al., 2009a), is that positive user experience leads to increased e-retention. Optimizing interactional richness therefore makes it possible to create a positive user experience, which is a prerequisite for staying on a website long enough to complete the intervention. Figure 1 proposes two potential moderators influencing the effect of media richness and information richness on e-retention (mediated by user experience), as a richer website is not always a better website in terms of e-retention.

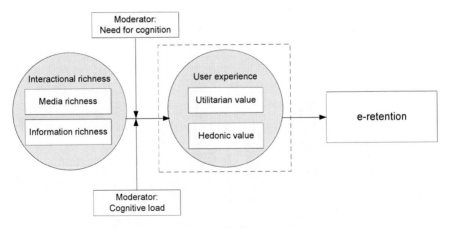

Figure 1. Integrative theoretical framework regarding e-retention.

These moderators, inspired by psychological theories, relate to the individual (i.e., need for cognition) and the situation (i.e., cognitive load). The crucial next step proposed here is to derive and test hypotheses based on this newly developed theoretical framework. Furthermore, the theoretical framework I propose is definitely not limited to the field of health promotion, but can also be used in other fields, such as marketing (e.g., web shops) or educational sciences (e.g., e-learning).

NEED FOR COGNITION

Inspired by the elaboration likelihood model (Petty & Cacioppo, 1986), I firstly propose need for cognition (NFC) as a potential moderator. NFC is an easily measured personality variable reflecting the extent to which people engage in and enjoy effortful cognitive activities (Cacioppo, Petty, & Morris, 1983). The elaboration likelihood model distinguishes between central route and peripheral route processes. Central route processes are those that require a great deal of thought and are related to high NFC. Peripheral route processes, on the other hand, rely on peripheral cues (e.g., attractiveness of the message source) and are related to low NFC (Cacioppo, Petty, Kao, & Rodriguez, 1986). Peripheral cues might thus be more effective in retaining visitors with a low NFC (Petty & Cacioppo, 1986; Petty, Cacioppo, & Schumann, 1983).

Example

Offering a game in which participants had to crush virtual cigarettes led to an increase in e-retention in a 12-week psychosocial minimal-support treatment programme to give up smoking (Girard, Turcotte, Bouchard, & Girard, 2009).

Explanation

Offering a peripheral cue (e.g., the game) in an Internet-delivered intervention can be very involving and ultimately lead to processing via the central route.

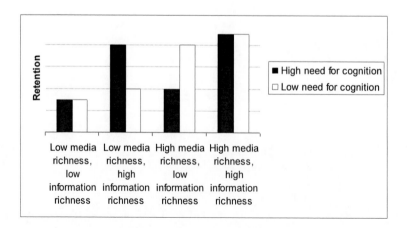

Figure 2. Hypothesis regarding need for cognition.

Hypothesis

If NFC is high, then information richness has a stronger effect on e-retention than media richness. If NFC is low, then information richness has a weaker effect on e-retention than media richness (Figure 2).

COGNITIVE LOAD

Inspired by the cognitive load theory (Paas, Renkl, & Sweller, 2003a), I secondly propose cognitive load (CL) (i.e., the load on working memory) as a potential moderator. CL can be distinguished into intrinsic CL (referring to the information on the website), extraneous CL (referring to the way in which it is represented), and germane CL (referring to the individual processing the information) (Sweller, Van Merrienboer, & Paas, 1998); these forms of CL are additive (Paas et al., 2003a).

Example

The germane CL for a cancer patient who is making a trade-off between benefits and harms across treatments is known to be very high (Stacey, Samant, & Bennett, 2008). An Internet-delivered intervention that aims to increase media richness (and thus extraneous CL) by offering peripheral cues might be counterproductive, leading to a decrease in e-retention (e.g., people leaving your website untimely).

Explanation

Whereas intrinsic CL cannot be directly influenced by design, extraneous CL can (e.g., through interactional richness) (Paas, Tuovinen, Tabbers, & Van Gerven, 2003b). A high CL might overburden working memory capacity (Kalyuga, Chandler, & Sweller, 1999) and therefore decrease e-retention.

Hypothesis

If CL is high, then higher media richness has a negative effect on e-retention. If CL is low, then higher media richness has a positive effect on e-retention. Overall, information richness has the strongest effect on e-retention (Figure 3). This hypothesis is counterintuitive, because it states that an increase in media richness does not necessarily increase e-retention. This stresses the need to investigate potential moderators of the effect of media richness and information richness on e-retention.

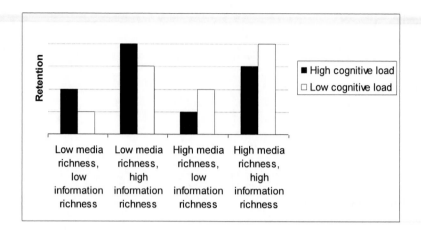

Figure 3. Hypothesis regarding cognitive load.

CONCLUSION

The proposed integrative theoretical framework provides a theory-driven solution for a practice-based problem; high rates of attrition in Internet-delivered interventions. The crucial next step is to test hypotheses based on this newly developed theoretical framework.

REFERENCES

Ballantine, P. W. (2005). Effects of interactivity and product information on consumer satisfaction in an online retail setting. *International Journal of Retail & Distribution Management, 33*, 461-471.

Bennett, G. G., & Glasgow, R. E. (2009). The delivery of public health interventions via the Internet: actualizing their potential. *Annual Review of Public Health, 30*, 273-292.

Brouwer, W., Oenema, A., Raat, H., Crutzen, R., De Nooijer, J., De Vries, N. K., et al. (e-pub ahead of print). Characteristics of visitors and revisitors of an Internet-delivered computer-tailored lifestyle intervention implemented for use by the general public. *Health Education Research*.

Cacioppo, J. T., Petty, R. E., Kao, C. F., & Rodriguez, R. (1986). Central and peripheral routes to persuasion: an individual difference perspective. *Journal of Personality and Social Psychology, 51*, 1032-1043.

Cacioppo, J. T., Petty, R. E., & Morris, K. J. (1983). Effects of need for cognition on message evaluation, recall, and persuasion. *Journal of Personality and Social Psychology, 45*, 805-818.

Chiou, W.-B. (2008). Induced attitude change on online gaming among adolescents: an application of the less-leads-to-more effect. *CyberPsychology & Behavior, 11*, 212-216.

Christensen, H., Griffiths, K. M., & Farrer, L. (2009). Adherence in Internet interventions for anxiety and depression: systematic review. *Journal of Medical Internet Research, 11*, e13.

Crutzen, R., De Nooijer, J., Brouwer, W., Oenema, A., Brug, J., & De Vries, N. K. (2008a). Internet-delivered interventions aimed at adolescents: a Delphi study on dissemination and exposure. *Health Education Research, 23*, 427-439.

Crutzen, R., De Nooijer, J., Brouwer, W., Oenema, A., Brug, J., & De Vries, N. K. (2008b). Qualitative assessment of adolescents' views about improving exposure to Internet-delivered interventions. *Health Education, 108*, 105-116.

Crutzen, R., De Nooijer, J., Brouwer, W., Oenema, A., Brug, J., & De Vries, N. K. (2009a). A conceptual framework for understanding and improving adolescents' exposure to Internet-delivered interventions. *Health Promotion International, 24*, 277-284.

Crutzen, R., De Nooijer, J., Brouwer, W., Oenema, A., Brug, J., & De Vries, N. K. (2009b). Effectiveness of online word of mouth on exposure to an Internet-delivered intervention. *Psychology & Health, 24*, 651-661.

Crutzen, R., De Nooijer, J., Brouwer, W., Oenema, A., Brug, J., & De Vries, N. K. (in press). Strategies to facilitate exposure to Internet-delivered health behaviour change interventions aimed at adolescents or young adults: a systematic review. *Health Education & Behavior.*

Crutzen, R., De Nooijer, J., & De Vries, N. K. (2008). How to reach a target group with Internet-delivered interventions? *The European Health Psychologist, 10*, 77-79.

De Wulf, K., Schillewaert, N., Muylle, S., & Rangarajan, D. (2006). The role of pleasure in web site success. *Information & Management, 43*, 434-446.

DeLone, W. H., & McLean, E. R. (2003). The DeLone and McLean model of information systems success: a ten-year update. *Journal of Management Information Systems, 19*, 9-30.

Evers, K. E., Cummins, C. O., Prochaska, J. O., & Prochaska, J. M. (2005). Online health behavior and disease management programs: are we ready for them? Are they ready for us? *Journal of Medical Internet Research, 7*, e27.

Eysenbach, G. (2005). The law of attrition. *Journal of Medical Internet Research, 7*, e11.

Giddens, A. (1984). *The constitution of society: outline of the theory of structuration.* Cambridge: Polity press.

Girard, B., Turcotte, V., Bouchard, S., & Girard, B. (2009). Crushing virtual cigarettes reduces tobacco addiction and treatment discontinuation. *CyberPsychology & Behavior, 12*, 477-483.

Glasgow, R. E. (2007). eHealth evaluation and dissemination research. *American Journal of Preventive Medicine, 32*, S119-S126.

Glasgow, R. E., Vogt, T. M., & Boles, S. M. (1999). Evaluating the public health impact of health promotion interventions: the RE-AIM framework. *American Journal of Public Health, 89*, 1322-1327.

Goetzel, R. Z., Anderson, D. R., Whitmer, R. W., Ozminkowski, R. J., Dunn, R. L., & Wasserman, J. (1998). The relationship between modifiable health risks and health care expenditures: an analysis of the multi-employer HERO health risk and cost database. *Journal of Occupational & Environmental Medicine, 40*, 843-854.

Kalyuga, S., Chandler, P., & Sweller, J. (1999). Managing split-attention and redundancy in multimedia instruction. *Applied Cognitive Psychology, 13*, 351-371.

Kim, J., Fiore, A. M., & Lee, H.-H. (2007). Influences of online store perception, shopping enjoyment, and shopping involvement on consumer patronage behavior towards an online retailer. *Journal of Retailing and Consumer Services, 14*, 95-107.

Koufaris, M. (2002). Applying the technology acceptance model and flow theory to online consumer behavior. *Information Systems Research, 13*, 205-223.

Liu, Y. (2003). Developing a scale to measure the interactivity of web sites. *Journal of Advertising Research, 43*, 207-216.

Mathwick, C., Malhotra, N., & Rigdon, E. (2001). Experiental value: conceptualization, measurement and application in the catalog and Internet shopping environment. *Journal of Retailing, 77*, 39-56.

Mathwick, C., Malhotra, N. K., & Rigdon, E. (2002). The effect of dynamic retail experiences on experiental perceptions of value: an Internet and catalog comparison. *Journal of Retailing, 78*, 51-60.

Mummalameni, V. (2005). An empirical investigation of web site characteristics, consumer emotional states and on-line shopping behaviors. *Journal of Business Research, 58*, 526-532.

Muylle, S., Moenaert, R., & Despontin, M. (2004). The conceptualization and empirical validation of web site user satisfaction. *Information & Management, 41*, 543-560.

Myung, S.-K., McDonnell, D. D., Kazinets, G., Seo, H. G., & Moskowitz, J. M. (2009). Effects of web- and computer-based smoking cessation programs. *Archives of Internal Medicine, 169*, 929-937.

Neville, L. M., O'Hara, B., & Milat, A. J. (2009). Computer-tailored dietary behaviour change interventions: a systematic review. *Health Education Research, 24*, 699-720.

Paas, F., Renkl, A., & Sweller, J. (2003a). Cognitive load theory and instructional design: recent developments. *Educational Psychologist, 38*, 1-4.

Paas, F., Tuovinen, J. E., Tabbers, H., & Van Gerven, P. W. M. (2003b). Cognitive load measurement as a means to advance cognitive load theory. *Educational Psychologist, 38*, 63-71.

Petty, R. E., & Cacioppo, J. T. (1986). *Communication and persuasion: central and peripheral routes to attitude change*. New York, NY: Springer-Verlag.

Petty, R. E., Cacioppo, J. T., & Schumann, D. (1983). Central and peripheral routes to advertising effectiveness: the moderating role of involvement. *The Journal of Consumer Research, 10*, 135-146.

Portnoy, D. B., Scott-Sheldon, L. A. J., Johnson, B. T., & Carey, M. P. (2008). Computer-delivered interventions for health promotion and behavioral risk reduction: a meta-analysis of 75 randomized controlled trials, 1988-2007. *Preventive Medicine, 47*, 3-16.

Rafaeli, S. (1988). Interactivity: from new media to communication. In R. P. Hawkins, J. M. Wiemann & S. Pingree (Eds.), *Advancing communication science: merging mass and interpersonal processes* (pp. 110-134). Newbury Park, CA: Sage.

Song, J. H., & Zinkhan, G. M. (2008). Determinants of perceived web site interactivity. *Journal of Marketing, 72*, 99-113.

Stacey, D., Samant, R., & Bennett, C. (2008). Decision making in oncology: a review of patient decision aids to support patient participation. *CA: A Cancer Journal for Clinicians, 58*, 293-304.

Sweller, J., Van Merrienboer, J. J. G., & Paas, F. G. W. C. (1998). Cognitive architecture and instructional design. *Education Psychology Review, 10*, 251-296.

Van den Berg, M. H., Schoones, J. W., & Vliet Vlieland, T. P. M. (2007). Internet-based physical activity interventions: a systematic review of the literature. *Journal of Medical Internet Research, 9*, e26.

Van Oppen, C. A. M. L. (2007). *From rags to richness*. Maastricht: Maastricht University.

Vandelanotte, C., Spathonis, K. M., Eakin, E. G., & Owen, N. (2007). Website-delivered physical activity interventions: a review of the literature. *American Journal of Preventive Medicine, 33*, 54-64.

In: Health Psychology
Editor: Ryan E. Murphy, pp. 155-166

Chapter 10

LEISURE AND DEPRESSION IN MIDLIFE: A TAIWANESE NATIONAL SURVEY OF MIDDLE-AGED ADULTS

*Luo Lu**

Department of Business Administration, National Taiwan University, Taiwan

ABSTRACT

We aimed to explore middle-aged people's subjective leisure experiences, and to further examine associations of such experiences with their depressive symptoms in a Chinese society--Taiwan. Known correlates of depression such as demographics, physical health and social support, were taken into account. Face-to-face interviews were conducted to collect data using structured questionnaires from a national representative sample of community older people ($N = 1143$, aged 45-65). Using hierarchical multiple regression, we found that (1) being female, had lower family income were demographic risk factors of depression; (2) worse physical health, lack of independent functioning in ADL, and disability were related to more depressive symptoms; (3) greater social support was related to less depressive symptoms; (4) having controlled for all the above effects of demographics, health, and social support, positive leisure experiences in terms of satisfaction and meaningfulness were independently related to fewer depressive symptoms. The benefits of meaningful leisure pursuits for successful midlife transition and prospective ageing were discussed.

In the Western popular media during the 1980s and 1990s, "midlife crisis" was a buzz word and a catchy topic of discussion. Almost universally, midlife is marked by a string of major life events, such as empty nest, menopause, and retirement. However, after concerted efforts, Western researchers were generally cautious whether the so-called midlife crisis is a widely recognized experience among middle-aged adults, they did agree though that midlife

* Correspondence concerning this article should be addressed to Prof. Luo Lu, Department of Business Administration, National Taiwan University, No.1, Sec. 4, Roosevelt Road, Taipei 106, Taiwan, ROC. Tel: +886-2-33669657. Fax: +886-2-23625379. E-mail: luolu@ntu.edu.tw

may be accurately portrait as a period of transition and readjustment (Hunter & Sundel, 1989). Systematic research on midlife transition for the Chinese people is lacking, thus the present study aimed to explore potential psychosocial factors facilitating a successful transition in middle life among the cultural Chinese population in Taiwan. Specifically, we focused on the largely overlooked benefits of leisure experiences on well-being, over and beyond those of employment, physical health and social support. As studies on midlife leisure and depression are non-exist in Taiwan, we used a large national representative sample to establish the baseline and ensure generalizability of our research findings.

Research on leisure with Chinese people in general and middle-aged adults in particular is in the rarity, partly because hardworking has always been a highly regarded Confucius virtue. However, with economic development, material abundance, and the shortening of statutory working hour (now 40 per week), Taiwanese people are learning to "improve quality of life with leisure" (Lu & Hu, 2002). Thus, against this transition of cultural mandate on a "good way of life", understanding the subjective experiences of leisure of middle-aged Chinese people will not only shed light on some interesting issues in leisure research, but also contribute to better leisure policies and management to promote healthy living in midlife and preparation for a successful ageing.

SUCCESSFUL MIDLIFE TRANSITION: CONSOLIDATING THE GAINS IN LIFE

Midlife is undoubtedly a phase of fully functioning in adult life. A Taiwanese study (Lee, 1999) found that middle-aged adults are expected to take care of both their young and old, acting as pillars in family life. They are also expected to perform at peak in their career roles to provide for their families and to earn senses of achievement for themselves. However, in the eyes of the Taiwanese people, midlife is also a period of transition towards the impending older age (Lee, 1999). Middle-aged adults start to worry about deterioration in health and various manifestations of ageing. They are also mindful of inevitable losses in life, for instance, launching of their young and departing of their old in the family. Earlier research did reveal that if a sense of psychological homeostasis can not be achieved during this transition period, crises may set in (Hunter & Sundel, 1989). These so-called midlife crises can take forms of burnout, premature withdraw from work, change of careers, feeling of loneliness in family life, perceived conflict between work/career and family life, feeling of low energy and weakening, anxiety over ageing and death, perceived discrepancy between aspiration and achievement, sense of loss and worthlessness. If these issues are not resolved satisfactorily, the bubble may burst and midlife depression may set in (Goldstein, 2005; Kertzner, 2007).

Examining midlife issues from clinical perspectives, Goldstein (2005) noted that the lifetime risk for major depression among middle-aged Americans is increasing. She further reviewed relevant evidence to illuminate one possible pathway to midlife depression: narcissistic injuries to self-esteem associated with ageing, particularly in those with pre-existing vulnerabilities. In accordance with the cultural emphasis on the independent self in the West, Goldstein is primarily interested in a question posed by self psychology: how individuals maintain a homeostasis of the self in the face of challenging life circumstances and specific to the current context, the vicissitudes of middle age.

However, the notion of self in a collectivist Chinese culture is very different from that of in the individualistic West (Markus & Kitayama, 1991). Instead of focusing on the independence and striving of the self, the Chinese self is defined in its interdependence with important others such as the family, and complete through dutifully accomplishing its social obligations (Lu, 2007; 2008). Thus, midlife is more likely viewed by the Chinese people as a period of consolidating life's gains through taking pivotal roles both in family life and at work, as voiced by Taiwanese adults of a wide age range (Lee, 1999). The same author found in an earlier study (Lee, 1997) that middle-aged Taiwanese experienced their life in a generally positive and active manner. Indeed they chose to focus more on fulfilling duties of parents, children, workers, and society members, not on individual losses. Thus in balance, it may be more accurate to portrait midlife for a Taiwanese adult as a transition rather than a crisis. An understanding in pathways to such a successful transition is now imperative.

LEISURE: THE INCREMENTAL VALUE BEYOND OTHER RESOURCES FOR A SUCCESSFUL MIDLIFE TRANSITION

In order to achieve a successful transition in midlife, personal and social resources need to be mobilized. Our purpose of the present study was to examine the incremental value of leisure participation over and beyond some known protectors. Social support is a valuable social resource and a known protector against depression. Research on social support has already accumulated a large body of empirical evidence supporting various theoretical formulations such as stress-resources models (Hobfoll, 1989; Holahan & Moos, 1986), the convoy model (Kahn & Antonucci, 1980), and the support-efficacy model (Antonucci & Jackson, 1987) for a wide age range of adults. Although there has been no research focusing on social support and midlife transition, results from a series of studies on young Taiwanese adults do underline the pivotal role of social support during another life transition: parenthood (Lu, 2006a; b). Thus, social support as social resources may also facilitate a successful midlife transition, including reduced likelihood of depression.

While friends and families are the most prevalent source of social support for adults facing a life transition (Lu, 2006a; b), leisure may be one additional way of obtaining support. This is because many popular leisure activities among adults involve sociability which may serve to enhance one's social embeddedness. For instance, a recent nationwide survey revealed that watching TV (usually with family) and getting together with friends are among the top 6 most frequently engaged leisure activities for Taiwanese adults of all ages (Fu, Lu, & Chen, 2009). Unlike the social forms in "the political, the economic, the purposive society of any sort," leisure exemplifies a form of sociable gathering that is "society without qualifying adjectives, because it alone presents the pure, abstract play of form" (Simmel, 1971, p. 127). Joining in activities with others reflects the social organization of leisure, strengthens interpersonal relationships, and enhances a sense of belonging among the participants (Cheek & Burch, 1976). Leisure-related social support has indeed been found to buffer the stress-illness relationship for the Americans (Iso-Ahola & Park, 1996).

Recent studies on aging also shed light on how leisure contributes to successful ageing by means of sociability. As verified in Western societies, leisure activities *per se* may enhance physical and subjective well-being among older adults, but the sociability aspect of such activities makes a more substantial difference (Litwin, 2000; Duay & Bryan, 2006; Harahousou, 2006). Likewise, a recent study in Taiwan also suggested that satisfaction with and meaningfulness gained from leisure activities help to prevent depression among older people, after controlling for social support and physical health (Lu, 2009). Thus, participation in leisure activities may facilitate successful life transition partly via its instrumental gains in enabling people to join and maintain social networks, and partly via enjoyment of leisure *per se* (Lu & Hu, 2005).

Limited research on the leisure life of middle-aged adults has suggested that leisure-related physical activity in midlife may be beneficial for people against the risk of dementia in older age, even when they were physically active at work (Rovio et al., 2007). Another prospective study revealed that greater participation in midlife cognitive activities was associated with a 26% risk reduction for dementia onset, and the protective effects were most robust for activities that were often cognitive and social in nature (Carlson, Helms, Steffens, Burke, Potter, & Plassman, 2008).

Various leisure theories have provided us with frameworks to understand the benefits of leisure. For instance, Beard and Ragheb (1980) purported that leisure could gratify basic human needs and generate satisfaction pertaining to six aspects: psychological (e.g., interesting activities), social (e.g., getting to know people), physical (e.g., getting exercise, keeping fit), educational (e.g., learning new things), relaxation (e.g., relaxed, rewind), and aesthetic (e.g., beautiful surrounding). Existing leisure research has confirmed that various leisure activities could indeed generate short-term benefits including positive mood, physical fitness and immediate satisfaction, as well as long-term effects of happiness, mental health, physical health, and social integration (e.g., Argyle, 1996; Lu & Hu, 2005). One in-depth interview study with Taiwanese college students further revealed that leisure also served an important function of structuring time (Lu & Hu, 2002), which should be important for middle-aged adults who are preparing for a withdraw from work. We thus hypothesize: *Leisure participation would be associated with less depression symptoms for middle-aged people in Taiwan, and this association would remain even after controlling for social support and physical health.*

METHOD

Samples and Procedures

Data for this present study were drawn from the "Needs, services and value preferences for older life among different generations" (Lin & Wang, 2008). This first-time nationwide survey in Taiwan followed rigorous procedures in sampling design, survey fieldwork, data cleaning, and data archiving. The survey adopted three-stage stratified Probability Proportional to Size (PPS) sampling with household registration data. The survey fieldwork relied on well-trained interviewers who made home visits for face-to-face interviews using structured questionnaires to collect data from community-residing adults in Taiwan, aged between 45-64 (Middle-aged Group) or above 65 years old (Older Group). Only one participant was interviewed in each household surveyed. The survey was conducted in January 2007. The two survey samples were confirmed representative of the national population in terms of age, sex, education attainment, and residence regions (Lin & Wang, 2008). The present study used data from the Middle-aged Group.

Our sample ($N = 1143$) was 46.8% men, with a mean age of 56.19 years ($SD = 5.42$). Most had elementary school education (34.47%), followed by senior high school education (23.62%), with an average formal education of 9.64 years ($SD = 3.65$). The majority of them (84.86%) were married with living spouses. Almost all (91.78%) had religious affiliations, the majority (86.18%) being that of Taoism/Buddhism.

INSTRUMENTS

Demographic Information

Participants' demographic information was recorded, including sex ($1 = M, 0 = F$), age, marital status ($1 = married, 0 = single$), education attainment (converted to years of formal education), religion ($1 = yes, 0 = no$), family income, and paid work ($1 = yes, 0 = no$).

Social Support

Five items were adopted from Functional Social Support Scale (Hanson et al., 1989). The scale has been used in Taiwan showing good reliability, construct validity, and criterion validity in predicting health and well-being of community people (Lu & Chang, 1997; Lu & Hsieh, 1997). Material and tangible support (3 items: "Are there anyone who gives you money/allowance?", "... who can help you in emergencies?", "... who helps with daily life activities"), and emotional support (2 items: "...who you can consult for personal problems?", "...whom you can trust and confide?") were rated ($1 = Never, 4 = Always$). Following the scoring procedure suggested by the scale developers, a higher aggregated score indicated more social support. In the present study, internal consistency alpha was .62 for this scale.

Physical Health

Three indicators of health were used in the survey. *Self-perceived health* was rated ($1 = Very bad, 4 = Very good$). *Independence in daily functioning* (ability in dressing, eating, etc. $1 = yes, 0 = no$) was enquired. Finally, *disability* or difficulty in performing activities of daily living was assessed (Nagi, 1976). Each item was rated ($0 = Very difficult, 3 = Not at all difficult$). In the present study, internal consistency alpha was .86 for this scale. We aligned the direction of scoring for higher scores to represent *better* physical health.

Leisure Participation

A checklist of 10 types of leisure activities was provided, including TV/radio, newspaper/magazine, chess/cards, visiting relatives/friends/neighbors, computer/internet, gardening/plants, interests/hobbies, concerts/plays, movies/shopping, and walking. Having checked participation in these activities, participants were then asked to rate their overall *leisure satisfaction* (*1 = Very dissatisfied, 4 = Very satisfied*).

In addition, eight items were adopted from Beard and Ragheb's (1980) Leisure Satisfaction Scale, tapping aspects of psychological (e.g., interesting activities), social (e.g., interacting with people), physical (e.g., keeping fit), educational (e.g., learning new things), and relaxation (e.g., relaxed) experiences. The frequency of each specific experience was rated (*1 = Almost never, 4 = Often*). Scores were then aggregated to indicate *leisure meaningfulness*. In the present study, internal consistency alpha was .87 for this scale.

Depression

Common symptoms of depression were measured by 11 items from the CES-D adopted for the Chinese people (Cheng & Chien, 1984). Sample items are "Don't feel like eating, bad appetite", and "Feeling sad and miserable". Respondents rated each item (symptom) on a 4-point scale (*0 = never or very seldom, 3 = almost always*). A higher total score indicated a higher level of depressive symptoms. In the present study, internal consistency alpha was .82 for this scale.

RESULTS

Before testing our hypothesis, we computed Pearson correlations among all research variables (Table 1). Sex (female), marital status (single), (fewer) education years, (lower) family income, and (no) paid work were demographic correlates of depression. All three indicators of physical health and social support negatively correlated with depression. Finally, both leisure satisfaction and leisure meaningfulness negatively correlated with depression. All relations were in the expected direction.

We then conducted hierarchical regression analysis to test our hypothesis (Table 2). At the first step of regression, we entered demographic variables of sex, age, marital status, education years, religion, family income, and paid work. Second, we entered three physical health indicators. Third, we entered social support. Finally, at step 4 we entered overall leisure satisfaction and perceived leisure meaningfulness.

The results reported in Table 2 show that sex and family income were consistently related to depression (Model 1 and 4): females and those with lower family income were more likely to be depressed. Those with better self-reported health, ADL independence, and less disability on the Nagi index were less likely to be depressed (Model 2 and 4). Social support had a consistent negative relation with depression (Model 3 and 4). Having controlled for effects of demographic variables, physical health, and social support, perceived leisure meaningfulness and avowed leisure satisfaction still had negative relations with depression (Model 4). Thus our hypothesis was supported. The combination of demographics, physical health, social support, and leisure participation explained a total of 34% of variance on depression, among which leisure had an independent contribution of 3%.

Table 1. Intercorrelations among research variables.

	1.	2.	3.	4.	5.	6.	7.	8.	9.	10.	11.	12.	13.	14.
1.Sex	1.00													
2.Age	.00	1.00												
3.Marital status	.11	***-.05	1.00											
4.Education yrs	.18	***-.27	**.07	*1.00										
5.Religion	-.04	.04	.02	-.24***	1.00									
6.Family income	.00	.00	.09	**.24	-.06***	1.00								
7.Paid work	.23	***-.37	**.03	.20	-.02***	.11	*1.00							
8.Health	.06	*-.15	**.08	**.22	-.05***	.26	.16***	1.00						
9.Independent functioning	.02	-.06	.01	.06	.00*	.06	.10*	.14**	1.00					
10.NAGI	.10	***-.14	**.11	**.18	-.02***	.22	.27*	.36	.58**	*1.00				
11.Social support	-.08	**.05	.19	**.03	.04	.20	-.10*	.07*	-.03	.00	1.00			
12.Leisure satisfaction	.06	*.03	.04	.07	-.06*	.12	.04*	.21	.04**	.10	.11*	*1.00		
13.Leisure meaningfulness	.01	-.03	.10	**.28	-.06*	.25	.05*	.27	.10**	.25*	.23*	.31*	1.00	
14.Depression	-.09	**.01	-.13	**-.13	.03*	-.36	-.12*	-.40*	-.09**	-.34*	-.26*	-.23*	-.35**	1.00

Notes: Sex: 1 = M, 0 = F; Marital status: 1 = married, 0 = single; Religion: 1 = yes, 0 = no; Paid work: 1 = yes, 0 = no; Independent functioning: 1 = yes, 0 = no.
* $p < .05$, ** $p < .01$, *** $p < .001$.

Finally, though we had no formal hypothesis about the preferences of leisure activities, we nonetheless looked at the frequency of middle-aged people's participation in various types of leisure. Results revealed that TV/radio (89.9%), visiting relatives/friends/neighbors (53.3%), newspaper/magazine (46.5%), and gardening/plants (28.9%) were the four most popular leisure activities. Other activities all had participation rates below 20%: interests/hobbies (19.6%), walking (19.0%), computer/internet (18.9%), movies/shopping (16.5%), chess/cards (10.1%), and concerts/plays (9.7%).

Table 2. Hierarchical regression predicting depression symptoms.

Step	Predictors	Depression (Model 1) ΔR^2	β	Depression (Model 2) ΔR^2	β	Depression (Model 3) ΔR^2	β	Depression (Model 4) ΔR^2	β
1	Sex		-.06 *		-.05		-.06 *		-.06 *
	Age		-.02		-.06		-.05		-.04
	Marital status		-.09 **		-.06		-.02		-.02
	Education yrs.		-.02		.03		.03		.06
	Religion		.00		.00		.01		.01
	Family income		-.34 ***		-.25 ***		-.21 ***		-.20 ***
	Paid work	.15 ***	-.07 *	.15 ***	-.01	.15 ***	-.03	.15 ***	-.03
2	Health				-.26 ***		-.25 ***		-.21 ***
	Independent functioning				-.10 **		-.10 **		-.09 **
	NAGI			.12 ***	-.25 ***	.12 ***	-.25 ***	.12 ***	-.23 ***
3	Social support					.04 ***	-.20 ***	.04 ***	-.16 ***
4	Leisure satisfaction								-.08 **
	Leisure meaningfulness							.03 ***	-.15 ***
	Total R^2	.15		.27		.31		.34	
	Final $F_{(df)}$	20.74*** $_{(7, 807)}$		27.83*** $_{(10, 803)}$		30.16*** $_{(11, 802)}$		27.60*** $_{(13, 799)}$	

Notes: Sex: 1 = M, 0 = F; Marital status: 1 = married, 0 = single; Religion: 1 = yes, 0 = no; Paid work: 1 = yes, 0 = no; Independent functioning: 1 = yes, 0 = no.
Standardized coefficients β and F are taken from the final equation.
* $p < .05$, ** $p < .01$, *** $p < .001$

DISCUSSION

The purpose of the present study was to explore whether middle-aged people's leisure pursuits were associated with their well-being, over and above the effects of some known correlates in a Chinese society--Taiwan. We used depressive symptoms measured with a standardized instrument as the indicator for well-being in the present study. With the advantage of a large representative national sample, we could compare our results with the existing literature in the West.

Female sex as a risk factor for depression has been well-documented in the Western literature (Nolen-Hoeksema & Rusting, 1999) and confirmed among the Taiwanese people (Lu & Hsieh, 1997; Lu &Wu, 1998). Furthermore, Butler and Lewis (1982, p.11) synthesized Western findings to conclude that "demographic data show conclusively that an increasing life expectancy follows in the wake of increasing income and status". Our current findings of female sex and lower family income (also a proxy for lower status) as predictors of depression corroborate these existing literature. One recent Canadian study (Etowa, Keddy, Egbeyemi, & Eghan, 2007) found that the middle-aged black women were under increasing risk of depression (using CES-D as the measurement). These women viewed midlife depression as the consequence of a complex set of circumstances and stressors that they face, resulting from the double jeopardy of being women and black (a minority status). At midlife, Black women frequently recognize the importance of greater self-care and the need to pay more attention to their health, but their daily experiences of racism, among other things, lead to accumulated stress and undermine their ability to cope and make healthy life choices. Lower status women in Taiwan may face similar challenges in midlife, though racism is not prevalent. We can compile a demographic profile of middle-aged persons who may run the risk of depression—female and lower income. The added value of our present study is that we were the first to simultaneously consider effects of physical health/disability, social support, and leisure, to confirm the above demographic risk profile for midlife depression. In other words, as we have identified middle-aged people who are at risk of depression or a negative outlook, when other important factors are taken into account, we can then better target our care resources to prevent health hazards and depressed emotional well-being.

More importantly perhaps, we have found that leisure pursuits in middle age were related to well-being, even after controlling for effects of demographics, health/disability, and social support. Although leisure pursuits were not the strongest predictor of depression, its contributions were largely independent from those of health/disability and social support (comparing Model 3 and 4 in Table 2). Previous research has firmly established the protective effects of social resources, such as social support and social integration (e.g., Antonucci & Jackson, 1987; Hanson et al., 1989; Holahan & Moos, 1986; Kahn & Antonucci, 1980). We have extended the list of protectors to include leisure pursuits, which is so far largely overlooked in Chinese studies of midlife transition. Our results compliment Western findings of leisure benefits on enhancing quality of life in middle age and reducing risks of dementia in older age (Carlson et al., 2008; Rovio et al., 2007). More importantly, our results were obtained after controlling for effects of social support, thus taking out any potential confound between leisure as a means of sociability (Fu et al., 2009) and social support as a function of social embeddedness (Hanson et al., 1989). Thus, our results serve to underline the importance of including leisure as a means of engagement with life, along with personal resources (e.g., self-care healthy behaviors) and social resources (e.g., social support) in the promotion of successful life transition.

Beard and Ragheb (1980) purported that leisure is beneficial because it could gratify basic human needs pertaining to six aspects: psychological (e.g., interesting activities), social (e.g., getting to know people), physical (e.g., getting exercise, keeping fit), educational (e.g., learning new things), relaxation (e.g., relaxed, rewind), and aesthetic (e.g., beautiful surrounding). These six aspects constituted our measure of leisure meaningfulness, which turned out to be a significant predictor of depression. Inspecting the middle-aged people's reported list of possible leisure pursuits in the present study, we noted that the most popular leisure engagement was TV/radio, a solitary leisure that tops the list of leisure pursuits for Taiwanese in a recent national survey (Fu et al., 2009). Although watching TV has been found to be a low arousal and sometimes boring activity (Lu & Argyle, 1993), TV (and radio) does provide a bridge of connecting people to the outside world, especially when social participation is constrained by low status, health/disability or location of residence (e.g., rural area). Lu and Argyle (1993) did find that the committed watch of selected TV programs such as soap operas was related to happiness, mostly due to psychological satisfaction generated by identifying with and learning from characters in these dramas. Thus, we may infer that watching TV and listening to radio help to keep middle-aged people, especially those of lower status, staying in touch with life, learning new things, and identifying with others in the society. Reading newspapers/magazines which ranked the third popular leisure in the present study possibly serves the same functions.

The second popular leisure pursuit for middle-aged people in the present study was social in nature: visiting relatives/friends/neighbors. In a close-knit Chinese society, people tend to have relatives and friends living nearby. In Taiwanese rural areas, older people habitually get together in front of the village temple to chat and drink tea. Such casual social gatherings help to strengthen community bonds and satisfy social needs.

In the present study, gardening was the fourth popular leisure pursuit. It is also the only one involving physical exertion and working outdoor. Gardening is generally regarded as a hobby which can generate a strong sense of achievement (Lu & Argyle, 1994) and aesthetical enjoyment (Argyle, 1996). Leisure-related physical activities such as gardening in midlife were found even prospectively to reduce the risk of dementia in older age for U.S. male twins (Carlson et al., 2008). Taken together, it is understandable that these often engaged leisure pursuits have encompassed benefits relating to psychological, educational, social, physical, relaxation, and aesthetic needs for middle-aged people. Leisure pursuits thus may play an integral part in promoting active engagement with life and successful midlife transition.

However, readers should still keep in mind that the present study has certain limitations. First, the study design was cross-sectional, thus no causal conclusions are legitimate. Second, this study was essentially a secondary data analysis. Contrary to our hope, some variables were measured with single or fewer than desirable number of items; some were not included. For instance, it would be helpful if we had a complete index of time use to link time spent on various leisure pursuits with their benefits on well-being. This information would then help us better plan and educate middle-aged people in their leisure engagement. Third, our interviews were conducted using structured questionnaires. Future studies may consider employing qualitative methods to explore middle-aged people's conceptions and lived experiences of successful midlife transition in greater depth, including leisure and other life domains, so that a fuller and richer understanding of midlife issues can be achieved from middle-aged people's own perspective.

ACKNOWLEDGMENT

The empirical study reported in this paper was financed by a grant from the National Science Council, Taiwan, ROC, NSC95-2420-H-008-001-KFS. In writing up this paper, the author was supported by another grant NSC97-2420-H-002-200-KF3.

REFERENCES

Antonucci, T. C., & Jackson, J. S. (1987). Social support, interpersonal efficacy, and health: A life course perspective. In L. L. Carstensen & B. A. Edelstein (Eds.), *Handbook of clinical gerontology* (pp. 291–311). New York: Pergamon Press.

Argyle, M. (1996). The social psychology of leisure. London: Penguin Books.

Beard, J. G., & Ragheb, M. G. (1980). Measuring leisure satisfaction. *Journal of Leisure Research, 12,* 20-33.

Butler, R. N., & Lewis, M. I. (1982). *Aging and mental health.* Louis, MO: CV Mosby.

Carlson, M. C., Helms, M. J., Steffens, D. C., Burke, J. R., Potter, G. G., & Plassman, B. L. (2008). Midlife activity predicts risk of dementia in older male twin pairs. *Alzheimer's & Dementia, 4,* 324-331.

Cheek, N. H., & Burch, W. R. (1976). *The social organization of leisure in human society.* New York: Harper and Row.

Cheng, T. A., & Chien, C. P. (1984, May). Epidemiology of depression: CES-D survey in Taiwan. Paper presented at The Third Practice Congress of Psychiatry, Seoul, South Korea.

Duay, D., & Bryan, V. (2006). Senior adults' perceptions of successful aging. *Educational Gerontology, 32,* 423-445.

Etowa, J., Keddy, B., Egbeyemi, J., & Eghan, F. (2007). Depression: The 'invisible grey fog' influencing the midlife health of African Canadian women. *International Journal of Mental Health Nursing, 16,* 203-213.

Fu, Y. C., Lu, L., & Chen, S. Y. (2009). Differentiating personal facilitators of leisure participation: Socio-demographics, personality traits, and the need for sociability. *Journal of Tourism and Leisure Studies, 15,* 187-212.

Goldstein, E. G. (2005). When the bubble bursts: Clinical perspectives on midlife issues. Hillsdale, NJ: The Analytic Press.

Hanson, B. S., Isacsson, S. O., Janzon, L., & Lindell, S. E. (1989). Social network and support influence mortality in elderly men. *American Journal of Epidemiology, 130,* 100-111.

Harahousou, Y. (2006). Leisure and ageing. In Rojek, C., Shaw, S. M., & Veal, A.J. (Eds.), *A Handbook of Leisure Studies* (pp. 231-249). New York: Palgrave Macmillan.

Hobfoll, S. E. (1989). Conservation of resources: A new attempt at conceptualizing stress. *The American Psychologist, 44,* 513-524.

Holahan, C. J., & Moos, R. H. (1986). Personality, coping, and family resources in stress resistance: A longitudinal analysis. *Journal of Personality and Social Psychology, 51,* 389-395.

Hunter, S., & Sundel, M. (1989). *Middle myths: Issues, findings, and practical implications.* Newburg Park, CA: Sage.

Iso-Ahola, S. E., & Park, C. J. (1996). Leisure-related social support and self-determination as buffers of stress-illness relationship. *Journal of Leisure Research, 28,* 169-187.

Kahn, R. L., & Antonucci, T. C. (1980). Convoys over the life course: Attachment, roles, and social support. In P. B. Baltes & J. O. G. Brim (Eds.), *Life-span development and behavior* (Vol. 3, pp. 253-286). New York: Academic Press.

Kertzner, R. M. (2007). Review of when the bubble bursts: Clinical perspectives on midlife issues. *Journal of Nervous and Mental Disease, 195,* 183-184.

Lee, L. J. (1997). *Adults' middle life experiences.* Tech report for the National Science Council NSC 85-2413-H-004-004.

Lee, L. J. (1999). Adults' perceived images of life experience and personaliy traits of middle-aged and older adults. *Bulletin of National Chengchi University, 78,* 1-54.

Lin, W. Y., & Wang, Y. C. (Eds.) (2002). *Needs, services and value preferences for older life among different generations: Users' manual.* Taipei, Taiwan: National Science Council.

Litwin, H. (2000). Activity, social network, and well-being: An empirical examination. *Canadian Journal on Aging, 19,* 343-362.

Lu, L. (2006a). The transition to parenthood: Stress, resources and gender differences in a Chinese society. *Journal of Community Psychology, 34,* 471-488.

Lu, L. (2006b). Postnatal adjustment of Chinese parents: A two-wave panel study in Taiwan. *International Journal of Psychology, 41,* 371-384.

Lu, L. (2007). The individual- and social-oriented self views: Conceptual analysis and empirical assessment. *US-China Education Review, 4,* 1-24.

Lu, L. (2008). The individual- and social-oriented Chinese bicultural self: Testing the theory. *Journal of Social Psychology, 148,* 347-374.

Lu, L. (2009). Leisure pursuits, social support, and depression among Chinese older people: Evidence from a Taiwanese national representative sample. Manuscript under review.

Lu, L., & Argyle, M. (1993). TV watching, soap opera and happiness. *Kaohsiung Journal of Medical Sciences, 9,* 350-360.

Lu, L., & Argyle, M. (1994). Leisure satisfaction and happiness as a function of leisure activity. *Kaohsiung Journal of Medical Sciences, 10,* 89-96.

Lu, L., & Chang, C. J. (1997). Support, health and satisfaction among the elderly with chronic conditions in Taiwan. *Journal of Health Psychology, 2,* 471-480.

Lu, L., & Hsieh, Y. H. (1997). Demographic variables, control, stress, support and health among the elderly. *Journal of Health Psychology, 2,* 97-106.

Lu, L., & Hu, C. H. (2002). Experiencing leisure: The case of Chinese university students. *Fu Jen Studies: Science and Engineering, 36,* 1-21.

Lu, L., & Hu, C. H. (2005). Personality, leisure experiences and happiness. *Journal of Happiness Studies, 6,* 325-342.

Lu, L., & Wu, H. L. (1998). Gender-role traits and depression: Self-esteem and control as mediators. *Counselling Psychology Quarterly, 11,* 95-107.

Markus, H. R., & Kitayama, S. (1991). Culture and the self: Implication for cognition, emotion, and motivation. *Psychological Review, 98,* 224-253.

Nagi S. Z. (1976). An epidemiology of disability among adults in the United States. *Milbank Memorial Fund Quarterly, 54,* 439-467.

Nolen-Hoeksema, S., & Rusting, C. L. (1999). Gender differences in well-being. In D. Kahneman, et al. (Eds.), *Well-being: The foundations of hedonic psychology* (p.330–350). New York: Russell Sage Foundation.

Rovio, S., Kareholt, I., Viitanen, M., Winblad, B., Tuomilehto, J., Soininen, H., Nissinen, A., & Kivipelto, M. (2007). Work-related physical activity and the risk of dementia and Alzheimer's disease. *International Journal of Geriatric Psychiatry, 22,* 874-882.

Simmel, G. (1971). Sociability, translated by Everett C. Hughes, In D. N. Levine (Ed.), *Goerg Simmel on Individuality and Social Forms* (pp. 127-140). Chicago: University of Chicago Press.

INDEX

C

Q

R